Royal Air Force
BEAM BENDERS
80 (Signals) Wing
1940-1945

Midland Publishing
Limited

Beam Benders
No 80 (Signals) Wing, RAF
1940-1945

© 1997 L.M. Brettingham and D.C. Brettingham

Design concept and editorial layout
© Midland Publishing Limited
and Stephen Thompson Associates

First published 1997 by
Midland Publishing Limited
24 The Hollow, Earl Shilton
Leicester, LE9 7NA, Great Britain
Tel: 01455 847815 Fax: 01455 841805
E-mail: midlandbooks@compuserve.com

ISBN 1 85780 040 0

Worldwide distribution (except North America):
Midland Counties Publications (Aerophile) Limited
Unit 3, Maizefield, Hinckley Fields
Hinckley, Leics., LE10 1YF, Great Britain
Telephone: 01455 233 747 Fax: 01455 233 737
E-mail: midlandbooks@compuserve.com

North American trade distribution:
Specialty Press Publishers & Wholesalers Inc
11481 Kost Dam Road
North Branch, MN 55056, USA
Telephone: 612 583 3239 Fax: 612 583 2023
Toll free telephone: 800 895 4585

Printed in Great Britain by Redwood Books
Trowbridge, Wiltshire

No.80 Wing badge artwork by
Mary Denton-Boomsma SHA

Royal Air Force
BEAM BENDERS
80 (Signals) Wing
1940-1945

Laurie Brettingham

CONTENTS

INTRODUCTION

The story contained in this book occurred over 50 years ago and the comprehensive recall of events displayed by the contributors does their memories full credit. The people listed below have generously given time and considerable effort to providing information and/or illustrations and to each I offer my thanks and gratitude. Ranks, decorations, and professional qualifications are not included: Maryse Addison, Eira Andrews, Bill Baguley, Gordon Barrow, Gerry Beaumont, H D Bickley, Peter Bramham, Daphne Brettingham, Walter Brettingham, Cecil R H Broadhurst, Phil Butler, E B Callick, Don Campbell, Frank H Churchill, Philip Colehan, Ivor Cole, Martin Derry, R S Diggins, Mamie Dray, L G Dunbar, Vic Flowers, Joan Francis, Godfrey Frank, Ralph Gabriel, Peter Giles, Gertie Goldstraw, Jack Gray, Peter Green, Ernest Hackney, Peggy Hanton, John Harvey, Tony Hastings, Jack Haworth, Harold Hughes, Ken Humphries, John Kent, Tom Kilvington, David Leete, Jack Leng, Cyril Lister, Betty Lonsdale, Robin Looser, Bob Lowson, Norman Mackenzie, H Manton, Ken Maxey, Eric Masters, Arthur McAughtry, Monty Meatyard, J H H Merriman, George Morley, Bob Morrow, Nancy Moss, Ken Myers, Pamela Northrop, Bob Oakes-Monger, Wilf Pafford, Eric Palfreman, O R P Phillips, Len Pittendrigh, the late Paddy Porter, Colin Prior, W Priestnall, Louise Rogers, George Rose, Eric Rostron, Joe Russon, Robert Sage, R W Schoop, Brenda Scott-Tucker, Richard Shotton, Alfred Simmonds, Bryan Simmons, H J Skinner, Jennifer Smeed, B B Smith, John Stevenson, Bill Stickland, W E Thomson, Fred Vincent, John Whitehead, Charlie Wilton.

Special thanks are also gratefully given to John Whitehead for his relevant and informative advice concerning the Operations Room at Radlett; he was patience personified. Norman Mackenzie carefully retraced the steps of his evasion through France and Spain, often providing tangible evidence of his journey. John Harvey not only provided information about his work as a Special Wireless Operator looking for the enemy beams, but generously gave the author many pages of detailed notes, written after the war, describing his experiences. Len Pittendrigh was a great help with the origin and activities of the Anti-Jamming Unit and Robert Sage provided new information on Operation *Trinity*. All exercised considerable understanding when dealing with a non-technical mind! John Kent and Alfred Simmonds were particularly helpful with the *Starfish* chapters, and Ivor Cole provided information about civilian life in wartime Radlett.

I am indebted to my brother, Walter Brettingham, and to the following for their contribution towards the illustrative material: Bill Baguley, L G Dunbar, Peter Giles, Bob Lowson, Eric Palfreman, Len Pittendrigh, Alfred Simmonds, John Stevenson.

At the Ministry of Defence Steve Clarke, Air Historical Branch (Publications Clearance) gave helpful advice. I am also grateful to the Crown Copyright Administrator, Clive Rowsell, for permission to reproduce extracts from the official records. Peter Trevitt of the Defence Research Agency, Malvern, was also very helpful. The Department of Aviation Records at the RAF Museum at Hendon, and the Imperial War Museum, Duxford, kindly provided me with facilities to enable me to photograph some of their exhibits. The following publishers have kindly allowed me to quote from books to which they hold copyright (full details in the Bibliography): Cassell, *The Last Ditch*; Coronet Books, *Most Secret War*; Harper-Collins, *The Diving Eagle, A Ju 88 Pilot's Story*, and *Secret Sunday*; HMSO, *SOE in France*; Oxford University Press, *Echoes of the Great War*, *The Diary of Rev Andrew Clarke, 1914-1918*; and Random House UK, *MI9, Escape and Evasion* and *Pantaraxia*.

Magazines were also a source of useful information. I gratefully acknowledge the permission of all to reproduce parts of their articles (full details in the Bibliography): *Eng Inf*, the BBC engineer magazine; *FlyPast*; *QRV*, the Journal of the RAF Amateur Radio Society; *RSS Newsletter*; and *The Scots Magazine*.

Lastly, I would like to thank my wife, Daphne, for her help and support during the writing of this book. Throughout she has been a constant encouragement and produced administrative order from chaos in the recording of information as it became available. Unless otherwise stated, she is responsible for the illustrations.

Laurie Brettingham

March 1997   Welwyn Garden City

SOURCES & BIBLIOGRAPHY

British Telecommunications plc archives
Post Office Radio Branch, Dollis Hill

The Institute of Royal Engineers, Chatham
History of the Corps of Royal Engineers: Volume III, 1952
The Indian Sappers and Miners: Lt Col E W C Sandes, 1948

Public Record Office, Kew
AIR 26/280 Setting up of No 80 Wing
AIR 26/582 Organisation and Functions of No 80 Wing
AIR 27/853 Operational Record Books No 109 Squadron
AIR 41/3 *Decoys & Deceptions*, Air Historical Branch (1) Air Ministry, first draft
AIR 41/46 Historical Report, No 80 Wing RAF,1939-45, Air Historical Branch

Royal Air Force Museum
The Second World War 1939-45, RAF Signals,Volume 7, Radio Counter Measures.

Telecommunications Research Establishment
TRE, Radio War, Robert Cockburn, 1945: addendum, E B Callick, June 1995

Newspapers and Magazines
BBC magazine *Eng Inf*: No 51, Winter 1992-93
Dollis Hill (RSS) *Newsletters*: Nos 43 (July 1991); 44 (Oct 1991); 46 (Apr 1992); 47 (July 1992)
Daily Telegraph: Obituary Air Vice-Marshal Addison, 7th July 1987
FlyPast: August 1984
Practical Wireless: January 1988
RUSI Journal: February 1947
QRV - Journal of the RAF Amateur Radio Society: Autumn 1993
The Scots Magazine: January 1989

Books
Annual Obituary, 1987: St James' Press, 1978
Bomber Harris: Dudley Saward; Cassell, 1984
Bomber Offensive: Sir Arthur Harris; Collins, 1947
British Intelligence in the Second World War: F H Hinsley with E E Thomas, C F G Ransom,
    R C Knight; Vol.1, HMSO, 1979
Cover of Darkness: Roderick Chisholm; Enfield Press, 1976
Deception in World War II: Charles Cruickshank; Oxford University Press, 1979
Diving Eagle (The): A Ju 88 Pilot's Diary: Peter Stahl; William Kimber 1984
Duel in the Dark: Peter Townsend; Harrap, 1986
Echoes of the Great War, The Diary of Rev Andrew Clark: James Munson (ed); OUP 1985
Enemy is Listening (The): Aileen Clayton; Hutchinson, 1980
Fight Another Day: J M Langley; Collins, 1974
First Pathfinders (The), The Operational History of Kampfgruppe 100, 1939-41: Kenneth
    Wakefield; William Kimber, 1981
From a Cat's Whisker Beginning: Norman Cordingly; Merlin Books,1988
Great Escape (The): Paul Brickhill; Arrow Edition, 1979
History of the 17th Light Anti-Aircraft Regiment, RA, 1938-45 (The): Lt Col H S Eeles;
    Courier House, Tunbridge Wells, Kent, 1946
In Full Flight: Roger Spooner; MacDonald, 1965, reprinted Wingham Press, 1991
Instruments of Darkness: Alfred Price; William Kimber, 1967
Joe: An Autobiography of a Trenchard Brat: Joe Northrop; Square One Publications, 1993
Last Ditch (The): David Lampe; Cassell, 1968
Luftwaffe Bomber Units 1939-41: Jerry Scutts; Osprey, 1978
Luftwaffe War Diaries (The): Cajus Bekker; translated/edited by Franz Ziegler,
    MacDonald, London, 1966.
Masquerade; The Amazing Camouflage Deceptions of World War II: Seymour Reit;
    Robert Hale, 1978
MI9, Escape and Evasion, 1939-45: M R D Foot and J M Langley; Bodley Head Press, 1979
Mission Improbable: Beryl E Escott; Patrick Stephens Ltd, 1991
Most Secret War: Professor R V Jones; Hamish Hamilton, 1978
Pantaraxia: Nubar Gulbenkian, (autobiography); Hutchinson,1965
Pathfinders: Air Vice-Marshal D C T Bennett, Frederick Muller, London, 1958
Post Office Goes To War (The): Ian Hay; HMSO, 1946
Saturday at MI9: Airey Neave; Coronet Books, 1971
Royal Air Force 1939-45, Volume 1, The Fight at Odds: Denis Richards; HMSO, 1953
Second World War (The): Winston S Churchill; Volume 2, Cassell, 1949
Secret Sunday: Donald Darling; William Kimber,1975
Secret War (The): Brian Johnson; BBC, 1978
Soldier at Bomber Command: Charles Carrington; Leo Cooper/Heineman, 1987
Spitfire On My Tail: Ulrich Steinhilper and Peter Osborne; Independent Press, 1989
Strategic Air Offensive Against Germany 1939-45 (The): Sir Charles Webster and
    Noble Frankland; HMSO, 1961
These Remain: Sir John Slessor; Michael Joseph, 1969
Tizard: Ronald W Clark; Methuen, 1965

Chapter One

SETTING UP

Large streams from little fountains flow,
Tall oaks from little acorns grow.
David Everett (1796-1813)
(Lines Written for a School Declamation)

In November 1939, a communication was left at the British Embassy in Oslo. An anonymous well-wisher had given information concerning current German scientific activities likely to be used in the war. Some two months earlier at the outbreak of war, Dr (later Professor) R V Jones[1] had been attached to Air Intelligence to investigate new techniques being employed in air warfare by the Germans. After examining what became known as the 'Oslo Report', despite doubts about its authenticity in some quarters, he considered the disclosure indicated a beam could be used to attack targets in the UK. He urgently sought further information. The RAF's 'Y' Service, which monitored Luftwaffe radio signals; the code breakers at Bletchley; the interrogators of enemy air crew who had been shot down over Britain; and the examination of crashed enemy aircraft – were all to prove helpful.

[1]
A detailed account of the events of this period is given in Chapter Eleven, 'The Crooked Leg' of Professor Jones' book, *Most Secret War* (Coronet Books, 1979 – see the bibliography).

Gathering the Intelligence

In March 1940 a document taken from the wireless operator of a crashed Heinkel He 111 belonging to Kampfgruppe 26 [KGr – Battle Group] showed an entry 'Radio beacon Knickebein from 0600 on 315°'. Dr Jones deduced that *Knickebein* was a beam along which an aircraft could fly to an already decided target. In June he met Group Captain L F Blandy (Head of 'Y' Service) in London, who showed him a piece of paper on which was written, translated from the original German, 'Kleve Knickebein is directed at position 53° 24´ North 1° West'. This was a decoded *Enigma* signal which seemed to confirm his thoughts about Knickebein, with the interpretation that a beam was running from Kleve in West Germany. This had been picked up by a monitoring aircraft over Britain. [*Enigma* was an ingenious code machine developed by the Germans and 'broken' by MI.6 cryptographers at the evacuation headquarters of MI.6 at 'Station X', Bletchley Park.]

Dr Jones urged those aiding him in his quest for information to be alert for further clues. One German prisoner of war (PoW) was overheard talking to a comrade stating that the equipment was actually in his aircraft and would never be found by the British. When a search was carried out the only item capable of receiving the beam was the blind landing receiver. Jones contacted the Royal Aircraft Establishment at Farnborough and was told by Squadron Leader Cox-Walker that this particular piece of apparatus was much more sensitive than it would need to be just for blind landings.

So that was it. I now knew the receiver, and the frequencies to which it would be tuned, and, therefore, on which the Knickebein must operate.[2]

[2]
Most Secret War,
R V Jones, p.137
(*ibidem* – ibid – in
the same place of
reference).

Satisfied that there had to be two beams, a 'director' beam along which the pilot flew and a side or 'cross' beam which intersected it and indicated the target area, Dr Jones continued his investigations. Another piece of luck occurred. In addition to locating the transmitter at Kleve, a second at Husum, south of Bredstedt in Schleswig-Holstein, was found.[3] It seemed certain the enemy had a navigational aid which enabled the Luftwaffe to find their targets in the United Kingdom with ease at night and during daylight in poor visibility. By the mid-summer of 1940 the problem had been identified. Now it was necessary to provide the means for combating it.

[3] Ibid p.143.

Strong support was forthcoming from Downing Street. With the country's fortune at low ebb and invasion a distinct possibility after the fall of France, Prime Minister Winston Churchill was ready to consider anything worthwhile for the defence of Britain. At a Cabinet Meeting on 21st June 1940, Churchill, on hearing the facts currently available from Dr Jones, ordered an intensification of interest by the Air Ministry into the beams; appropriate counter-measures should also be implemented. His keen interest added impetus to activities already taking place at the Air Ministry.

The staff at the Air Ministry charged with these investigations had not been idle. By mid-June a considerable amount of information had been accumulated and there was reason to hope that the beams could be located and some form of counter-measures taken against them. A meeting of the Night Interception Committee on 16th June decided to form 'a ground watching organisation and also to employ aircraft specially equipped for investigating beams.' The following day it was decided that the recently disbanded Blind Approach Training and Development Unit (BATDU) which had the only personnel sufficiently trained in beam flying, would be quickly reformed to provide the air arm of the unit.[4] Its first task on 18th June, was to investigate 31.5 megacycles (Mc/s, more often currently referred to as megahertz – MHz), believed by 'Y' Service at Cheadle to be the waveband being used by the Luftwaffe for the navigational beam; Wing Commander Blucke was placed in charge. The investigations were carried out by aircraft from RAF Wyton (augmented by some from BATDU at Boscombe Down, on Salisbury Plain). A number of 'Watcher' stations were set up along the East and South Coasts.[5]

[4]
Public Record Office
(PRO) file
AIR 41/46, para 5.
Air Historical Branch
(AHB) History of
No 80 Wing.

[5] PRO AIR 26/580.

The creation of this new organisation was the responsibility of Air Commodore O G Lywood, the principal Deputy Director of Signals at the Air Ministry. He consulted an old colleague, Wing Commander E B Addison (see end of chapter), a signals officer of considerable experience and ability and gave him limited information about Dr Jones' extraordinary findings concerning *Knickebein*. Addison suggested a counter-measures organisation. Air Commodore Lywood agreed and gave him the job of setting up a radio counter-measures (RCM) section at the Air Ministry. Its primary function was clear, 'to provide an actual counter-measures organisation against German navigational aids. The investigation of the methods would remain under the Deputy Director of Signals 'Y' Service.'[6] At the same time a small section was set up in the Filter Room at Fighter Command to assist.

[6] Ibid.

The rapid expansion of enemy radio navigation systems particularly those operated from France, Belgium and Holland, which were now in enemy hands, soon made it obvious that the RCM would have to be very large indeed. A separate formation, using the Radio Counter-Measures Unit at the Air Ministry as its nucleus, was formed. As a temporary measure the headquarters of the new organisation was quickly established in a government building, the Road Research Laboratory at Garston, near Watford in Hertfordshire (at the time alternative Fighter Command Administration HQ should Bentley Priory be put out of action) and placed under the local command of Wing Commander C S Cadell.[7] The entire organisation was under the direction of Wing Commander Addison as it was considered the overall supervision of this work was better carried out under single control.

In September 1940[8] an air investigation section, the Wireless Intelligence Development Unit (WIDU) was formed at Boscombe Down from BAT&DU personnel under the command of Wing Commander Blucke with a detachment under Flight Lieutenant Robert Sage at Wyton.[9] (See Chapters Six and Seven for more information about this unit.)

Control

As the availability of equipment and jamming stations increased the question was posed; Who should control these activities? Initially it was Fighter Command who had an overall knowledge of enemy air activity over Great Britain. Later it was decided that a separate organisation with its control room and staff fed with information from 'Y' Service and the Filter Room at Fighter Command would be more effective:

It soon became apparent that radio counter-measures would be required on an ever increasing scale, involving a very much greater organisation than had originally been envisaged.[10]

Thus was the genesis of the RCM Unit which would be directly responsible to the Air Ministry. As the man who could claim credit more than any other for bringing it into existence wrote at the war's end: *From a small beginning it rapidly grew into a vast and complex organisation whose eventual role covered the offensive, as well as the defensive, side of ground RCM.*[11]

After a few months at Garston the HQ moved the short distance to Radlett where, under the command of the recently promoted Group Captain Addison it was officially named No 80 (Signals) Wing. Accommodated firstly, in October 1940, in a requisitioned country hotel, Aldenham Lodge, it moved its Operations Room a year later to larger premises at 'Newberries', a disused golf course, some half a mile away.

In the early stages of its existence the operations of No 80 Wing were necessarily defensive. With Europe over-run by the rapidly advancing German Army the victorious invaders had plenty of captured airfields from which to launch raids on Britain. This they did to great effect. However, as the tide of war turned, RCM took their place in the offensive against Germany in Continental Europe, their usefulness increasing by the day. With the Luftwaffe continually trying new radio aids, counter-measures were expanded in an attempt to combat them. At the end of 1943 the work had reached such proportions, in the air as well as on the ground, that No 100

[7]
Enquiries have been made by the author to find the exact location without success. One who served there feels sure it was in the grounds of what is now the Building Research Establishment – letter from John Whitehead to author, dated 24th June 1993.

[8]
Another source quotes the WIDU formation date as 30th October 1940.

[9]
In the work quoted in note [5] (*opere citato* – Op cit).

[10]
Op cit [4], para 36.

[11]
Op cit [4]. Foreword to the AHB History by Air Vice-Marshal E B Addison.

(Bomber Support) Group was formed with its HQ at Bylaugh Hall, near Dereham, Norfolk; Air Vice-Marshal Addison was appointed to command the unit. It eventually comprised 14 squadrons, with fighters as well as bombers. No 80 Wing became a segment of this Group, continuing to provide ground counter-measures as distinct from those undertaken in the air.

Air Vice-Marshal E B Addison CB CBE

Edward Barker Addison was born in Cambridge on 4th October 1898. In the First World War, aged 17 years, he became an Air Mechanic in the Royal Flying Corps and was promoted to Corporal in 1917; a year later he was commissioned in the newly-formed Royal Air Force.

At the conclusion of the war he studied natural science at Sidney Sussex College, Cambridge, graduating with a BA in 1921, being awarded his MA five years later. Whilst at Cambridge he met a French student, Marie-Blanche Rosain, whom he later married. They had a son and daughter.

Rejoining the RAF after university, Addison served in India from 1923 until 1926 when he became a signals officer in the Far East. Recalled to the Air Ministry in London in 1940 he took command of the RCM Unit set up to take part in what became known as 'The Battle of the Beams'. This unit shortly afterwards became No 80 (Signals) Wing where he stayed, in command, until returning to the Air Ministry in April 1942 where he eventually became Director of Signals. In December 1943, No 100 (Bomber Support) Group was formed to provide offensive RCM against the Luftwaffe. Addison assumed command of this large unit and contributed greatly with his extensive technical knowledge to the bomber offensive against Germany.

[12]
Annual Obituary 1987, St James' Press: *Daily Telegraph,* 7th July 1987.

He retired from the RAF in 1955 and entered industry, later acting as a consultant for the Vocational Guidance Association. He became a Fellow of the Institute of Electrical Engineers in 1966, and was awarded the CBE in 1942; the CB in 1945 and the US Legion of Merit in 1947. He died on 4th July 1987.[12]

Air Vice-Marshal E B Addison CB CBE

Chapter Two

MEASURES AND COUNTER-MEASURES

Let it work
For 'tis sport, to have the engineer
Hoist with his own petard.
Shakespeare: *Hamlet*, III, iv.

As the new beam appeared, how were the controlling beacons to be nullified? Professor Lindemann, (later Lord Cherwell), friend for 20 years and Scientific Adviser to Winston Churchill, using information received from his former student Dr R V Jones at Air Ministry Intelligence, explained to the Prime Minister 'in lucid homely terms' the two options available.

The first was to 'jam' the beams so that their signals could not be received by the enemy aircraft. A radio beam is highly directional and is used principally for putting an aircraft on a target; bringing it back to base, or locating it from the ground.

The second method was to 'mask' the enemy's transmitting beacons by picking up and repeating the German signals. A radio beacon radiates in all directions and is used by aircraft for fixing its position. It needs two beacons to obtain a 'fix' and also needs to know their geographical locations. To summarise, the Luftwaffe used the beams for attacking targets, with the beacons being principally used for getting home. The enemy aircraft would not be able to distinguish between the signal from its home beacon and the echo from the interfering station in the United Kingdom, thus confusing the direction finding of the crew.[1] The method was to be given the official abbreviation of 'Meaconing' (from *M*asking *B*eacon).

Radio counter-measures (RCM) received high-level approval and three men were to share the main responsibility for implementing them. Dr Jones, Scientific Adviser at the Air Ministry, acquired and evaluated the intelligence received from various sources, and advised concerning the beams; Wing Commander Addison set up and dealt with the operational tactics; Dr (later Sir) Robert Cockburn, headed a small team at the Telecommunications Research Establishment, dealing with the research and development of the technical equipment required.

Knickebein ('Crooked Leg')

The first navigational beam used by the Germans, had its origin in the Lorenz blind approach beam which had been used since before Second World War by both the RAF and the Luftwaffe for assistance in landing in adverse weather conditions. Two radio beams were radiated almost in the same direction and slightly overlapping. Looking down the beams with one's back to the transmitting aerial array the left hand beam transmitted

[1]
Letter from
Professor
Lindemann to
Prime Minister
Winston Churchill,
10th August 1940;
Cherwell Archives.

'dots', while its partner on the right carried 'dashes'. With each beam while dashes were being radiated dots were not, and vice versa. In the area where the beams did overlap, the dots and dashes would combine to produce a steady tone. This region was called the 'equi-signal' zone and formed the beam along which (in the case of *Knickebein*) a pilot found his way to a target; or (in the case of the Lorenz blind approach system) gave the pilot the line of his final run-in back to base. (See Figures 1 and 2.)

Fig.1
Lorenz Beam for blind landing. In the 'steady note' zone (cross hatched), the 'dots and dashes' beams overlapped, they interlocked exactly to produce a steady note.

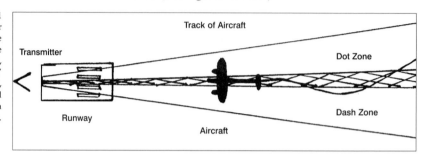

Fig.2
Sample map of *Knickebein* Beams.

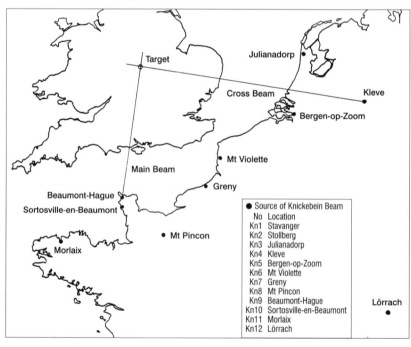

For *Knickebein*, to provide an approach beam was only half the battle. Some sort of signal was needed to indicate the point along the approach beam at which the bomb load had to be released in order to stand a chance of landing in the target area. This was achieved by providing a cross beam from a transmitter on a different site which intersected the approach beam more or less at right angles. It was a simple system, easy to operate. Its strength was that it could be operated by all Luftwaffe crews. Its weakness was its vulnerability to interference.

Arrangements were made for listening watches to be carried out not only by aircraft, but also at certain ground sites along the east and south east coasts of England where receivers were installed at the top of 300ft radar towers. Harry Spencer, a Telecommunications Research Establishment (TRE) scientist remembers:

Bob Light (seconded from the Post Office) and I were sent off to Ottercops Moss near Hexham to monitor 'Knickebein' beams. Our mission was so 'hush-hush' that we were not told our destination, but given a rail warrant to Newcastle, where a WAAF driver appeared from nowhere and took us to Usworth, a Fighter Command station. To our surprise, we were held under arrest until our identities were confirmed by some high level 'phone calls. We were then taken next morning to a brewery at Hexham where we were off-loaded onto a dray making its weekly trip, which included a village near Ottercops.

And so we started our watch. We had a tiny garden shed (with floor) lashed to the top of a 300ft mast. It kept the weather out, and had a power supply sufficient for a light and our receiver, a Hallicrafters S.10. By nightfall I had rigged up a dipole using the curly technique developed by E C Corke of EMI, in which two quarter wavelengths of wire are wound in spaced spirals round a broomstick and connected at their inner ends to a twin-wire feeder cable. This provided reasonable accuracy for measurements of the transmitter's bearings …

It was very cold up there. After a week or two, an RAF Corporal was attached to me so that he [eventually] could take over the work. Feeling cold at night (even though he'd recently come from Narvik) he soon scrounged a one-bar electric fire and a mile drum of signal cable to make enough parallel lines to transmit useful power up the tower. He then 'found' a Swan kettle, a coil of rope and a bucket. Until you've tried it, you have no idea of the effort required to haul a bucket up 300ft. The Corporal 'came by' a pulley and length of scaffolding, which made it much easier. From the top of the tower no habitation was visible for miles, so how he found all the bits and pieces remains a mystery. Later on he was joined by an LAC. After training and testing, they took over.

Whilst we were installing ourselves at Ottercops, Vic Russell, another TRE scientist, had been sent to a similar mast-top shack at West Beckham, near Sheringham in Norfolk, to watch for more southerly beams. One morning he said that during the night one leg and footing of his tower had been blown away by a bomb, and that the CO had forbidden him to come down because of 'possible unbalancing of the structure which could lead to its collapse'. How long it took to prop up the tower with a jury-rig I do not know. I can only hope that it was measured in hours! [2]

[2]
The Radio War, An Addendum, June 1995 by E B Callick to the TRE Report by Robert Cockburn.

The success of these tests led to an extension of the ground-based listening network over the southern half of the country. On 24/25th June 1940 one of the tower listening stations reported that beam-type signals were being heard on 31.5 M/cs. The existence of a beam laid over this country had been established a few nights previously during a flight by an aircraft of the reformed Blind Approach Training and Development Unit (BAT&DU).

Early Counter-Measures

In addition to the listening arrangements primitive steps were taken to produce countermeasures against the beams. The absence of suitable jamming transmitters tested the initiative of the planners. As an emergency measure it

was decided to adapt electro-medical (diathermy) apparatus as crude jammers. A Harley Street specialist in their use who had volunteered his help,
suddenly found himself involved in accelerated promotion and, as Flight
Lieutenant Heald, was sent around the hospitals to 'acquire' some of the
sets. Two of these were modified to cover the 30 Mc/s. frequency band as
crude jammers without keying facilities and were installed in vehicles containing receivers for intercepting the beam signals. Based at Wyton in
Huntingdonshire and Boscombe Down in Wiltshire, they could be despatched to any specified target area when required. Top priority communication was set up with Fighter Command HQ at Bentley Priory, Stanmore, in
Middlesex, where any reports from the listening stations were examined by
a small body of radio experts specially formed for this purpose, subsequent
action being taken on their advice.

Airborne tests of transmissions from these first simple diathermy sets indicated they were ineffective both in range and jamming effect. More sets, of a
different pattern, were obtained from hospitals, and 12 of the most suitable
were selected and modified. These were installed in police stations on or
near the East and South Coasts of England to form a jamming screen, the
police getting their instructions from RCM Control. Four had been set up at
Chichester (Sussex), Henley-on-Thames, Eye (Suffolk) and at East Dereham
in Norfolk, by 10th July 1940, the remainder being installed shortly afterwards in other parts of the Country.

I always felt ridiculous when asking the duty copper, 'Will you please switch on
your "Aspirin"?' an RCM Controller later wrote.[3] (The *Knickebein* beams were
a 'headache' for the RCM Organisation and thus the counter-measures were
code-named *Aspirin*!)

[3]
Letter to author from
John Whitehead,
18th February 1993,
PRO AIR 26/580.

In addition to these sets, five fixed Beam Approach beacons at airfields and
three portable ones were taken over and adapted for jamming. These were
superior to the diathermy sets having greater power and being already fitted with good quality audio frequency modulation.

The beam pattern details used by the Luftwaffe was shown diagrammati-
cally on tracing cloth; this was placed on a map with the centre of the diagram on the site of the *Knickebein* Station transmitting the signal. The cloth
was rotated until the characteristics obtained at the various ground stations
fitted those of the diagram. When they co-incided the direction of the main
beam was determined and there was an immediate indication from the map
of the cities or towns over which the beams passed. When the process was
repeated for the second *Knickebein* the proposed target area could be ascertained. This method was found to be reliable and was of great value in determining the enemy's choice of target for the night. Any information thereby
obtained was promptly passed on to the Duty Air Commodore at Fighter
Command HQ.[4]

[4] PRO AIR 41/46
(part 1), p.6.

During the month of August 1940, two more *Knickebein* transmitters were
identified by aircraft of BATDU at Dieppe and Cherbourg, both operating on
30 Mc/s. From radar plots it seemed that the Kleve and Dieppe transmitters
were being used for heavy raids on London with Dieppe and Cherbourg
coming into use for the raids on the Midlands and Portsmouth. As the
enemy established these further *Knickebeins* it became obvious that to try to

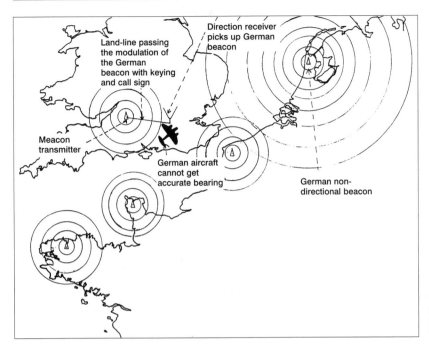

Direction receiver picks up German beacon

Land-line passing the modulation of the German beacon with keying and call sign

Meacon transmitter

German aircraft cannot get accurate bearing

German non-directional beacon

Fig.3
Example map of 'Meaconing'.

ensure complete jamming of the signals over Britain more higher powered counter-measure transmitters and additional listening stations would be needed.

Enemy Beacon System

It was well known before the war that the Luftwaffe was keen on the use of radio for navigational purposes; they had erected a great number of medium frequency beacons throughout Germany. When they overran France and the Low Countries in 1940, this radio system was extended to assist the Luftwaffe in their attacks on the UK.

The second part of Professor Lindemann's explanation to Churchill now came into being. The No 80 Wing History relates:

In order to render the beacons less useful to the enemy, a system of 'masking' was put into operation. This consisted briefly in the provision of transmitters sited in this country, the frequency of which could be changed rapidly to keep track of the enemy's beams. The transmitters were designed to re-radiate the enemy beacon signals and so render them unsuitable for direction finding processes over key areas in the UK. The system used was one earlier devised by the Radio Branch of the Post Office Engineering Department to prevent illicit radio beacons being used by enemy aircraft over certain areas of the United Kingdom.[5]

The principle was more subtle than plain jamming, since, being a re-radiation of the original beacon signal, there was no frequency difference and no difference in 'keying', only a different point of radiation:

Thus the effect of meaconing could not be detected in an aircraft fitted with normal receiving equipment. Hence false or indifferent bearings were obtained without the air operator realising fully that counter-measures were being used. (See Figure 3)

[5]
For a fuller description of the contribution made by the Radio Branch of the Post Office Engineering Depart see the 'Dollis Hill' section of the Outstations chapter.

The provision of a comprehensive scheme of these Meacons to cover the whole country moved on apace, a major factor in the progress being the first class co-operation between the Radio Counter-Measures Section at the Air Ministry, and the Post Office Engineers. The first Meacon was ready for service in July 1940 at Flimwell (near Tunbridge Wells, in Kent) and by the end of August of that year 15 sets of equipment at different sites, Harpenden, (to the north of London, in Hertfordshire), Templecombe (Somerset), Henfield (Sussex), and Petersfield in Hampshire, were in use operationally.[6]

[6] Op cit ⁴, p.7-8.

Additional sites became operational shortly afterwards near vital target areas such as London, the industrial areas of the Midlands, Liverpool, South Wales, Bristol, and the main ports of the east and south coasts. As the installation of these good quality transmitters progressed the need for the employment of the emergency inspired diathermy sets lessened and they were withdrawn from the police stations and transferred to some of the newly established sites.[7]

[7] Ibid p.11.

The effectiveness of the Meacons depended on crucial support and help from other organisations:

The successful operation ... was not only dependent on the skilled manipulation of the equipment employed, but relied to a major degree on a precise knowledge of the German 'Systems' of call-signs and the frequencies allocated to his beacons, together with their radiated powers and localities ... and the supply of rapid intelligence from the 'Y' Service when systems were changed, played a very important part throughout the European War in the operational control of Meaconing.[8]

[8] Ibid p.8.

Late in the summer of 1940, it became obvious that the enemy was aware his signals over the UK were being interfered with. The power of the enemy beacons was frequently reduced and changes of frequency and call-signs were made at odd times – often to the detriment of German aircrews. Frequent requests were made for direction finding 'fixes' and there were often complaints from them that their direction finding (D/F) sets were out of order.[9]

[9] Ibid.

The first record of the enemy being obviously aware of the counter-measures against *Knickebein* came on the night of 24th/25th September 1940, during a raid on London, when the frequencies were changed whilst the raid was in progress.

In an effort to 'counter' the counter-measures, the period of transmission of the German beams was much reduced and they finally were not turned on until the raiding aircraft had crossed the English coast.

This caused problems for the 'watchers' of 80 Wing: *This procedure called for a high standard of efficiency in all the sections of the counter-measures organisation. It also rendered difficult, and often impossible, the prediction of the target from the beam intersection as it was necessary to switch on the jammers immediately the enemy signal became active.*[10]

[10] Ibid p.12.

The beginning of September 1940 had seen the commencement of a period of intense enemy night activity over Britain, only slackening in May 1941, when the Luftwaffe was transferred to the Eastern Front for the attack on the Soviet Union. During this time additional radio navigational aids were brought into operation by the Luftwaffe. These included two narrow beam systems employing the *X-Gerät* and *Y-Gerät* (*Gerät* being interpreted apparatus or system) which were capable of being used for blind bombing of individual targets with much greater accuracy than was possible with the *Knickebein* system.

X-Gerät (Code-named *Ruffians*)

In the middle of August 1940, 'Y' Service stations on the Kent coast in the south of England intercepted a new signal with beam-type characteristics on 74Mc/s. As the frequency was not covered by any known German receiver the initial report was not taken seriously. By the end of the month, however, further signals on the frequency were heard. From information received from ground watcher stations, and investigations by Wireless Intelligence Development Unit (WIDU) aircraft, beams were established which appeared to originate in the Calais, Le Havre, and Cherbourg areas.

Although these beams differed from *Knickebein* in radio frequency and other characteristics they were sufficiently similar to suggest they might be used for navigational purposes, the *X-Gerät* beams were code-named *Ruffians*. (See Figure 4)

By September considerably more information had been obtained from intelligence sources and further investigational flights:

It then appeared that these beams were connected with the X-Gerät which was a new system of blind bombing for use by aircraft of a specialist enemy squadron (KGr100). The system was optimistically believed to have an accuracy of the order of 10 to 20 yards over London. It consisted of fine (narrow) and coarse (wide) approach beams, and fine and coarse cross beams originating in the Cherbourg and Calais areas respectively. By a process of deduction, Air Scientific Intelligence at the Air Ministry

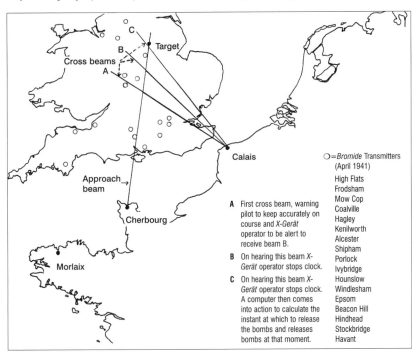

Fig.4
X-Gerät Beam.

Cross beams

Target

Approach beam

Calais

Cherbourg

Morlaix

○ = *Bromide* Transmitters (April 1941)

High Flats
Frodsham
Mow Cop
Coalville
Hagley
Kenilworth
Alcester
Shipham
Porlock
Ivybridge
Hounslow
Windlesham
Epsom
Beacon Hill
Hindhead
Stockbridge
Havant

A First cross beam, warning pilot to keep accurately on course and *X-Gerät* operator to be alert to receive beam B.

B On hearing this beam *X-Gerät* operator stops clock.

C On hearing this beam *X-Gerät* operator stops clock. A computer then comes into action to calculate the instant at which to release the bombs and releases bombs at that moment.

proved that the time of flight between two fine cross beams, directed across the fine approach beams, would give the ground speed of the aircraft along the line of approach, and this in conjunction with the position of the second fine cross beam relative to the target would be sufficient to give the correct instant of bomb release at a given height. These deductions were later confirmed. If the expected accuracy was attained here was a system of blind bombing which was an even greater threat than 'Knickebein'.[11]

The supposition proved to be correct:

Proof that the threat was an extremely serious one was produced later by the Air Warfare Analysis Section of the Air Ministry. This department carried out an investigation after an attack on Birmingham by KGr100, on the night of the 26/27th October 1940. By correlating the bomb plots with the direction of the beams it was shown that as regards 'line' in particular, the accuracy of the system was of an extremely high order.[12]

When steps were taken to institute a counter-measure for the new system it was found that existing transmitters were not suitable. After modification, the output power was too low to be effective. As a temporary measure a Gun Laying Pulse transmitter was borrowed from the Army and modified; and an emergency transmitter was produced at short notice by the Royal Navy Signals School, Portsmouth, to cover the frequency band. The former was installed at Hagley, near Birmingham, the latter at Birdlip, in Gloucestershire, the sites being chosen to cover the approach route from Cherbourg to the Midlands, as this area had been subjected to attacks by aircraft using the new system. Both transmitters were in operation by the first week of November. Two others, at Kenilworth (Warwickshire), and Kidsgrove, near Stoke-on-Trent, were installed by 8th November. These were augmented later in the month by jammers (also Gun Laying Pulse Transmitter) to cover Liverpool, Manchester and London. Each of the transmitters was sited close to the line from Cherbourg to the Luftwaffe targets in the UK since it had become apparent that, at that time, the Cherbourg beam was always used for the approach to the targets. (This changed when two more *Ruffian* transmitters were established at Morlaix). The counter-measures transmitters were code-named *Bromide*.

Early success for the counter-measures had not been anticipated owing to the number of frequencies used simultaneously in this system, and the limited number of jammers available. Another difficulty, not always appreciated by critics of the RCM work carried out by No 80 Wing, was also present. The nature of the work required the training up of personnel speedily and, it was hoped, efficiently, to the required standard for a particular task. Given the speed of action necessary at the outset, difficulties were often encountered in counter-measures work. They existed on this occasion:

The personnel available for operating the jammers were unskilled in the handling of the complicated equipment with the precision and speed necessary for its efficient use. The monitoring of the jammers to ensure that these were on the exact frequency of the enemy signal also proved to be a difficult problem.[13]

Shortly after the installation of the transmitters, however, good fortune favoured the watching organisation. As the result of the Meaconing of an enemy beacon, an aircraft from KGr100 which was known to use the *X-Gerät*,

[11]
Kampfgruppe 100 (KGr: Battle Group) – the German Pathfinder and Fire-raiser unit, based at Vannes, on the Brest Peninsula, which preceded the main Luftwaffe bomber force in attacks on the UK at this time.

[12] Op cit [4] p.13.

[13] Ibid p.14.

crashed into the sea off the English coast. Skilful interrogation of the surviving crew members – the observer had been killed in the crash – by Squadron Leader Felkin's team at Trent Park, Cockfosters, to the north of London, elicited an admission from the navigator that they had been hopelessly lost. This was caused by the wide divergence in readings between his master compass and D/F repeater compass, due to a masking station reproducing the characteristic signal of the Luftwaffe beacon he had been using. Valuable information was also obtained from pieces of apparatus recovered from the aircraft which included two receivers and a 'clock' (a key component of the *X-Gerät*) used for computing the ground speed of the aircraft.

Additional listening stations were set up in the Bournemouth area, on the south coast, since the approach beams from the Cherbourg group of transmitters passed over this district and early warning of an attack could be thus obtained. Mobile receivers were also used in this area, specified routes being patrolled when *Ruffian* signals were heard. As soon as the equi-signal was heard its exact position was telephoned from local General Post Office (GPO) boxes (later radio telephone links were established) to the main Bournemouth station who passed it on to the Operations Room at Radlett.

By the end of 1940 after analysis of ground listening station reports, and investigative flights, a picture built up of the *Ruffian* beam systems, the transmitter sites which had been named after German rivers. These had been harder to fathom than *Knickebein* as there were many more subsidiary beams. At the same time it was discovered that the Luftwaffe was using frequencies in the band 66.5 to 71.1 Mc/s. for the approach beams and 71.5 to 75 Mc/s. for the cross beams. Early in the New Year two more *Ruffian* transmitters became operational from Morlaix on the Brest Peninsula in Northern France, which were used for attacks on the West Country and South Wales. The beams from these transmitters were used for the approach to a target with Cherbourg being used for cross beams.

With 17 well-spaced *Bromide* transmitters taking on their three transmitters the Germans quickly realised their transmissions were being interfered with and took evasive action. As with the *Knickebein* transmissions they delayed laying the beams until the last possible moment or transmitted 'spoof' (false) signals. Also, in an effort to assist their aircrews to identify the correct beam signal, a Morse letter was superimposed on it at regular intervals. Later, all the transmitters available to the enemy at the three sites were switched on simultaneously so that nine frequencies were active at the same time, with rapid changes of frequency being made during attacks. These changes seemed to come as the leading aircraft of KGr100, made their final approach to the target.

Identification of the beams became more difficult. With the Cherbourg beams being used as either approach or cross beams it made target prediction almost impossible. They could be approach beams for the Midlands or cross beams for attacks in the West of England. In an effort to counteract this, Morlaix and Cherbourg were jammed by *Bromides* in Devon, Bristol and Wiltshire, while the Calais beams were jammed by the London group of stations, supplemented by units in the Midlands and the Northern *Bromides*. Close co-operation between all jammer and watcher stations was necessary to overcome the enemy's action. A special landline communication system from No 80 Wing HQ at Radlett, and certain selected watcher and *Bromide* (transmitter) stations meant that it was usually possible to follow such a change of frequency within three to four minutes.[14]

[14]
Ibid paras p.16-17.

A report by the Air Warfare Analysis Section of the Air Ministry in February 1941, claimed that since 15th November 1940, the effectiveness of the *X-Gerät* system had deteriorated seriously. This view was later supported by the interrogation of a captured Luftwaffe crew:

Evidence that this deterioration had been caused by radio counter-measures was obtained from the crew of a KGr100 aircraft which crashed on 13th March 1941. It was stated by them that by 1940 it had definitely been assumed that the interference to the beams had been caused by counter-measures. In December and January the interference to the pilot (approach) beams was described as very serious, and again when disturbances on the cross beams first began to be experienced. This later statement is interesting in that it was not until about the middle of January that sufficient transmitters became available for jamming cross beams in addition to those for the approach beams.

Further support to the claim that radio counter-measures against the 'Ruffians' were effective was given by a detailed analysis of an attack on St Athan airfield in Glamorganshire on 28/29th April 1941. On this night the cross beams were adequately jammed, but owing to the small number of transmitters in the West Country it was not possible to give full coverage to the approach beams. The result was that the enemy was able to make an attack which was extremely accurate in line but had an error of one mile in range.[15]

[15] Ibid.

Ruffian transmissions continued to be made but there was a steady decline in the use of the system by the Luftwaffe over Britain due, no doubt in part, to the opening of the Eastern Front in Russia in May 1941, but also to the effectiveness of the counter-measures. The *Ruffian* system was not used for attacks on the UK after June 1941 until April 1942, and, even then, its use thereafter was spasmodic. After mid-November, no further signals were heard.

Y-Gerät

In November 1940 signals were heard with the dot-dash characteristics of beam-type transmissions in the 40 Mc/s frequency band. Investigations indicated that the rate of 'keying' was 180 per minute, much higher that those connected with the *Knickebein* and *Ruffian* beams.

It was clearly a different system. (See Figure 5). Messages were also being passed by radio telephony in the same band to aircraft. One message instructed an aircraft to drop its bombs as the weather was getting bad. It also added 'We are accompanying you; follow the beam from the emergency aerodrome.' On another occasion, an aircraft was informed that the beam was being turned and was instructed to turn itself and make a new approach, later being told, 'Measurements impossible, carry out task on your own.' Some time afterwards 'Y' Service heard two signals on different frequencies in the same band with the same modulation frequency which appeared to be interlocked, one of these being from an aircraft.

The information thus gathered gave direct support to the Air Scientific

Intelligence Reports issued by Dr Jones in July 1940 and January 1941, that the Germans were developing a system known as *Wotan II* (*Wotan I* was the *X-Gerät*), for making a distance measurement along a beam which could be used for bombing. *Wotan II* referred to the *Y-Gerät* and was given the code-name *Benito*, in 'honour' of the Italian dictator, Benito Mussolini.

Early in January 1941, some progress had been made into the investigation of the new system, but it had not then been fully understood. Listeners found that the human ear heard the same characteristics whether tuned into the beam or not. The difference could only be detected, visually, on a cathode ray oscilloscope. The accuracy of the range measurement was thought to be of the order of 90 yards but other details of the beam were not known. It was different from *Knickebein* and *X-Gerät* in that when the signal changed from dots to dashes (and vice versa) it did not pass through an equi-signal.

The new beam was found to be coming from Poix, near Amiens, in Northern France, and Cassel, 15 miles south of Dunkirk, and at Beaumont, on the Cherbourg Peninsula. It was also established that the bombing was being carried out by a specialist unit, KG26 (*Kampfgeschwader* – Battle Wing), in much the same manner as KGr100 had been employed for *X-Gerät* operations.

This new bombing system had been developed by Dr Hans Plendl, a German scientist, who had previously worked on the *X-Gerät*. It used a single beam (no cross beams) and navigation along it was controlled from the ground station which sent out pulses which were picked up and re-radiated to the ground station by a receiver/transmitter carried in the aircraft. Thus, at any instant, the position of the aircraft along the beam was known.

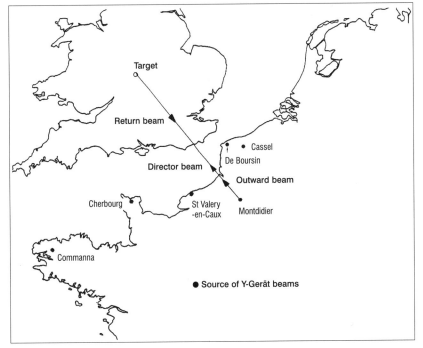

Fig 5
Example map of
Y-Gerät beam.

At the appropriate time the ground station would give the instruction for the aircraft to drop its bombs. The 'drop bombs' signal consisted of three dots, two dashes, and three dots, ie the letters SMS in Morse Code. This was always transmitted at a slow speed.[16]

[16]
Letter to author
from J Russon,
21st January 1994.

German aircrew were not at all happy about being controlled from the ground and sometimes the verbal exchanges between ground and air revealed anxiety and anger – particularly when the aircrew were certain that their aircraft was not where the men on the ground said they were. Sometimes the ground controller became very 'bossy'; on one occasion an instruction from him to a pilot to, 'Synchronise your engines!' brought a very sharp retort.

John Whitehead was a Squadron Leader working on intelligence in Group Captain Addison's office at Radlett at this time. He remembers the period as a worrying time for the Counter-Measures Unit: *... by the time that it (Y-Gerät) came into large scale operation, we had a counter-measure ready but, if my recollection is correct, it required several months of effort to discover how the thing worked. Fortunately, the enemy spent some time trying it out by sending out single aircraft by night to bomb a target in an area remote from other activity and then putting up a photo 'recce' 'plane the next day to obtain a precise record of where the bomb(s) fell.*

No 80 Wing ground stations along the South Coast reported unusual signals whenever this activity was on, their nature being 180 dots per minute, quite different from the dots and dashes of the other beam systems which had frequencies of 60 to the minute. No 80 Wing aircraft sent up to investigate confirmed these findings and reported that no beam could be found. Whenever they flew the result was the same. The recurrence rate of the dots was so high that it was impossible to detect changes of length of the dots – if there were any.

[17] Op cit [3].

[18] Ibid.

The only thing to do was to study a visual impression of the signal. Accordingly, an aircraft equipped with the necessary gear, including a cathode ray oscilloscope, and a route along which to fly was sent on investigation flights. From this it was learnt that the enemy pilots must have a visual display unit on board to be able to keep their aircraft on the beam.[17]

[19]
Later in the War
both Blumlein and
Browne were killed
in a flying accident.
On 7th June 1942
Handley Page
Halifax II V9977, in
which they were
travelling carrying
out experiments on
H2S radar
equipment, crashed
near Ross-on-Wye.
There were no
survivors. (*Aircraft
for Airborne Radar
Development. Fatal
Accidents 1936-1967
Report.* Annex 5.)

During this period a suggestion by John Whitehead was taken up:
Now that we knew how 'Benito' worked it was time for the next step. Group Captain Addison said, 'What about counter-measures?' Prior to joining the RAF I had worked for EMI on research and development and I knew a little about the TV transmitter which they had installed at Alexandra Palace, in North London. I said to him, 'Ally Pally could be used as a jammer or meacon. It works on the same band.' He said, 'Who shall I speak to?' and I replied, 'Either A D Blumlein or C O Browne.' He spoke in a very guarded manner to Browne who said, 'Ally Pally' is closed down for the duration of the war. It would be ideal for what you want; and we could make it look upwards for you if you want.' He had spotted immediately what Addy was getting at.[18, 19]

The BBC transmitter at Alexandra Palace had been used for the first public transmission of television a few years earlier. Although closed for the duration of the war, it was still being manned on a 'care and maintenance basis', the engineer in charge being Wilf Pafford.

The advice was heeded. Dr Cockburn's team in the Telecommunications Research Establishment (TRE) at Swanage, designed a type of *Meacon* in which the enemy aircraft ranging signal (which was a re-radiation of the enemy ground signal) was picked up on a broad band receiver and the modulation superimposed on a medium power transmitter tuned to the radio frequency of the German ground range station. In this way the range indications at enemy ground stations would be confused.

The first installation of this counter-measure, to which the code-name *Domino* was given, was set up to protect London from enemy aircraft covering the *Benito* station at Cassel, near Calais. As mentioned above, use was made of the BBC television sound transmitter at Alexandra Palace, in North London. The receiver was placed at a disused BBC station in Swains's Lane, Highgate, where a high fidelity cable was already available to Alexandra Palace for passing the various tones to the transmitter. The receiving equipment was later moved to a higher site at Parliament Hill as it was found that receiving conditions were not good at Swain's Lane. The equipment was ready for operational use by the middle of February 1941. At the end of this month a second *Domino* installation was completed on Beacon Hill near Boscombe Down about eight miles north of Salisbury, thus making both the Cherbourg and Cassel controls subject to counter-measures simultaneously. In addition, another counter-measure, code-named *Benjamin*, operated against the easily jammable electronic bearing analyser of the *Benito* system.

Dr (later Professor) Ewart Farvis, a peace-time lecturer in structural engineering, called up in the national emergency like so many other scientists made a major contribution to the new counter-measures. He did outstanding fieldwork in monitoring the enemy beam transmissions and later led the counter-measures at Alexandra Palace. He was later congratulated by Cockburn on producing 'an almost undetectable jammer design'.[20]

During this period the Luftwaffe used the *Benito* system on a small scale over the UK, presumably to test it under operational conditions. This was a mistake. On several occasions the fact that the aircraft of KG26 were the only aircraft engaged in these operations enabled good indications to be obtained of the tracks followed by these aircraft and the bomb plots. However it did show that the system was capable of enabling aircraft to bomb with remarkable accuracy and to obtain great precision in grouping.

There were early indications from intercepted enemy messages passed from enemy ground stations to the aircraft that the system was not working smoothly. On one occasion, out of 89 aircraft in action, 27 were told to carry on and undertake their tasks independent of ground control, 44 were not heard to receive a bombing signal, and only 18 were given the 'bomb drop' signal. There was not, however, conclusive proof that this was entirely due to the counter-measures as it was exceedingly difficult to differentiate between the tracks and bomb plots of KG26 and units not using the *Y-Gerät* who were also involved in the attack.

Attacks using *Benito* became heavier in March 1941; 18 aircraft (out of 36) working within the range of their ground stations received bombing signals. However the counter-measures were being felt:

During an attack on London on 9th March, a change of air and ground ranging

[20]
'Alexandra Palace, The Battle of the Beams 1940-41 ' by Jack Gray, in the BBC Magazine *Eng Inf No 51,* Winter 1992/3.

frequencies was made during the course of the operation. These changes were at once followed by the two 'Domino' stations. A second incident took place two days later when a bombing attack was made on the 'Domino' station at Beacon Hill and the station suffered a 'near miss'. As a result, this 'Domino' was not working on the following night when nine aircraft operated with the Cassel control and eight with Beaumont. The Cassel aircraft were covered by the Alexandra Palace 'Domino', while the Beaumont aircraft were 'uncovered'. None of the Cassel aircraft received their bombing signals, whereas most of the Beaumont aircraft appeared to perform their task satisfactorily.

However it was clear from later information that the counter-measures were beginning to bite: *Information was received from the interrogation of the crews of three aircraft of KG26 brought down on the night of 3rd/4th May 1941 that the whole of KG26 were losing confidence in the 'Y' System owing to the troubles which were being experienced. These troubles were attributed by them to English jamming and had become progressively worse since March.*[21]

[21] Op cit [4] p.22.

An example of the accuracy of the *Benito* system was displayed on three successive nights when a lone aircraft attacked an aircraft factory in Buckinghamshire. On the first night the stick of 16 bombs fell short of the target, the last bomb falling just outside the factory wall. On the second, similar hits were made by the bombs which landed virtually in the craters created on the first. On the third night the stick of bombs fell parallel to the first two nights and only a few yards away. The 16th bomb apparently stuck in the rack before its release and landed just outside the far wall of the factory![22]

[22] Op cit [3].

WIDU Christmas card for 1940. By the time the NAAFI had this on sale, the WIDU had changed title to 109 Squadron, so they had to make do with what they had! Note that the title is 'Intelligence' – not 'Investigation' – as some sources have suggested.
Bill Baguley

ROYAL AIR FORCE
WIRELESS INTELLIGENCE DEVELOPMENT UNIT

Chapter Three

HEADQUARTERS

We were not aware
that the work was secret,
not until after the war.
Ivor Cole

Garston

Given the urgency of the times and the desperate state of the nation's resources (it was only weeks after the evacuation of the remnants of the British Army from Dunkirk) the HQ at Garston, intended to be only a temporary measure, was hastily put together.

Located in *Radium*, the alternative Fighter Command Administration HQ, at Garston, Watford, in the Hertfordshire countryside to the north of London, the accommodation was, according to one officer who was employed there 'very rudimentary and Spartan'. The Operations Room was situated in a very large garage on the site which formerly must have housed large vehicles and earth moving equipment. In one corner was a small glass office, outside which were situated tables and telephones and a table carrying a large map of the UK upon which the movements of enemy aircraft could be plotted from information received from the Operations Room, at Fighter Command HQ, at Stanmore.[1]

[1]
John Whitehead,
in a letter to
the author
14th February 1993.

Aldenham Lodge, Radlett

After a couple of months the unit moved to more permanent accommodation at Aldenham Lodge Hotel, Radlett, said to have once been a favoured haunt of the famous aviatrix, Amy Johnson, who ten years before, had distinguished herself by making solo journeys to Australia and South Africa. Situated some 15 miles north of London along the old Roman road to St Albans and beyond, the location had been chosen due to its proximity to the London/Birmingham GPO Trunk Cable which, in the days before direct-dialling, assisted considerably the communications with many remote out-stations. It was also within easy access of the Air Ministry and Fighter Command HQ, at Stanmore. Radio experts were recruited for technical appointments from the BBC and given RAF ranks, to augment RAF Signals personnel already drafted to the HQ.

The requisitioned property had a varied history whilst occupied by the RAF. The cockroaches which occupied the old hotel kitchens were a constant menace and seemed to have been remembered by all. There must have been great consternation in July 1944, when the first floor room which housed the stationery stock, and which was grossly overloaded, collapsed onto the Accounts Section below causing serious injury to one WAAF. This resulted in her medical discharge, and slight injuries to several others. Against these experiences could be set the fact that the swimming pool of the hotel, a resource not usually to be found on RAF camps, was available to all and much used. In addition an unknown artist had been given permission to brighten up the interior of the mansion by painting gigantic murals on the walls of the canteen, the theme being 'The Four Seasons'.

The arrival of No 80 Wing (21 officers and 200 other ranks), under Group Captain Addison, in Radlett, (pre-war civil population 3, 188 in the 1931 census), must have disturbed the tranquillity of the village. (See Figure 6.) Hitherto most of the activity was confined to the main street, its 'through' traffic, and commuters using the railway station:

The village was a quiet place generally at this time. Apart from the RAF presence there were wounded servicemen at Shenley Hospital and they were regularly to be seen walking or limping about. There was very little traffic except for 'Queen Mary' trailers constantly bringing Handley Page Hampden and Halifax aircraft airframes to Radlett Aerodrome to be assembled. In the evening a large exodus of workers from Handley Page was apparent in the village.[2]

[2]
Ivor Cole, in a letter
to the author
15th December 1991.

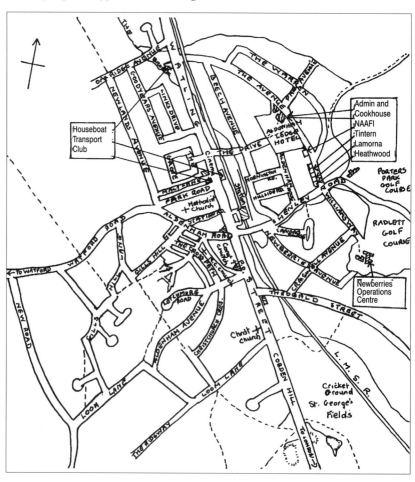

Fig 6
Wartime Radlett.

WAAFs in garden
at 'Heathwood'.
Mamie Dray

Armed posts were established at every entrance to the village. In addition to Aldenham Lodge, other large houses were requisitioned as quarters for the personnel of the unit. 'Heathwood', in The Avenue, became a WAAF hostel, initially in what had been the chauffeur's flat above the garage, later taking over the whole house. Two other houses, 'Tintern' (which with 'Heathwood' housed the Ops Room Clerks, 'Special Duty' and other shift workers) and 'Lamorna', (where the HQ Staff were billeted) were also taken over. All RAF personnel were billeted elsewhere in, or just outside, the village. 'Howard's Garage' in Watling Street, became the first motor transport (MT) section.

Without a unit medical officer at the beginning, the sick were placed under the care of a local GP, Dr Forbes Simmers, a former Royal Army Medical Corps Captain, who had his surgery in Watling Street. Hospital cases were accommodated at the Military Hospital in the nearby village of Shenley. In February 1941, an RAF Medical Officer was posted to the Wing and, in the following December, the RAF Sick Quarters, originally in Aldenham Lodge, moved to 2 Beech Avenue, another requisitioned house.

Local residents, it seems, took the occupation of the village in their stride. One such person recalls youthful employment connected with the new arrivals: *We were not aware that the work was secret, not until after the war. When I delivered newspapers to 'Newberries' they were left in the guardroom. As youngsters I don't think we were aware of security, only the presence of the RAF Police. In fact, life went on as normal, which was pretty quiet anyway.*[3]

[3] Ibid.

By the end of September 1941, the personnel of the Wing (including those at the outstations) was now over 2,000 and there had been 122 outstations built since the inception at Garston in June 1940; eighty-five were still operational, 37 had been closed down or amalgamated with other outstations.[4]

[4] PRO AIR 26/580.

'Newberries'

The HQ at Aldenham Lodge expanded rapidly and all sections could no longer be contained comfortably in the building. In October 1941, a year after moving to Aldenham Lodge the Operations Room and workshops moved the short distance to 'Newberries'. Administration was still undertaken at Aldenham Lodge.

Central to the establishment was the Operations Room which received reports from Watcher stations, intelligence, and the 'Y' Service, and gave orders for the various types of jamming at outstations . It also gave instructions, for the lighting of the *Starfish* decoy fires and lights (with one or two exceptions – see Chapter Eleven), and the deployment of its air arm, the Wireless Intelligence and Development Unit (WIDU), later known as 109 Squadron.

No 80 Wing HQ worked throughout in close liaison with Fighter Command HQ, through their Liaison Officers who, in addition to being responsible for closing down BBC stations and beacons when enemy activity dictated, were responsible for keeping Radlett informed of the movements of enemy aircraft making attacks on this country. This was accomplished by passing a running commentary of the information from Stanmore to Radlett.[5]

The Liaison Officers also worked closely with senior engineers at the BBC: *Low powered transmitters were dotted all over the country and a number of 'portable' transmitters were mounted on lorries. During an air raid alert instructions would go out to the fixed transmitters – the pre-war ones the Luftwaffe had pinpointed on their maps of Britain - either to switch off altogether or to reduce power, and broadcasting would then continue on various combinations of the new and old transmitters. Reception on the ground would be hardly affected, but aircraft 'homing' would be impossible. Throughout the war this system operated effectively, and the BBC never helped the Luftwaffe home onto their targets.*[6]

[5] PRO AIR 41/46 (Part 1) p.10.

[6] *The Last Ditch*, by David Lampe, p.39, (Cassell, 1968).

No.80 (Signals) Wing HQ, Ops room and Signals room at Aldenham Lodge.
Mamie Dray

Chapter Four

OPERATIONS ROOM

Go and bid the watchman stand at his post to give tidings of all he sees…
How goes the night, watchman?
How goes the night?
Isaiah xxi 6.

Accommodation for the pivot of No 80 Wing, the Operations Room, ranged, during the Wing's existence, from the grimy practicality of a garage at Garston, through the vermin-infested confines of the Aldenham Lodge Hotel (cockroaches in the kitchen and rats behind the skirting boards!), to the palatial ballroom at 'Newberries'. Locations changed but never the function. A key, sensitive area, this was the central position from which all the combative activities of the Wing emanated.

The lay-out of the Ops Room at Aldenham Lodge and 'Newberries' was much the same (See Figures 7 and 8), but the room at the latter was slightly larger, with a raised platform for the Controller. At Aldenham Lodge a large coal-fired grate was set into one of the walls. Its usefulness is fondly remembered:

In winter time, and on occasions when aircraft plots on the map and other signs indicated that the enemy was well on his way home, a couple of WAAFs would organise tea, and toast with peanut butter, by courtesy of that coal fire. It was great! [1]

[1]
Letter from
John Whitehead
to the author,
14th February 1993.

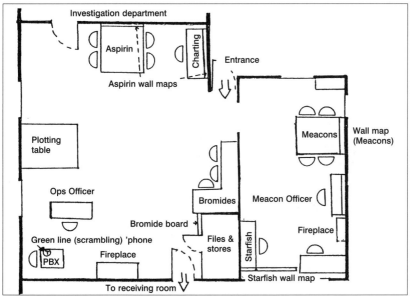

Fig.7
Plan of Ops. Room
at Aldenham Lodge.

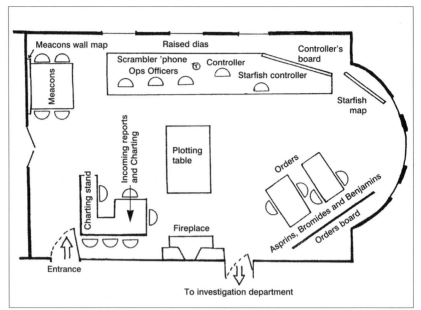

Fig.8
Plan of Ops. Room
at 'Newberries'.

The 'listening' (or 'monitoring') room housed some receivers and various instruments, eg a cathode ray oscilloscope. It was here that the characteristics of enemy signals were investigated with a view to establishing their purposes. The 'ante-room' was for relaxation when the occasion allowed it, or for discussions on tactics and policy.

In a prominent position in the room was an aircraft plotting table with a large map of Great Britain thereon and a WAAF in attendance; she was telephone-linked with the No 80 Wing Liaison Officer who was posted in 'The Hole' (the Operations Room at Fighter Command HQ, at Bentley Priory, Stanmore, Middlesex). Nearby, in a corner of the room, was a green telephone for use by the CO, the Controller, and the Scientific and Intelligence Officers, which was used for the transmission and reception of 'scrambled' (secret) messages.

In September 1940, four Liaison Officers with technical knowledge and experience of signals work had been appointed on a 24 hour watch basis from No 80 Wing to Fighter Command. It was their duty to relay to Radlett the details of every enemy aircraft plotted on the Fighter Command HQ plotting table, which was then transferred to the Radlett table with any other information they thought would be useful. One of their early tasks was to keep a special watch on aircraft from *Kampfgruppe* (KGr) 100 ('X' System) and *Kampfgeschwader* (KG) 26 ('Y' System) of the Luftwaffe; these groups preceded the main enemy attacks. The practice of KGr100 and KG26 was to 'meander' to within 20 or 30 miles of the target and then fly absolutely straight for it.

The No 80 Wing Liaison Officers maintained close contact with Liaison Officers from other organisations also at Fighter Command HQ. For instance the representative of the Ministry of Home Security, who sat next to the No 80 Wing Officer in the Stanmore Operations Room, could supply up-to-date information on potential targets (obtained from the Key Points Intelligence Branch at the Home Office), and there was close liaison between the No 80 Wing officers and those of 'Y' Service, the RAF wireless monitoring organisation. Fighter Command HQ provided weather forecasts.[2] So, unwittingly, did the Luftwaffe Meteorological Service. They were very reliable![3]

[2]
PRO AIR 41/46,
Appendix 'F'.

Group Captain Addison frequently visited the Operations Room and constantly astonished his staff by his habit of 'walking in just as everything was hotting up. It was amazing how often he did it - every time.' Working under the Group Captain were three Wing Commanders, each responsible for a watch, whose function was to exercise 'a general and discreet oversight'. Usually, the Wing Commander (Ops) and/or the CO would wander in to learn how things were going and would watch 'from the side lines' in order to be on hand if any help was requested. They did not stay long unless a lot was happening but they were always easily found if the occasion required it.

[3]
Letter from
John Whitehead
to the author,
9th May 1994.

The operational running of the watch was the responsibility of the Controller, a Squadron Leader, liaising with the other Operations Officers responsible for their particular sectors (*Starfish*, Meacons etc,) and the Scientific Analysis and Intelligence Section. It was an awesome responsibility considering the possible consequences one mistake could cause.

The Operations Officers worked three shifts: 0800 to 1400 hours, 1400 to 2200 hours and 2200 to 0800 hours. Of the three watches the last almost invariably carried the greatest burden, although in winter enemy activity increased during the second half of the second watch as well.

The Scientific Analysis Section carried a staff of three, Squadron Leader Cox-Walker, Flight Lieutenant George Baillie, and civilian Reggie Wells, an elderly, senior BBC Radio Engineer. The last-mentioned was a 'thinking type', and a very effective one. One WAAF noticed that Mr Wells, 'pottered round the Ops Room recording figures in a small notebook. He was a benevolent figure of the absent-minded professor type, who managed to stay calm and unruffled when all hell was breaking out around him, with 'phones ringing and instructions flying at periods of maximum activity!'[4] Cox-Walker is described as 'a decidedly practical person'. George Baillie was 'a bit of each.' A quiet and gentle-man, bald and a little plump, he looked 'a slim replica of Mr Micawber'. A good description of the way he must have operated is given by someone who worked under him at the Radio Warfare Establishment at Watton, Norfolk, just after the war:

[4]
Letter from
Jennifer Smeed
to the author,
31st March 1993.

Of course, Mr Baillie was a much superior person to myself (a 'Sprog' Pilot Officer), and so one scarcely had any direct conversation with him, but I did attend meetings where he was …and I always remember he would sit throughout long arguments and discussions about how some effect was achieved, or some project pursued, with eyes closed, or looking up at the tiny piece of sky available through the skylight, arm outstretched along the top of the radiator beside him - as if oblivious to the proceedings, and then suddenly come out with a most cogent summary of the situation, and a proposal of what should be done next![5]

The three members of the Scientific Analysis Room did only investigative work and were not involved with the minute-by-minute, day-to-day

[5]
Letter from Godfrey
Frank to the author,
25th March 1993.

running of the Ops Room. They had no authority in the Ops Room but needed to have a regular presence there. This scientific trio worked very well as a team. Results of their observations led to experiments involving investigative flights by 109 Squadron (and its predecessors), and routine observations from the ground, all related to enemy radio navigation systems and methods of countering them. They were all well liked and did a good job.

Work in the Operations Room was very WAAF intensive and selection of the right staff for work in this important area was paramount. It is rumoured that, certainly in the early stages, this was carried under the personal vetting of the CO, Group Captain Addison. Those chosen performed with efficiency. Fifty years on John Whitehead, a Squadron Leader employed as an Operations Room Controller at that time, recalls:

All ranks of WAAFs were exceptionally good at their jobs, and their womanly intuitions stood them in good stead and when signals of great importance reached their particular 'phones they would call directly across the room to me instead of routing the message formally through their immediate bosses. A frequent instance which often comes to mind is the call of one Marjorie Hawke that 'F4G is on the air.' 'F4G' was the call sign of the KGr100 ground station. Its transmission indicated that aircraft were taking off and that it was attempting to contact them as an initial check that communications were OK. Otherwise a quiet and reserved girl, she was really 'set alight' when passing this message on. On my acknowledgement she would settle back to her usual quiet ways.[6]

[6] Op cit [1].

One of their number, Jennifer Smeed, gave an indication of how they were recruited:

The WAAFs in the Ops Room were known as Clerks, Special Duties. Some came from abroad, two were from Canada, three from Argentina and one had come from Brazil. All were British by birth. The early arrivals, who became NCOs, had been plotters at other RAF stations but the rest of us were recruited at our initial training units, not for any high academic achievement or radio knowledge, but having a reasonable level of intelligence and telephone competence, and, above all, the ability to keep completely silent as soon as we left the Ops Room, about the work going on there.[7]

[7] Op cit [4].

One of these early arrivals was Nancy Moss (née Hunn), who, with other personnel, was later mentioned in despatches for services to 80 Wing:

I joined up on 19th September 1939. Posted to Uxbridge I helped to plot the Battle of Britain. In September 1940 some of us were sent to 80 Wing at Garston. The work was very different from 'plotting' and new to us. We were billeted in the road leading up to Garston Ops Room site. It (Garston) was a barn-like place and we had just a part of it, not a big area. No 80 Wing was only just developing then, the work was mostly on 'meacons'. Later, when we moved to Radlett, we did other things. Our Flight Sergeant was Wade Thomas and there were four sergeants, Stronach, Bell, Hatfield, and myself. Each sergeant was in charge of a watch. I was in 'B' Watch.[8]

[8]
Interview by
the author with
Nancy Moss,
1st August 1995.

The job necessarily called for unsocial hours. There were four watches (each consisting of a Sergeant, Corporal and four/five Aircraftwomen, and were six hours in length. Lettered from 'A' to 'D' starting at 6am., thus covering the whole day, the girls moved forward one watch each day. After the fourth day they were granted 48 hours off duty. Jennifer Smeed (née Baines) describes the work:

I was on 'D' Watch under a Sergeant who was older than most of us, Mary Stronach; she was strict but kindly. We had periods of frenzied activity when all the 'phones were ringing followed by periods of quiet, when we knitted and chatted. We were known on the 'phone by initials (I was 'Johnnie Beer' in the telephone code then in use) and we knew the men at the listening stations only by their code initials - we never met although we were in regular communication. Only in the last five or so years have I discovered that a friend of ours over many years was, in fact, 'Apple Willie' from Louth Outstation![9]

[9] Op cit [4].

Above left:
Ops Room WAAFs, 'B' Watch. *N Moss*

Above right:
WAAFs marching through Radlett, during War Weapons Week, 1942. *N Moss*

For the communication of operational instructions from and to outstations, the Operations Room was divided into two Sections, 'Reports' and 'Orders':

'Reports' Section dealt with all incoming information, including that from the 'Y' Service Monitoring Station at Cheadle. Five Clerks (Special Duties) worked under the supervision of an Operations Officer. Three of them continuously received telephone reports; one maintained a permanent log and the fifth charted information for future analysis.

'Orders' Section dealt with the outgoing orders for implementing radio countermeasures. Operations Officers and the Scientific Analyst assessed the information which was passed onto 'Headache Control' for 'Orders' to be issued. There were four Clerks (Special Duties) in this Section. Each had a telephone extension from the Ops Room PBX (telephone exchange). Any action taken was displayed on 'Orders' boards making use of display plaques which could be kept up to date by moving them around as fresh information came in. Four boards were used, each of which was divided into three vertical sections for the counter-measures *Aspirin (Knickebein)*, *Bromide* ('X' System) and *Benjamin* ('Y' System). Each Clerk was responsible for one board and, therefore, a particular number of outstations. (See Figure 9) The general method of operating was as follows:

Observing any directions on the Controller's Order Board, the Clerks contacted the sites required, and passed the appropriate instructions in the following form:

'Orders here. On TX [Transmitter] 1, line up and standby on 31.3. The time is now 2125.' Or...

'Orders here. On TX 1, *Radiate* on 31.3. The time is now 2125.'

The details of all instructions were logged and 'Standby' was shown on display plaques placed on the boards which had the frequency printed black on a white background. *Radiate* was shown on the back of the plaque with the colours reversed. Familiarity with the names of the various outstations enabled discrimination to be used while 'watching' the Controller's Order Board and this avoided unnecessary duplication of telephone calls.[10]

There were two WAAFs to a table, sitting opposite each other. If one girl was absent, or had to leave her post for some reason, the other would then cope with both telephones, sometimes with great difficulty, but always, according to one observer, with great calmness. There was always a WAAF NCO in the Ops Room who would help out in any part of the room in which difficult situations arose. (See Figure 10.) At times the noise of telephone bells ringing all together became almost unbearable, but the problem was finally solved when someone suggested loading each bell with a lump of well masticated chewing gum. This not only reduced the noise but also lowered the pitch of the sound to a more musical level.

Additional telephones were connected directly from the 80 Wing switchboard to the more vitally important outstations (ie, those most often needed in a hurry); these lines did not go through the usual telephone exchanges. If Ops Room personnel requested such a call, the connection was plugged in at once and the person making it needed only to talk to set the bell (or light) working at the other end, a special arrangement having been activated by the electric current variations generated by the voice of the person calling.

[10]
PRO AIR 41/46,
Appendix 'E'.

Fig.9
'Orders' Board in
Ops. Room.

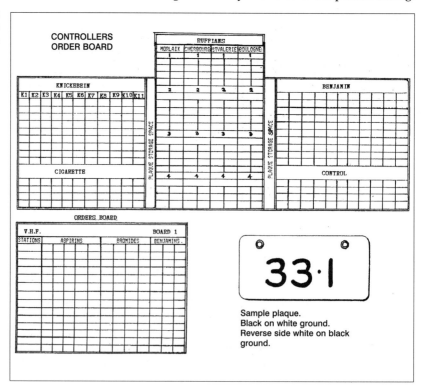

Sample plaque.
Black on white ground.
Reverse side white on black ground.

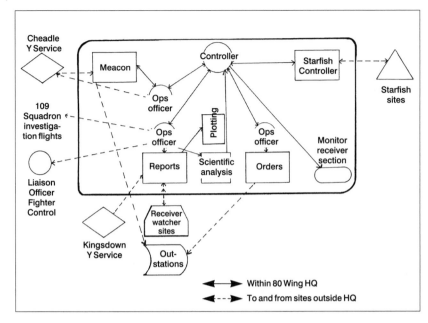

Fig.10
Chart indicating
flow of information
to and from Ops.
Room.

The Controller, with the vital help of the Operations Officers, assimilated information from all sections of 80 Wing Headquarters and outside sources and used this to plan and execute appropriate radio counter-measures. Orders Section issued the Controller's instructions to outstations who implemented the counter-measures. The Controller also gave final instructions to *Starfish* Control.

Receiver Watcher Sites sent information of signals received to Reports who passed this immediately to the Operations Officer, and sometimes directly to the Controller. This information was sifted by the Operations Officer together with that received from 'Y' Service. *Knickebein* and *Ruffian* reports were sent to the Scientific Analysts for target predictions and the formation of plans for investigation flights by 109 Squadron. Crews were interrogated on their return from these flights. The frequency and source of the *Benito* Beam and the range the signals were active were given to the Controller. He also received the results of the Scientific Analysis and any proposed flight plan. The Controller could instigate flight plans himself when he thought it appropriate. Target predictions were passed to the Liaison Officer Fighter Command who sent filtered information of all tracks of enemy aircraft to 80 Wing Headquarters where it was plotted. Meacon Control received enemy beacon activity reports from 'Y' Service. Outstations were allocated and ordered to mask the beacon. The *Starfish* Controller maintained close liaison with *Starfish* Sites and prepared a plan for suitable action using information obtained from the Plotting Table and from the Scientific Analysts.

Usually a response would come immediately from the other end. Technically these were known as 'voice operated relays' ('relay' in this instance meaning 'switch').

At times of high enemy activity over the UK, when the pressure on 80 Wing was therefore high, a 'highest priority facility' could be used without questions being asked. Priority was given over VIPs on occasions. It is said that on one occasion the Prime Minister, Winston Churchill, was highly indignant at being kept waiting until he found out the reason for it. By dialling 'London Trunks 12' and asking for whichever outstation was required they were connected immediately. This system could also operate in reverse from an outstation, as Bob Oakes-Monger, a wireless mechanic at Louth (Lincs) outstation remembers, 'If we wanted Radlett we used to ask for "London Trunks 12". If we weren't put through in 30 seconds we had to report it.'[11]

[11]
Interview by
the author with
Bob Oakes-Monger,
21st January 1993.

During the busiest period of 80 Wing's defensive activities (September 1940 to May 1941), 105 GPO Exchange Lines, 63 GPO Trunk Subscriber Circuits (including 'voice operated relays' on certain sites) and 74 'tied lines' (combined GPO and RAF network) were used at Radlett and the out-stations. This extensive use of the public network was the only possible solution to the difficult problem of providing instantaneous contact with remote outstations. In addition there was a teleprinter connection between Radlett and the 'Y' Service Station at Cheadle, also with Fighter Command HQ at Stanmore. A staff of 27 WAAFs, all of whom were vetted (due to the highly secret nature of the work), was required for the maintenance of the communications at Radlett, 19 being telephonists and six (all NCOs) teleprinter operators.[12]

[12]
PRO AIR 41/46,
Appendix 'H'.

Work in the Ops Room varied according to conditions prevailing at any given time but a basic method of working seems to have evolved. One-time Controller, John Whitehead, describes a usual day in the Ops Room; per-sonal experiences of 'Meaconing'; and other counter-measures.[13]

[13] Op cit [1].

A Typical Watch in 80 (Signals) Wing Ops Room

As far as I am able to recall the watch times during my tour of duty at Radlett (September 1940-September 1942) were as follows: 0800-1400 hours; 1400-2200 hours; 2200-0800 hours. The three watches were covered, I believe, by four Controllers so that a steady shift rotation was experienced by each Controller.

Other groups of Ops Room personnel had different shift patterns. For instance, the WAAF Clerks (Special Duties) operated on a basis of four equal shifts per day from 0001 hours to 2359 hours.

The logic behind the use of several shift patterns was that several small discontinuities in the Ops Room each 24 hours was to be preferred to one large one during the same period. The logic was certainly sound as far as the smooth running of the Ops Room was concerned, but sometimes caused alarm and despondency among people of a particular watch system who were dating others operating under a different system!

The Controller firstly studied the log book covering the period of the pre-vious watch and maybe the one before that. All being well, the morning passed comparatively peacefully, with perhaps only sporadic bouts of activ-ity. The receiving stations 'phone in, when necessary, to report changes in the characteristics of the enemy beam signals which are being received; beam signals going off and coming on; and any signals which were unusual. In fact, anything which might be considered relevant or mysterious. The outstations, both receiving and transmitting, would also put in requests for spares, and these would be sent out by despatch rider.

During the first half of the Second World War, at around midday, we would receive from Station 'X' at Bletchley Park a copy of the Luftwaffe High Command instructions to their beam transmitters for the setting up of the aerials on to the target(s) for that night, the information having been acquired by Bletchley through the courtesy of the *Enigma* de-coding machine.

We hung onto this information for as long as was prudent. It was held strictly within the confines of Ops Room until the last possible moment for security reasons and then passed on to the emergency services and hospital authorities in the general area of the target in as guarded and vague manner as we dared. 'We think you might be receiving some unwelcome attention tonight. We're not sure, but its possible. Please be prepared - in case.' was the gist of what we said. The Fire Service, in particular, was exhorted to make maximum efforts to put fires out and let us know as soon as that had been done in order that we could usefully deploy the *Starfish* sites. (Decoy fires – see Chapter Eleven.)

The outstations carried on normally with their monitoring of enemy signals. Ultimately some would report the reception of beam-type signals, and those who possessed specially equipped vans would send them out in an endeavour to locate the position of the beam or, if it was not laid within a reasonable distance, to report any variations in the nature of the signals received. This information, when put together, would usually enable us to deduce a possible position of the beam.

We could send up an aircraft, armed with our rough, (sometimes very rough!), information to find the beam and then fly along it to determine its compass bearing, and to note landmarks beneath the beam, eg towns, so that we would have a fair chance of identifying the target area. The signals which were received by the aircraft when flying just off the beam on either side would indicate whether the beam which had been found was an approach or a cross beam. For the *Knickebein* and the *X-Gerät* (rivers) system the approach beam had dots to the left and dashes to the right as the aircraft was flying towards the target, and in both cases the approach to the cross beam was through dashes. The 'Y' system, was quite different. In practice, the combination of ground station and aerial observations gave very good results. When *Enigma* failed to provide information, it proved a very adequate alternative.

One or more of our listening stations on the South Coast would report the reception of the call sign 'F4G'. This was the signature of the ground station at the Luftwaffe all-weather airfield at Vannes in the Brest Peninsula, the home base of *Kampfgruppe* 100 [KGr100], the 'pathfinders' and fire-raisers. The reception of this call-sign meant that their aircraft were airborne, and sure enough, within a minute, an aircraft would be heard responding to the German ground station; it would not be long before the first radar plots would be reported.

It was at this point that the authorities in the target area would be warned that they could expect an attack in 'n' hours and/or minutes, and at the same time all our beam jammers would be alerted. Thereafter the Ops Room would be working flat out receiving and acting on all reports from our outstations and other agencies, and igniting decoy fires should the occasion demand it.

A *Knickebein* Experience –
The Day the Italians Raided London (or Said They Did!)

This took place during my Aldenham Lodge days, in 1941, and during daylight: as a Flight Lieutenant I was in charge of the 1400-2200 hours watch. *Knickebein* beam activity was all quiet when suddenly our listening room and several outstations reported Lorenz beam-type signals on 31.6.megacycles per second. This I knew from experience was from the beam transmitter at Kleve, in Germany, close to the Dutch border. The figure of 31.6 Mc/s was unique; all the others operated on 30, 31.5 or 33.3 Mc/s. Kleve was the odd one out.

Analysis of the signals received by the other receiving stations in the south east of the UK revealed that the beam was directed over London and so I immediately set about bringing all the *Aspirins* around the Capital into action – about five I think. I was horrified to discover that all but one were unable to operate.

The outstation able to function was on Ide Hill, between Sevenoaks and Westerham in Kent. I knew this particular *Aspirin* 'looked' south in order to deal with the *Knickebeins* based in north east France and also that it was housed in a vehicle. Talking to the NCO in charge of the site I discovered that to turn the vehicle round presented no technical problem and so I instructed him to arrange for radiation to the north, ie, to cover East London and the River Thames about as far east as Gravesend. This he did.

I then telephoned around the out-of-action *Aspirins*, discovered their needs and then arranged for the required spares to be taken to them at once by despatch riders. While all this was going on, aircraft had been plotted leaving the Low Countries heading westwards towards London. The raiders had been identified as Italian Air Force aircraft.

At this point Group Captain Addison, the 80 Wing CO, walked into the Ops Room. Clearly astonished at the high level of activity in the room on a bright, sunny afternoon when hostile enemy action would normally have been nil, I gave him a brief resumé of what had happened, informed him of the steps I had taken, and showed him the entries in the log book. He said nothing, but looking very perturbed and quite angry, turned and walked away to the other side of the room where he stood with his back to me studying the *Knickebein* map.

After several seconds, I plucked up courage and crossed the room to stand behind him and said, 'Excuse me, Sir, what would you have done had you been in my position?' He turned, smiled slightly, and said, 'I would have done exactly what you have done.'

When I returned to the plotting table I noticed that the plots indicated the Italian aircraft were in the Thames Estuary. They were in the neighbourhood of Gravesend. On reaching this position they turned and returned to base. Later in the day the Italian domestic radio announced that units of the Italian Air Force had successfully raided London in broad daylight with devastating results! The Radlett plotting board showed only 'enemy aircraft' but I imagine that the Italian bombers must have met opposition from our own aircraft plus 'ack-ack' fire. Nevertheless, I like to think that the Ide Hill *Aspirin* had something to do with their retreat.

Meaconing

A 'Meacon' was simply a radio relay station made up of a receiver which was tuned to the frequency of the beacon with which it was intended to interfere, the output of the receiver being fed into a transmitter, located some distance away on another site, which would then re-radiate an exact copy of the German signal simultaneously. Any aircraft attempting to use the German beacon for navigation purposes would then get a faulty bearing, the degree of error depending on its distance from the beacon and its meacon. The nearer it was to the Meacon, the greater would be the error.

The beauty of the system was its simplicity. The Meacon just had to be left running and it would get on with its job. If the beacon's call sign happened to be changed, the meacon would automatically respond perfectly.[14]

Meaconing often demoralised Luftwaffe aircrew. I can recall more than one occasion when some 30 plus aircraft signalled frantically back to their bases that their navigation systems had gone haywire while operating over England. Some plots revealed lost aircraft leaving the country in a north easterly direction when the route home was south easterly.

The Luftwaffe became so worried about the effect of the meaconing that the German domestic radio stations were brought into action as beacons. For example, Radio Bremen transmitted a Morse 'B' superimposed on its programme at regular intervals as a means of identification, but there were times when the 600 or so kilowatts of this station were insufficient to swamp the effect of the Meacon mimicking it some 400 miles away over England – to the consternation of Luftwaffe aircrews anxious to set a course for home. Inexperienced crews were known to signal to base that their compasses were faulty, and I can recall two nights when over 30 aircraft radioed that they were experiencing navigation difficulties. Our radar plots confirmed that their fears were justified.[15]

An Example of Effective Meaconing

This particular incident concerns a flight by a Luftwaffe bomber, a Dornier Do 217, with a trainee crew and their instructor on their first night flight. Their intended flight route was to take-off from their airfield not far from Paris, pick up the medium frequency beacon near Evreux (70km – 43 miles – WNW of Paris), then fly on to the medium frequency beam near Paimpol on the north west coast of France to the west of St Malo. From there they were to fly due west along the north of the Brest Peninsula out west over the Atlantic for a given distance then back by their outward route to base.

The first part of the journey went quite well (so they thought) although strong winds were encountered over the Atlantic. At the appropriate time they turned for home and took a bearing on the Paimpol beacon. In due course they were able to discern a coastline below them which was assumed to be the North Coast of the Brest Peninsula, their direction finder having confirmed that they were on the correct bearing from Paimpol. In actual fact they were in the vicinity of Ilfracombe and at that time Paimpol was being 'meaconed' by a Meacon in the West Country (near Templecombe). Upon reaching the vicinity of that Meacon they circled it. The duty officer there telephoned me in the Ops Room at Radlett to report that an unidentified aircraft was circling his site in the semi-darkness.

Having satisfied himself that his aircraft was over the Paimpol beacon the German instructor's next task was to obtain a bearing on the beacon at Evreux some 200km (124 miles) due east of Paimpol. A satisfactory reading

[14]
John Whitehead,
letter to the author,
15th December 1992.

[15]
John Whitehead,
letter to the author,
14th September 1993.

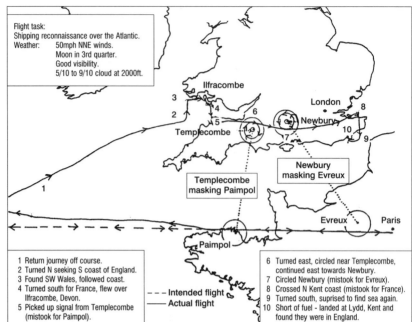

Flight task:
Shipping reconnaissance over the Atlantic.
Weather: 50mph NNE winds.
           Moon in 3rd quarter.
           Good visibility.
           5/10 to 9/10 cloud at 2000ft.

Ilfracombe

London

Newbury

Templecombe

Newbury
masking Evreux

Templecombe
masking Paimpol

Evreux   Paris

Paimpol

– – – Intended flight
———— Actual flight

Fig.11
'Lost over England'.
The Meaconing
effect.

1 Return journey off course.
2 Turned N seeking S coast of England.
3 Found SW Wales, followed coast.
4 Turned south for France, flew over
  Ilfracombe, Devon.
5 Picked up signal from Templecombe
  (mistook for Paimpol).

6 Turned east, circled near Templecombe,
  continued east towards Newbury.
7 Circled Newbury (mistook for Evreux).
8 Crossed N Kent coast (mistook for France).
9 Turned south, suprised to find sea again.
10 Short of fuel - landed at Lydd, Kent and
   found they were in England.

was obtained, but at that time Evreux was being 'meaconed' by a Meacon near Newbury, Berkshire, well to the east of the Templecombe meacon. Upon arriving there the German pilot circled the spot; again the manoeuvre was reported to me at Radlett. The German pilot then re-set his course to run further east for the run-in to base, but was soon astonished to find himself over a coastline. He convinced himself that he had unexpectedly flown to the north, and turned south. (He was, in fact, flying over the north Kent coast).

One can imagine his astonishment when, in a very short time, he found himself over the sea again; he forced himself to believe that it was the Mediterranean – some tail wind! Running short of fuel there was only one thing to do – turn back over land and make a forced descent. This was accomplished, even though the field he chose was equipped with hazards designed to prevent landings. The instructor and his crew were quite confident that they were in France. In fact they were at Lydd in Kent, a fact immediately apparent when a detachment of Home Guard appeared and took them in charge! (See Figure 11)

The Coventry *Blitz*

[16]
John Whitehead,
letter to the Author,
24th March 1993.

John Whitehead was Controller in charge of the Radlett Ops Room on the night of 14/15th November 1940, part of the *blitz* on Coventry.[16] Early in the period of mid-August to mid-November 1940, beam-type signals were first heard on the 70Mc/s band originating from the Calais and Cherbourg areas. The RAF 'Y' Service, including their 80 Wing watcher stations, did some detecting. By 24th September 1940 six beams had been identified – three at Calais; two on the Hague Peninsula; one on the Brest Peninsula.

During the beam activity, KGr100 aircraft were operational as follows:

13th August 1940 – Twenty aircraft attacked a target in Birmingham. Some bombs hit the target.

Then followed some training raids:-

September 1940 – Forty attacks by small numbers of KGr100, about half the attacks being on London.

October 1940 – The first raids in which incendiary bombs were used. KGr100 apparently practising at fire raising.

6th November 1940 – An aircraft of KGr100 crashed on the coast of southern England at Bridport, in Dorset, between the high and low watermarks and was recovered some days later while the Army and Navy squabbled over who was entitled to fish it out. Meanwhile the RAF was fuming with frustration, being aware of the importance of this particular aircraft and desperately wanting to examine its radio equipment. By the time the aircraft was eventually recovered, it was rather the worse for wear.

Then came the first big raid of Goering's 'Moonlight Sonata' (The 'Sonata' ceased after the second raid, which was on Birmingham during the next full moon period, when the Germans discovered that, although the moonlight helped their aircraft, it also helped the British night fighters.)

During the previous three months great efforts were made by all concerned in the field of counter-measures to make a full and detailed study of this new threat from every possible source of information, eg. radio listening, photo reconnaissance, prisoner of war (PoW) statements obtained under interrogation etc, and also the special communications sent out from Station 'X' at Bletchley Park as a result of decoded *Enigma* messages, plus the design and construction of jammers by the Telecommunications Research Establishment (TRE) at Malvern. The amount of investigation and preparation achieved during this time was remarkable.

By the 14th November four jammers were in place; one near Kenilworth, just south of Coventry (installed on 1st November) and three others were in place by 8th November, one near Hagley, to the west of Birmingham. The other two were at Kidsgrove (Cheshire) and Birdlip (Gloucestershire), and were not sufficiently near enough to affect the happenings at Coventry.

I was in charge of the Operations Room on the 1400-2200 watch. It was a clear, bright moonlight night. KGr100 aircraft led the attack and dropped incendiaries and flares on Coventry, followed shortly afterwards by other aircraft; the total (including KGr100) was 449. The area on fire was bombed with high explosives. There were many casualties among the population and great damage to the city.

Some Luftwaffe aircrew, who took part in the raid, when captured later in the war said that they could see Coventry clearly by the light of the flares and fires:

A red reflection is visible beyond the horizon before we even cross the coast - that must be the target! There is no need for navigation now and I vary my approach route to avoid areas with particularly massed anti-aircraft fire.[17]

I can't recall the precise details of all that happened during the watch, but I am sure it was much the usual routine – beam-type signals reported by watcher stations, exploratory flights by 109 Squadron aircraft, almost cer-

[17]
The Diving Eagle: A Ju 88 Pilot's Diary by Peter W Stahl (translated by Alex Vanags-Baginskis), p82; (William Kimber, 1984).

tainly very detailed information from Bletchley Park – all during the first part of the watch – and finally the radar plots received via HQ Fighter Command of enemy aircraft plus traffic between KGr100 and their ground station. All Meacons, *Bromides,* and *Aspirins* would be going flat out.

The order to switch on the Midland's *Bromides,* was given when I was sure that the aircraft were heading for the Midlands.

As mentioned elsewhere Group Captain Addison had the remarkable ability of arriving in the Ops Room at precisely the 'right' time. He asked particularly about the Midland's *Bromides,* and I said they had been switched on when the leading aircraft still had about 100 miles to go. He looked relieved, but neither he nor anyone else expected that they would have much effect, but they might spread the enemy's effort somewhat and so reduce the intensity a little on the actual target. It was a dreadful night for Coventry and its inhabitants with well over 500 dead and 800 plus seriously injured.

As will be imagined there was a great deal of discussion amongst the more senior Ops Room Staff and the CO in the days immediately following the raid. Criticism had been levelled at 80 Wing because the modulation frequency of the *Bromides,* was 1500Hz whereas that of the *Ruffian* beams was 2000Hz, which meant that our audible interference would not reach the enemy pilot's ears, or his on-course visual indicator, because the circuits feeding these instruments had been arranged to reject all audio tones *except* 2000Hz.

Before joining the RAF I had worked for five years at EMI and elsewhere on research and development involving radio receiver design and I put forward the view that the enemy pilots would have heard no signal at all on the final run up to the target. I was asked, 'Why?' I gave the following reasons:
- The Kenilworth and Hagley *Bromides* were on exactly the right frequency ie. the carrier wave of each was identical with that of the approach beam used by the oncoming aircraft.
- The two *Bromides* were much nearer the enemy aircraft than was the beam station far south on the Cherbourg Peninsula, and
- Our signals would overwhelm the enemy's signal and would thus virtually close down the enemy aircraft's receiver by operating its 'AGC to its fullest limit.[18]

[18]
AGC – automatic gain control, or automatic volume control. A device which automatically levels out unwanted variations in signal strength such as those known as 'fading'.

Group Captain Addison looked hopeful; the other two present had their doubts but I was subsequently proved correct. A KGr100 pilot who took part in the raid, taken prisoner later in the war said, without any prompting, that his approach beam signal disappeared on the run-in to the target and the run-in had to be concluded by guess-work.

The jamming cover was not enough for the job, and for that neither 80 Wing nor TRE were to blame. In addition, the conditions were perfect for bombing, a full moon, cloudless sky, and brilliant flares and fires. PoWs said that it was just like bombing in daylight. Follow up crews could see the flames as they were approaching over the South Coast, 150 miles away. For them navigation proved no problem.[19]

[19] Op cit [16].

The picture was very different five weeks after the Coventry raid when Birmingham was being attacked in indifferent weather conditions. By then, there were more *Bromides* in action and the jamming was very effective on both the *Ruffian* and the *Knickebein* beams. The result was that the attack lacked concentration and the overall damage was less than it would otherwise have been. From the enemy point of view the action must have been deemed a failure. A repeat attack on the following night suffered in the same way.

Kampfgruppe 100

At this time the results achieved by the Luftwaffe without the assistance of KGr100 were very poor. I remember on one occasion when Birmingham again was the target, that only 19 bombs fell in the whole of surrounding Warwickshire. KGr100, of course, was the only unit using the *X-Gerät*. The pilots and navigators of the *Gruppe* were highly skilled and could put themselves close to a target area by night without radio aids. I know of one instance to confirm quite a high degree of skill when, during a later raid on Birmingham when our jamming had been effective in that it blotted out the enemy beam and sometimes by chance created a spurious beam elsewhere, the pilot of the leading KGr100 aircraft radioed his base, 'Beam 15 kilometres to east of target', and then turned west, dropping his incendiaries right in the centre of the city. The following aircraft then 'homed' visually on to the resulting fires, with very sad results for Birmingham and its people.

The following anecdote describes the experiences of a KGr100 crew on their first operational flight:

Nervous, wondering what was in store for them, they set out on their first mission in a state of trepidation. Their worst fears were realised when, on beginning their run up to the target, an anti-aircraft shell went straight through the aircraft.

Mission completed, they turned for home but their troubles were not yet over. At 16,000ft above the New Forest, the aircraft began to break up.

One of the crew managed to bale out (I think he was the only one) and during the descent lost his Luftwaffe standard issue flying boots. As bad luck would have it, he landed in a pond in the New Forest. Drenched and bootless he hauled himself out of the pond to be confronted by a white ghost which subsequently materialised into a forest pony. He staggered away and in due course found what he was seeking – a road.

His next aim was to give himself up. This proved more difficult than expected. The first vehicle to come into view was an ambulance, driven by a lady. It stopped at his request, but when she realised what he was, she screamed, let in the clutch and sped away.

His success with several following vehicles was no better, but finally he was picked up and taken a few miles further along the road to captivity.

At his first interrogation the prisoner readily gave his name, rank and number and not so readily revealed that he belonged to KGr100 and was the "X-Gerät" operator. Beyond that he would not budge. He was adamant that he would not disclose details of the operation of the apparatus.

It was by good fortune that essential equipment from the crashed aircraft was discovered, and by even greater good fortune it was found to be intact - despite a fall from 16,000ft. At a further interview with the PoW the instrument was at first kept under wraps. He still proved unco-operative, but when it was finally put before him, he completely caved in and told all he knew.

Operations Room WAAFs

The WAAF personnel employed in the Ops Room were an integral part of the organisation. Some of them remember aspects of their time there:

Night Duty

We were very lucky to be have been posted to Radlett in such pleasant surroundings. Those going on night duty collected a soup plate of syrup or jam, another of margarine and some cheese together with bread. This was toasted over the open fire in the Ops Room when time allowed. If it was a quiet night, two or three would be allowed to go off duty on the understanding that they would be recalled if things got busy again...[20]

[20]
Eira Andrews,
letter to the author,
19th January 1993.

People

I worked on the Meacons ... Mr Wells, the Scientific Analyst, had the inner room where all the bits went on that we didn't know about ... Group Captain Addison was a very quiet man.

Secrecy

We constantly received exhortations from one particular RAF Officer to 'Keep it under your hat!'

Recruitment

I joined as a Radio Operator and when I went down to Gloucester for my recruit training on 5th June 1941, a WAAF Group Officer there had been asked by Group Captain Addison to pick 12 people for his unit. She said to me, 'Would you like this job, I can't tell you what it's about,' and that was that.

Aldenham Lodge

When we arrived at Radlett from Gloucester we could hardly get up the hill to Aldenham Lodge with all that kit and the blistering heat. At Aldenham Lodge we had cockroaches. I saw them come out of a tea urn overflow on one occasion. They were horrid.

'Newberries'

When we went into the rest room we had to bang a tray hard to get the rats to run back down their hole before we could sit down and eat our food and have a rest.

Home Comforts

I lived in Croxley Green, about eight miles from Radlett. I used to take six WAAFs home at a time and my poor mother's larder got smaller and smaller!

Off duty

We used to go for baths in some of the nearby houses (our hot water system was hopeless) and sometimes we played the 'rummy' card game with the owners. There were five of us to a room. I suppose there were 20 WAAFs in 'Heathwood'. We used to make fudge. One day when it was laid out on plates to set, an inspection took place. We had been on night duty and the curtains were drawn.[21]

[21]
Mamie Dray
interview
with the author,
27th August 1993.

Relations with HQ Staff

[22]
Brenda Scott-Tucker
letter to the author,
8th December 1993.

We might have appeared aloof to HQ Staff - it wasn't that. Security just worked out that way. Neither could we be posted – because we knew a lot! ... the Ops Room took little interest in the rest of the camp. Security was tight.[22]

Listening In

I was posted to the Ops Room at Radlett in early 1941. We received telephone calls from the many wireless outstations ranged around the East and South Coasts of England who were listening to German radio transmissions mainly on 30 and 31.5 Mc/s band, the 'Knickebein' band. They reported to us at regular intervals during the 24 hours as to whether they were receiving dots or dashes and on what frequencies. We logged these and pinned the result on a large map of the UK – blue for dashes and red for dots – so that at the end of the listening period there was a picture of the beam showing, when the two overlapped, a continuous note.

Meacon Control

In a small lobby off the main Ops Room (Aldenham Lodge), senior WAAF watch keepers operated a jamming system against the Luftwaffe homing beacons. This was known as 'Meacon Control' and involved passing instructions to one or more out-stations. Each station had a number of transmitters of varying strengths and the WAAFs known as 'Meacon Queens' became adept at knowing which transmitter could best cover the appropriate beacon. This became my favourite job in the Ops Room as you were away from the general hurly-burly of the main room! The operations were monitored by the large 'Y' Service wireless station at Cheadle.[23]

[23] Op cit [4].

Aldenham Lodge to the Rescue…

Sometimes incidents happened to Ops Room Staff, John Whitehead recalled, before they came on duty:

While stationed at 80 Wing I lived at 9 Aldenham Road, Radlett, very near its junction with Watling Street. My route to and from Aldenham Lodge took me along Watling Street a few hundred yards towards St Albans, until I reached The Drive (which I seem to remember was then an unmade road and not built on) where I turned right and up the hill to what was regarded as the back entrance to the Lodge area.

On this particular occasion I was going on duty for the watch commencing at 2200 hours and, when a little way up The Drive, I became aware of an aircraft flying very low. It was a moonlit night and, when the aircraft came into view, it was recognisable as a Wellington, flying at no more than about 700ft in circles, and clearly in trouble. Without more ado your intrepid hero rushed up the hill into Aldenham Lodge. Bursting into the Ops Room, I rushed up to the 'phone which was on the direct line to the 80 Wing Liaison Officer at Fighter Command HQ, explained the situation to him and asked if he could help. He said he thought he could.

Half an hour later he 'phoned back saying that he had put out an SOS in the Fighter Command Ops Room with the result that the 'Ack-Ack' (Anti-Aircraft) Army Liaison Officer also stationed there had responded by issuing instructions that every searchlight in the area should direct its beam to point in the direction of Northolt Airfield which was already being warned to receive the surprise visitor.

The 'Wimpey' touched down safely and thanks were sent to all who had been involved. Without wishing to emulate that Shakespearean big-head, Coriolanus who was prone to shout 'Alone, I did it!' whenever a wheeze came off, I must confess that I felt a little pleased with myself that night.[24]

[24] Op cit [3].

Chapter Five

HEADQUARTERS SUPPORT STAFF

Most of the time was taken up
with making equipment with a view to
try and stop the V-1s and V-2s.
Bill Stickland

Although emphasis of interest lies in the operational activities of 80 Wing, the work of the support services should not be overlooked. Telephone switchboards – vital, given the 'rapid communications' aspect of the work, the motor transport (MT) section which maintained and repaired the many vehicles needed with so many outstations, and feeding and accommodating the ever burgeoning staff at Radlett all played their part in the efficiency of the unit. With so many people passing through Radlett 'en route' to and from outstations there was plenty for the clerical staff to do and it requires little imagination in such an equipment-intensive operation to realise the necessity of providing adequate an workshop for its repair and manufacture. For such a high security enterprise the guarding of all the premises also required a great deal of attention. Therefore the ancillary trades had an essential contribution to make to the effectiveness of the Wing. In this chapter several of their number relate some of their experiences.

On Duty

Ken Maxey was transferred to Radlett in February 1941. Originally posted to the Air Ministry for 'Security Duties' in June 1940, he was sent to a building taken over by the Air Ministry in Bruton Street, Mayfair, in the West End of London. It was considered a good posting. Then the *blitz* began. 'From then on it became a nightmare, working every night, sometimes under a glass roof without any leave or even a weekend pass.' Thus he was employed until: *One night… there was a tremendous explosion and debris was flying about and the ceiling came down. When we pulled ourselves together we were like ghosts, covered in plaster dust and debris. One of us was knocked unconscious by a flying brick; he was the only one not wearing a tin hat. We got him to the hospital… a few minutes later Harry Roy, the band leader, arrived to check. He was warden on that particular section. He quickly produced a bottle of Scotch from his car, so the rest of the night passed reasonably well!*

After his London *blitz* experience Ken was posted, with two colleagues, to Radlett. He thought it paradise after London, 'We had a few air raid warnings and isolated bombs, but the worst incident I remember was a land mine falling in the grounds of Shenley Hospital.' Billeted about a half mile from Aldenham Lodge he initially imagined the Ops Room was being used for an early form of radar. Maxey later became the Sergeant in charge of the 12

Service Policemen at Radlett; there was little trouble:

Without doubt the two and a half years at Radlett were the best part of my six years war service. I am sure most of the personnel felt the same way. There was no excessive discipline and most 'toed the line'. We had an occasional 'Absence without Leave' which was dealt with by the Wing Commander but the officers in the administration wore 1914-1918 war ribbons and were 'Father Figures' to us.[1]

R S Diggins was involved during 1942 in maintenance work and guard duty at 'Newberries' before transferring to outstation work in the Eastern Area with the Fire and Gas Section . He visited the Ops Room from time to time in the course of his work:

One thing that on reflection does stand out in the memory is the security aspect in what was a big secret unit. On joining the unit neither I, nor anyone else on the non-technical staff, was ever told what the Wing was doing. Nor do I recall being told of the need for security. I was never told anything about the Ops Room or outstations by any of the radio operators/mechanics that one got to know quite well as a person by living with them on and off these units. They seemed naturally to keep the operational side of things to themselves. During the three years of visiting outstations no one told me directly what the unit was doing. The little I knew at the time was as the result of having to go into the Ops Room at Radlett, and seeing the 'Aspirin' and 'Bromide' boards, and then over a period of time putting two and two together and forming a rough idea of what was going on.[2]

Louise Rogers worked in the admin section at Aldenham Lodge with two typists. She was responsible for typing details of personnel and sending the information to the RAF Records Office, at Gloucester. She remembered the stationery store on the upper floor collapsing [qv]; wireless vans being dotted around the ground just prior to D-Day in June 1944 and receiving a reprimand from a superior for listening to the radio news on D-Day instead of getting on with her work. Victory for the Allies in Europe, (VE-Day) was celebrated by herself and a lorry-load of colleagues making a flushed, but happy, lorry journey between Radlett and St Albans calling at every public house on the route to drink the health of the Allied Armies.[3]

Workshops

Eric Masters worked some time in the Ops Room in 1942 after being declared unfit for further aircrew duties due to a flying accident. He spent most of the time in a plaster cast from his hip up to his neck and found it very difficult to crouch over a radio set for long periods. He spent some time at the outstation at Windlesham in Surrey but was brought back to Radlett at the Medical Officer's request due to lack of suitable medical facilities. He was employed in the extensive workshop which maintained and constructed a lot of the equipment used by 80 Wing. He described some of the work.

During the summer of 1944, shortly after the D-Day landings, a group of electronic engineers from a University in Boston, in the USA, brought to Radlett a radio transmitter designed and built by them. It had then been dismantled and shipped to Britain to be re-assembled over here under their supervision. They were a little bit dismayed on arrival in England to discover that the United States forces had no equivalent unit to 80 Wing over here, nor any experience of radio warfare. In retrospect it may be fair to say that the American High Command were too busy at this

[1]
Ken Maxey, letter to the author, 2nd December 1992.

[2]
R S Diggins, letter to the author, 7th November 1992.

[3]
Louise Rogers, interviewed on 17th November 1992.

stage of the war to be concerned with that kind of project. Whatever the reasons the Air Ministry made them welcome to our facilities at 'Newberries' and I was pleased to become a member of the crew to work with the American engineers.

The task was a big one and I had not worked on a transmitter of this size before. When completely assembled it took the whole of an RAF 60ft articulated lorry, one of the so-called 'Queen Mary's', normally used to transport our largest bombers. The trailer was fitted with a cabin for the whole of its length in which to house the transmitter, designed to jam enemy radio frequencies. On completion it was to be shipped across the Channel to France. I enjoyed the time spent working with the Americans. None had been to Britain since the outbreak of hostilities, they were astounded at the amount of damage to London and the fact that the civilians carried on seemingly unconcerned. We could have done with this equipment about four years earlier when 80 Wing was making do with borrowed diathermy machines from hospitals who could ill afford to let them go.

Shortly after this V-1s ('flying bombs') and V-2s (rockets) became a daily occurrence over London and the Home Counties and 80 Wing technical officers were keen to get hold of an intact V-1 in order to discover whether the alleged radio-control system could be interfered with in any way. In due course one, damaged but which had not exploded on impact, was delivered more or less intact (and, we hoped, in a 'safe to handle' condition!) to the workshops at 'Newberries'.

The V-1 radio-control system was a very simple and crudely constructed affair not actually designed to control the bomb whilst in flight as was previously thought but simply as a means of cutting off the fuel when it was estimated the device to be near enough to the target. It was, therefore, an indiscriminate method of bombing, but the target being London the bomb was hardly likely to miss. As the pulse transmitted in order to cut off the fuel was almost instantaneous it was virtually impossible for a counter-measure to be effective. Anyway the Germans abandoned the radio system shortly after this and relied upon a mechanical timer set at the time of launching. An interesting fact about the V-1 radio was that it had a trailing aerial of at least 100ft long, which unwound after launch - similar to our own bombers when transmitting on the lower frequencies. As for the V-2 there was no means of defence against this weapon once launched; the only hope was to bomb the launch sites.[4]

[4]
Eric Masters,
letter to the author,
17th November
1992.

Bill Stickland also worked in the workshop:

Most of the time was taken up with making equipment with a view to try and stop the V-1s and V-2s. I was making aerials to the specifications of the scientists who were on the staff and had drawn them. Some of the aerials were 8-9ft high, great tubular things.[5]

[5]
Bill Stickland,
interviewed on 21st
January 1993.

Off Duty

There was a marked contrast between life at Radlett HQ and on the outstations, with an even bigger dissimilarity when compared with usual RAF camps and aerodromes. The location was near to London and other largish centres of population such as St Albans and Watford and was blessed with a reasonable railway service to such places. Many personnel took advantage of the facilities. Those who stayed in the village had much to occupy them.

There was a local cinema. Opposite the fire station in Watling Street was the Radlett Hall, with a service canteen next door. The RAF virtually took over the 'Railway Inn' pub on the corner of Watling Street and Aldenham

Road, particularly on pay nights, where an RAF sergeant regularly played the piano. Saturday night dances were held in the Congregational Hall at the rear of the Church; an RAF band played there. Dances were also held at Aldenham Lodge. A Nissen hut was erected next to the commandeered house, 'Tintern', for use as a NAAFI. Personnel fed up with cookhouse food could visit local cafes, the Scotch Cafe in Watling Street being a particular favourite.

After three years in Bomber Command an air gunner/wireless operator, Eric Masters was transferred to Radlett. He found the transfer presented few problems in the pursuit of leisure:

The close proximity to London and St Albans with a good rail service provided a wide choice of entertainment. There was a billiards/snooker club nearby and two excellent public houses. One often met interesting people in both. The film studios at Elstree were only a few miles away and well known actors and actresses frequently drank in both pubs; they were always friendly and generous. During the warm summer days the swimming pool at Aldenham Lodge was available to everyone. On one particularly hot summer's night after a dance a mixed bathing party took place, the participants being unencumbered by clothing. The CO was not amused... Memories of candle-lit dinners at the Pea Hen Hotel in St Albans with a beautiful young girl after a visit to the cinema or theatre still linger in my mind after all these years. Some of the romances blossomed and became permanent but, as in most service units, others were transient affairs terminated by a posting or an undisclosed spouse.[6]

[6] Op cit [4].

Ken Maxey was co-opted onto the Sergeant's Mess Committee and occasionally served behind the bar when the Steward was absent: *'The Mess was well used by Senior NCOs and officers alike. It was convenient for the officers when coming off duty – their own Mess was half a mile away.'* A keen swimmer he obtained the permission of the CO for the swimming pool, which had been empty since the RAF had taken over, to be filled and used. Swimming began after the Medical Officer had chlorinated the water, 'unfortunately he overdid it and several of us came out with "Pink Eye".' Later Ken Maxey found himself in the Military Ward at Shenley Hospital suffering from pneumonia. Treatment by a new wonder drug, M&B 693, 'got me over the crisis but nearly killed me in the process. I was confined there for about eight weeks but was looked after extremely well.'[7]

[7] Op cit [1].

For some, Radlett was almost a home posting. Those whose families lived a short distance away often went home when off duty. They must have been supremely fit, the pedal cycle being the most usual means of transport. One WAAF used to cycle the 15 miles to her parents in Welwyn Garden City; on one occasion her 14 year old brother cycled the reverse journey to bring her a birthday cake on her 21st Birthday.[8] An RAF man kept a 250cc motor cycle going for as long as he could acquire petrol.[9] Another cycled every day to Harrow to visit his wife returning like most of the other Service 'Cinderellas' as the clock struck midnight.

[8] Op cit [3].

[9] Op cit [1].

There was the usual service 'lottery' of postings for personnel. One man whose home was in Radlett – his mother served in the canteen next to Radlett Hall – was posted, to Lincolnshire![10] Another, at the end of his wireless training, who asked specifically not to be posted to Radlett was posted - to Radlett!:

[10]
Bob Oakes-Monger, interviewed on 21st January 1993.

At the end of the course, I changed from ACH(UT), (Aircraft hand Under Training) to AC2 Skinner H J, Wireless/Electrical Mechanic, and was ready to join the struggle against Hitler. We all had to fill in a form asking where we wished to be posted, and I think I put down Orkney or Shetland, since I did not wish to be at the same station as my elder brother who was at Radlett. Lo and behold, in true RAF fashion, when the postings were read out I learned my destination was 80 Signals Wing at Radlett in Hertfordshire. When I arrived there the first person I bumped into in the Mess was my brother, Tim, who said I wouldn't be there long. He was right. I soon discovered that my presence was urgently required at a Detachment at Windlesham in Surrey which was, I discovered, near Sunningdale. I can remember little of Aldenham Lodge which was the Wing HQ. I think I spent one night in the Dormitory Unit on the Watford Road.[11]

[11]
H J Skinner,
letter to the author,
12th January 1993.

Chapter Six

AIR ARM ACTIVITIES

The heights by great men reached and kept
Were not attained by sudden flight,
But they, while their companions slept,
Were toiling upward in the night.
H W Longfellow (1807-1882) *The Ladder of Saint Augustine*

No 80 Wing was created as a ground controlled watching organisation. However, at the same meeting of the Night Interception Committee, in June 1940, which brought it into existence, a decision was also made to provide the new unit with an air arm. Specially equipped aircraft, with highly skilled specialist crews, were brought into use. The only personnel sufficiently trained in beam flying were the crews of the recently disbanded Blind Approach Training and Development Unit (BATDU *or* BAT&DU)).

On the 18th June 1940, to help combat the *Knickebein* menace, this unit was hastily reformed. In its life the airborne unit underwent many changes in title and establishment, and for a short time in late 1940 it was known as the Wireless Intelligence and Development Unit (WIDU). However its prime function, wide ranging operational activities in both defensive and offensive roles, remained unchanged. It formed an important part of the Wing.

By the end of 1940 the Air Arm had been increased to squadron strength and became known as 109 Squadron. In February 1941, co-incidentally with offensive attacks against the German beam transmitters at Cherbourg, a 'striking flight' was added to the establishment.

In August of the same year the squadron was increased to three flights which were employed respectively for:
1 Development of the OBOE technique
2 Investigations for the Telecommunications Research Establishment (TRE) and 'Y' Service
3 Radio counter-measures (RCM) investigation flights

No 1473 Flight
The squadron operated in this manner until July 1942 when the RCM Investigation Flight became 1473 Flight; the remaining flights being transferred to other duties unconnected with 80 Wing. In June 1943, improvement in aircraft height, speed and range and the transfer of extra personnel enabled other commitments to be undertaken which hitherto had not been possible due to the shortage of suitable aircraft.

In December 1943, with the war turning in the Allies favour, there was a growing need for investigations in connection with offensive counter-measures and 100 Group was formed to satisfy this need. No 1473 Flight became part of 192 Squadron in the new Group.

The Airborne Unit's Work

The first task for the airborne unit was to identify and plot the *Knickebein* beams on 30 Mc/s band. Avro Ansons were employed and, as the RAF had no suitable equipment, the US-manufactured Hallicrafters S.27 Receiver was used for this purpose.

The first beam was identified on 21st June 1940, by Flight Lieutenant Hal Bufton (pilot) and Corporal Dennis Mackey (Special Wireless Operator) on a flight from RAF Wyton. The early investigational routine flights were made during enemy operations against the UK in order to obtain beam settings to pass to the Operations Room at Radlett. It later became possible to obtain these settings from ground watcher stations. Flight tests were also made to ascertain the effectiveness of the *Aspirin* counter-measures and to identify new *Knickebein* beams as they became operational.

Robert Sage holding a Hallicrafters receiver used by 109 Squadron Avro Ansons to pick up enemy signal transmissions. Photograph taken at the Yorkshire Air Museum, 1993.
R Sage

Dennis Mackey, by then a Sergeant, was later killed in an aircraft crash at Oakington, near Cambridge, in November 1941, a week before he was due to be commissioned: *The aircraft, a Vickers Wellington, stalled on the circuit in bad weather. The cause of the crash was not clearly established. One version was that the ASI on this aircraft was reading 20 knots too high; said to be common knowledge amongst the Squadron crews. The second pilot was in control of the aircraft at the time: he was a recent arrival, and unaware of this defect. Another version is that flap failure was the cause of the accident. Robert Sage witnessed the whole distressing incident: 'I went out immediately to the crash site, there was no fire but amongst the crew and passengers were a complete [Short] Stirling crew being returned to Oakington from Boscombe Down and several GPO and TRE boffins who were important to the Trinity Operation. There were no survivors.'* Such was the secret nature of the work Dennis Mackey's parents had no knowledge of how he died until well after the war when they were visited by one of his wartime comrades. He was posthumously awarded the Air Force Medal in the New Year's Honours List 1942.[1]

Flights investigating *Ruffian (X-Gerät* or *Wotan I)* activity became a nightly routine. These flights were undertaken during periods of enemy activity and often under hazardous flying conditions, providing vital information often unobtainable from other sources to assist the Scientific Analysis Section at Radlett HQ then investigating this complex system. Pinpointing the beams at night to the high degree of accuracy required for this work was a most exacting navigational task.[2]

By December 1940 the existence of the *Y-Gerät (Benito* or *Wotan II)* beam was established. Some method of ground control was also discovered. Investigation flights by 109 Squadron showed two pinpoints of beam over Norfolk and a likely transmitter at Poix (near Amiens, in northern France). The flights indicated that some form of visual presentation was used.

Enemy tank-to-tank communications during the Libyan campaign of August 1941 were transmitted on 28-34 Mc/s. It was decided that the only practical way of interfering with these transmissions was by barrage jamming from airborne units using radio counter-measures. No 109 Squadron was given the task of designing, manufacturing and fitting the special aerial equipment to be used in conjunction with modified standard aircraft equipment into six 'Tropical Type' Vickers Wellingtons. The work was accomplished in a short time and, at times, bordered on the unorthodox:

A member of TRE gave technical assistance to the design... With the use of a Hoover motor it was eventually found possible to convert a general purpose transmitter to emit musical jamming tones over 28-34 Mc/s wavebands; the power came from an ASV (Air to Surface Vessel radar) alternator specially fitted into the aircraft... the hole through which the brass tube travelled was fitted with special steel rollers made to 109's specification by the local ironmonger.[3]

There were flight trials and then the aircraft were flown to Egypt, one of the crews being comprised of 109 Squadron personnel; the whole party was placed in the charge of an officer from 80 Wing. These aircraft were used extensively during the opening phases of the Libyan Campaign where, it is recorded, 'an appreciable measure of success was obtained.'

In December 1942, 1473 Flight carried out tests on an Armstrong Whitworth Whitley bomber equipped as an airborne signal station designed for

[1]
Letters to the author from R Sage, 27th November 1993 and from Bill Baguley November 1996, plus letter from John Harvey to Norman Mackenzie, 8th January 1990

[2]
PRO AIR 41/46.
Air History of No 80 (Signals) Wing, appendix 2.

[3] PRO AIR 26/580.

Part of the 109 Squadron investigative team in the Middle East. Sgt Dennis Mackey, who (with F/Lt Bufton) found the first *Knickebein* beam over Britain in 1940, joins fellow sergeants for a photograph at RAF Heliopolis, Cairo, in August 1941. Left to right: Mackey, Macfarlane, Adamson, Hazlewood and Mackenzie. *N Mackenzie*

use on Combined Operations overseas. It was to act as a Flying Repeater Station to relay wireless telegraphy (W/T) messages to distant stations, as an Emergency Ground Station to use in forward areas and as a semi-permanent Ground Signals Station. The trials 'proved in the main satisfactory. A report, with suggested modifications, was submitted to the Air Ministry.' It is not known whether it was used. In addition, many other miscellaneous activities were undertaken, some of which are listed below:

1   Investigation of enemy interference with *Splasher* (RAF Bomber Command navigational aid).
2   Examination of the effective range of Allied radio installations.
3   Investigation of a prisoner of war (PoW) statement that good bearings could be obtained on the supposedly 'masked' Droitwich BBC transmitter.
4   Flights were made to investigate the possible use of certain BBC transmitters as navigational aids to enemy aircraft launching V-1s.
5   Testing the effects of barrage balloons on VHF beams.
6   To determine whether terminal equipment at submarine cable stations radiated waves capable of being used as position indicators.
7   Assisting in *Window* (strips of aluminium dropped to simulate Allied aircraft on German radar screens) experiments.
8   Investigation of *Oboe* (RAF bombing aid) jamming for Pathfinder Force.
9   Observation flights in connection with *Starfish* (decoy fires).[4]

[4] Op cit 2

On the Offensive

In the November of 1940 it was decided that the WIDU should commence offensive action against the beam transmitters in the Cherbourg area. The unit had been engaged for some time seeking information about the *Ruffian* beams and had been working in close collaboration with the TRE, to produce a suitable technique for attacking purposes.

Two methods were considered to be practical; both would use the enemy beam for direction. The first would combine this with the 'cone of silence' (which was assumed to be vertically over the target), whilst the second combined with the observation of prominent landmarks thought, in good weather, to be easily identifiable due to the outline of the Cherbourg Peninsula.

The offensive began during the night of 14th November when two Whitleys attempted an attack on the transmitter during the large scale raid on Coventry. Both *Knickebein* and *Ruffian* ceased transmissions for a time. It was later established that at least one of them had received a direct hit. The attackers encountered considerable anti-aircraft (AA) fire and found it necessary to avoid two parallel lines of balloons which had been placed on one side of the transmitters to avoid their cables interfering with the beams.

Attacks continued throughout November and it soon became obvious to the enemy that the attackers intended to fly down the beam. Defensive measures built up, including mounted searchlights and AA guns, which could be rotated with the transmitters thereby keeping constant watch on the beam. To avoid this, care was taken when planning the flights to avoid routine procedure. Variations took place in the time of attack, and height and direction of approach, use being made of the subsidiary beams. No direct hits were sustained but 'there was ample evidence that the enemy was considerably embarrassed by these attentions.'[5]

At the end of the year WIDU became 109 Squadron, commanded by Wing Commander Hebden. An early entry in the Operations Record Book (ORB) of the Squadron indicates initial difficulties:

1.1.41. Wing Commander Cadell, Operations Staff No 80 Wing visits. Agrees to try to obtain our much awaited 'Captains of Aircraft' from the Operational Training Unit. Said the Air Ministry had been informed that none of our old flying crews are to be posted away until replacements are obtained. Our only serviceable Whitley 'de-bombed' on authority of Group Captain Addison. Special Identification Friend or Foe (IFF) fitted.[6]

Little progress was made with the acquisition of personnel during January 1941. At the end of the month another entry observes that the, 'Posting of aircrew to fill vacancies created by the revision of the Establishment continues to be affected.' Six months after Dunkirk, with the Battle of Britain still freshly etched in the memory, and the *blitz* at its peak, plus the need for these crews to be top quality specialists to carry out the work, it is perhaps, easy to see why.

Aircraft, it seems, were easier to obtain. At the beginning of December instructions were issued for eight Wellingtons to be issued to the new unit for operational work. In the next month eight Ansons and three Whitleys were added to the unit which now came under Technical Training

[5]
PRO AIR 41/46.
Air History of No 80 (Signals) Wing, part 1, paras 93-103.

[6]
PRO AIR 27/853
Operational Record Book, No 109 Squadron.

Command, Bomber Command not being prepared to accept responsibility for these aircraft.

Attacks on the enemy transmitters during the first three months of the squadron's existence were carried out by Whitleys. In February, however, a Striking Flight of four Wellingtons (with two reserves) was formed for this specific purpose. TRE had been developing more accurate methods of attack and crews had been trained under operational conditions to use them. In April, a new radar ranging device was used in two attacks which was thought to be promising but it was difficult to assess results with confidence.

The following month, as the result of collaboration between the Air Warfare Analysis Section at the Air Ministry, and the Scientific Analysis Section at 80 Wing HQ the exact position of the *Ruffian* transmitters at Morlaix was established and subsequently confirmed by photographic reconnaissance. Attacks were made on the 6th and 11th of May. After the latter raid one of the transmitters did not transmit for six days. The raid is described in the Squadron's ORB as 'successful'.[7]

The flights also provided valuable evidence of the efficiency of the BRO-MIDE counter-measures. During the period of operations (May/June) more than 50 attacks were made contributing greatly to beating the *Ruffian* system. The aircraft transported scientists (who were given RAF ranks and uniforms in case they were shot down over enemy territory and could therefore be expected to be treated as prisoners of war), special wireless operators, and others concerned with the negation of the enemy beams. Flights were also occasionally used for camouflage observation and checking on the efficiency of *Starfish* sites. Investigations made on these flights benefited RAF Bomber Command's later operations.

A considerable amount of flying for determining the directional frequencies of the beams was a regular feature of the daily operations. The crews constantly flew in danger of attack by the enemy who nearly always knew where the investigative aircraft were. Sometimes they were required to fly in foul weather when air operations would not normally be carried out. This entailed 'a high standard of flying and navigation' and was 'invaluable in obtaining the desired information.'[8]

The Squadron was kept busy. In the ten months from January to October 1941 they flew 716 flights, 298 being daylight operations and 418 at night. Midsummer saw them particularly active, making 78 night flights in May (on one occasion the CO, Wing Commander Hebden, himself went up), and 66 during June. Most of the flights during these two months, (laconically described in the official records as 'Trips on the 30s and 40sMc/s') were concerned with the *Ruffian* beams and their transmitters. *Ruffian* activity having virtually ceased by the end of June, attacks on the transmitters were discontinued.[9]

Aircrew Memories

Visibility standards were determined in vertical terms. For that purpose we had a 'Met' balloon tethered at 50ft and when that disappeared from sight we gave up![10]

Robert Sage was the last survivor of the five original, highly skilled pilots of the disbanded BATDU hastily reborn in the mid-summer of 1940 to assist

[7] Ibid.

[8] Op cit 5, para 77.

[9] Op cit 6.

[10] Wing Commander Robert Sage OBE AFC RAF, (Retd) in *Battle of the Beams* in *FlyPast* magazine (Key Publishing) August 1984. Much of the information in this section, unless otherwise noted, is taken from this feature with permission, or was later supplied by Wing Commander Sage to the author. Robert Sage died in May 1994.

in combating the German navigational beams. Recalled from an operational Handley Page Hampden squadron by 'an urgent order' he returned to Boscombe Down on 19th June. Briefed from various sources, he picked up an Anson and a new crew. The latter, four in number, consisted of first pilot (Sage), second pilot/navigator, wireless operator and air gunner. Sage made his first *Headache* flight on 22nd July 1940, and his last, after 138 operations from Boscombe Down and Wyton (where he subsequently commanded the Flight) on 29th October 1941:

We operated the Ansons at 13,000ft although any question of higher altitude was academic since the Anson was designed with Coastal Command crews in mind for skimming the wave tops. There were no refinements like cabin heating or oxygen, and the Cheetah engines had 'run out of breath' at 13,000ft anyway. I doubt whether our particular aircraft had ever been above 2,000ft before!

Without visual or electronic aids the crews of these aircraft depended largely on audio skills picked up by experience. To find the equi-signal of the enemy beams which, initially, were being used for training purposes, wasn't always easy. It would have taken much longer had it not been for the excellent advice given to the crews by the Scientific Analysis Section at 80 Wing HQ at Radlett, who gave them a good idea of what to look for.

In mid-August the Luftwaffe started night operations against the UK using both *Knickebein* and *X-Gerät*. This added urgency to the airborne investigations as it was necessary to identify the enemy's targets with great speed.

Like so many other aspects of 80 Wing's work the paramount need for secrecy brought its problems:

We were not very popular at our operating bases because of the intense secrecy surrounding our activities. We were not able to discuss them with the station staff at any level and we operated quite independently from the Station Operational Control, apart from the 'Met' Office. This of course led to rumour and suspicion.

In time, the detached unit at Wyton had its own staffed Operations Room in a caravan connected by land line to Radlett. Sage remembers only one occasion when he was required to invoke high-level support for the unit's activities over local opposition, at a fog-bound Coastal Command airfield in the north east of England.

Aircraft 'scare' stories were plentiful. The flight commander of the Wyton detachment recalls coming into land at Waddington on one occasion and lowering the hand operated flaps. Suddenly he found himself in a vertical bank amongst the station buildings:

Only one flap had lowered and I was extremely lucky to be able to recover and remain in contact with the airfield at very low level to make a landing. All the aircrew had turned out on the tarmac to witness the display of crazy flying!

The black-out at the home airfields was a big problem. With enemy raids always likely the Ansons could only use the Standard Beam Approach (SBA) and the aircraft landing light. At Wyton, currently being used as a day bomber station, in August 1940, one BATDU pilot returning from a night operation had the misfortune to strike a Bristol Blenheim on the ground and career into a second, causing serious aircraft damage but only slight personal injury. On another occasion at Boscombe Down an Anson piloted by an experienced pilot (one of the original BATDU pilots), attempting to land in fog without airfield lighting during an air raid, crashed killing all the crew.

The job was full of hazards. One relatively inexperienced pilot from the Wyton detachment was lost with his crew when their Anson flew into a barrage balloon cable near Birmingham. Here again secrecy gave rise to problems:

Considerable difficulties arose with the next-of-kin of one crew member who were determined to penetrate the secrecy surrounding the unit's role, but they could be told nothing.

The investigative flights by their very nature were often operating close to the enemy raiders (sometimes receiving very unwelcome attention from the British defences). In October 1940, Robert Sage remembered taking off from Wyton in thick fog and being 10,000ft above Suffolk monitoring the beams during an enemy attack on London:

The weather had kept all fighter aircraft on the ground so we were the only RAF aircraft airborne above East Anglia at this time. Suddenly an aircraft rose through the cloud ahead and below... it was a Heinkel 111... I decided to have a go, it was just a matter of full throttle and nose down. The Cheetah engines went faster than they had ever gone before... I managed to fire one short burst before the target disappeared back into the cloud.

On returning to Wyton the SBA receiver was found to be 'dead'. When cocking the gun Sage had accidentally knocked on the landing light switch which flattened the battery and left the aircraft with no communication with the ground:

I chose to come down by dead reckoning, but the cloud extended from 8,000ft down to around 200ft with fog beneath. There were many anxious moments before I managed to get a glimpse of the ground which enabled me to recognise a section of the A1 near Peterborough which I knew well.

A group at RAF Wyton, April 1942. Left to right: P/O E P Fernbank, F/Lt Robert Sage, a signals officer from 109 Squadron HQ at Boscombe Down, and a Post Office engineer who was working with 80 Wing. *R Sage*

Operation *Trinity*

At the beginning of the Second World War the German capital ships *Scharnhorst* and *Gneisnau* operated successfully together in the Atlantic against Allied shipping. By the time they had docked at Brest in February 1941 they had sunk 22 ships including the Royal Navy aircraft carrier, *Glorious*. In dock they became the target for many raids by the RAF. A plan was devised to bomb by beam.

The 'J' Beam (or narrow beam) was originally developed by George Baillie (*qv*) as one of the means of guiding bombers to small targets. It had been used in particular against *Ruffian* beam stations, and was similar to the SBA Lorenz type equipment. In order to obtain accuracy pilots flew along the edge of the beam and a pulse transmission, repeated back from the aircraft, measured the range. Bombing instructions could also be given in the transmission, and it was claimed that a suitably equipped aircraft flying at 10,000ft could have a useful range of about 125-150 miles.

At a Bomber Command Conference held on 6th November 1941, it was optimistically stated that it was hoped to bomb the warships with no more of an error than about 200 yards from 18,000 feet over 10/10ths cloud using the beam. No 80 Wing technicians emphasised that the ranging equipment was still experimental but Bomber Command gave approval for the plan to proceed and 3 Group allocated two squadrons of Stirlings (Nos 7 and 15) for the task. Special wireless operators were loaned from 109 Squadron for the operation, and experienced pilots from the same squadron acted as second pilots in the Stirlings.[11] Robert Sage was one of their number:

[11] PRO AIR 41/46, part 2, paras 79-82.

I took up position at Oakington on 9th November 1941 and made the first 'Trinity' training flight in Stirling N6090 with Flying Officer Parnell as captain. The policy was for the captain to make the initial take-off and climb and then to hand over control to me, in the first pilot's seat, to locate the 'J' Beam which were then pointed inland for experiment, and to practise flying on the dot edge, where experienced beam flyers had found there was greater sensitivity and accuracy.

Later test flights included ranging experiments using specially modified identification, friend or foe (IFF) sets, which received pulsed signals from radar stations on the South Coast. Because of the nature of audio scale of the signals the sets became known as 'Broody Hens'. They proved to be very unreliable operationally mainly because of a tendency to wander off frequency necessitating constant attention by the operator who had the doubtful privilege of trying to regain it by using a small screwdriver. This proved very impractical in flight, particularly when the aircraft came under fire.[12]

[12] Letter to the author from R Sage, 27th November 1993.

The first *Trinity* attack on 7th December 1941, with each aircraft carrying four 2,000lbs armour piercing bombs, was not the hoped for success. Of the five Stirlings taking part, three reported 'the track beam satisfactory' but the other two found it difficult to follow. Four of the aircraft reported heavy interference with 'Broody Hen' reception; all the signals were unintelligible, and the only aircraft able to receive both was unable to open its bomb doors over the target. Later, the suppression of radar transmission in south west England during *Trinity* operations reduced the interference. The unreliability of the 'Broody Hen' equipment was, according to official records, 'due mainly to it being worked at its extreme operational limit of range.' It was later replaced by other equipment with greater power and increased range.

Seven further attacks took place in December and early January 1942. 'The last three,' the unit history records, 'being hazardous, the enemy putting up a box barrage of great accuracy on the final run up to the target.'[13]

[13] Op cit [11].

Wing Commander Sage, who was awarded the AFC at this time, recalled the difficulties:

The tactics employed by the Stirlings involved a 15 minute final approach to the target at an accurate, predetermined, speed and height (15,000ft) in order for the ground radar stations back in England to calculate range and bomb release points. These tactics were quickly assessed by the German defence forces and anti-aircraft weapons were concentrated in the path of the approach beams giving a very hostile reception to the Stirlings.

In an attempt to counteract this, other units of Bomber Command concentrated sorties on the target at the same time as the 'Trinity' raids, many of these diversionary sorties being at lower altitude than the Stirlings.[14]

[14] Op cit [12].

The last raid took place on 26th January 1942. There were 40 individual attacks; 16 were successful from a technical point of view and there were 12 'Broody Hen' failures; no aircraft were lost.

On 12th February the two ships, accompanied by the cruiser *Prinz Eugen*, weighed anchor and slipped out of Brest. Aided by appalling flying weather, they sailed into the North Sea and, although damaged, eventually reached their German base.

Sage viewed the whole operation with mixed feelings:

It could be that the German decision to move the battleships, and therefore, their considerable threat to Atlantic shipping, was influenced by the, then, new potential threat of 'Trinity'. Some success for the operation might therefore be claimed in that respect. At any rate they remained contained in their German port and never again posed a threat.

Their departure also ended a year's embarrassing demonstration of the inaccuracy of Bomber Command's bombing techniques and the inadequacy of the armament designed for attacking armoured fighting ships.[15]

[15] Ibid.

Eric Rostron flew with Robert Sage on many of the operations as his air gunner:

...being a straight gunner I had no knowledge of what it was all about (or at least only the most rudimentary knowledge) and this applied all the time. The obvious reason being that if ever we got into enemy hands nothing could be extracted from us. We had flights every day, both during daylight and at night.

He remembered the escaping Heinkel He 111:

On the 30th January 1941, we were over Orfordness in Suffolk at about four in the afternoon. I had not seen the Heinkel and the intercom was not working... the first I knew about it we were diving down towards the Heinkel.

To my ever lasting regret the manual turret in the Anson when diving at high speed, is incapable of being turned to shoot forward. In consequence I did not fire one shot although I could see the enemy 'plane disappearing into the cloud.

and recalled a later trip over the Irish Sea:

[16]
Letter to the author
from E Rostron
2nd January 1994.

In June 1942 we went to Jurby, in the Isle of Man, and I remember throwing some metal objects out of the turret and trying to photograph them with a cine-camera. This, presumably, had something to do with the development of 'Window'.[16]

Navigator

After completing the excellent pre-war RAF training as a Trenchard 'Brat' at Halton, Joe Northrop fulfilled his ambition to become a pilot in August 1936. On 4th July 1940 Joe was a staff pilot in 'B' Squadron, No.17 Operational Training Unit (OTU) at Upwood when he was summarily posted with no explanation to a new unit at Boscombe Down. There he met a small group of people, several of whom he knew. None seemed to know why they were there. After talking to Roger Reece, Pat Hennessy and Goldsmith, Joe Northrop discovered that: *A common factor seemed to be that, with the exception of 'Goldie' and myself, all had passed through the BATDU set-up at Boscombe Down under Wing Commander Bobby Blucke shortly before the war.* [17]

Other pilots arrived including Robert Sage, George Grant (Canadian), Vic Willis, 'Butch' Cundall, Dudley Munro, Johnny Bull and Harcourt-Powell. The unit being formed was WIDU, the acting commanding officer was Hal Bufton. Joe Northrop and Goldsmith were initially there as navigators (later reverting to pilots). At the beginning Northrop crewed up with Robert Sage. It was easy, he found, to work with him: *We got on well together and quickly developed a mutual trust of each other in the air that was so vital in the peculiar circumstances under which we operated the searches.* [18]

With the acquisition of the knowledge that *Knickebein* was being used by the Luftwaffe for attacks on Britain, Sage and Northrop were sent to Wyton with a small detachment of aircraft and crews on 17th August 1940. The following night they began beam finding operations as far north as Spurn Head. As the enemy extended its beam activities: *Bobby Sage and I covered the target areas on our beam investigational flights and were helpless spectators of the bombing. During this period we lost 'Goldie' who had been with me on the St Athan Navigation Course and, like me, was acting as navigator on our second aircraft. His aircraft hit balloon barrage cables in the Midlands and all the crew were killed.* [19]

One of the Ansons was damaged by hitting the Chance light when landing in mist at Wyton, losing four to five feet of the mainplane. Northrop was very impressed by the prompt efficiency demonstrated by the Avro representative in speedily repairing the damage with a large tin of cold water glue and his tool kit!

Ground Support

Bill Baguley, a motor mechanic in civilian life, volunteered for the RAF at the outbreak of the Second World War. He became a fitter, and served at Boscombe Down and Wyton with the RCM unit:

I joined up on 5th September 1939 as a volunteer and reported to Cardington. I did my square-bashing at Martlesham Heath. In those days we formed fours. We had to wait for our courses and we were posted to various stations to assist in the hangars doing our jobs, until our courses came through. I was posted to 10 Flying Training School at Ternhill, Shropshire, on Ansons. I had been working on Ansons for about a month when I was called into the office one day and was asked about the remark 'Fit/Fit 2E U/T' on my docs. I told them the U/T meant I was 'under training'. The Flight Sergeant went purple when he found I hadn't done a course! I'd been signing certificates and all sorts of things! 'Get your kit together, you are posted.' he said.

They posted me to France and I flew over with other blokes in a Handley Page

[17] Joe, *The Autobiography of a Trenchard 'Brat'*, Joe Northrop, Square One Publications, 1993, p.129.

[18] Ibid, p.131.

[19] Ibid, p.133.

Harrow and when we got somewhere near Rheims we landed at an airfield there and for about three weeks I worked on repairing Bristol Blenheims. Then I was posted to a course at Halton. The Flight Sergeant there thought I was going to become a Fitter 1 and was very surprised when I told him that I wasn't even a Fitter 2 yet!

I was posted to Hednesford and was there when the Low Countries fell. I used to go home every weekend on my motorbike. Hednesford stank to high heaven. It was built on the edge of an escarpment and in the bottom of the escarpment was a pit. It used to smell of sulphur. You could go on parade in the morning with your buttons shining and ten minutes later they were blue! We had to live there!

After completing my Fitter 2E course at Hednesford towards the end of June 1940, I found I was posted to BAT&DU, Boscombe Down. We spent most of a day trying to find out what BAT&DU meant. Nobody could offer us a clue at all. When a course finished at Hednesford it was customary for the next entry to come into the billet and tip you out of bed. As a result of this horseplay I got a corner of a bed in the eye! My face was a mass of blood and they thought I'd lost my eye. I went down to the MO and he stitched it up and the following morning off we went to Boscombe Down.

When we got into London I had a great black eye and large pad of cotton wool and a bandage over it. As soon as we got on the Underground, people thought we had come through France (I think they were still evacuating from there at the time), and we were very popular wherever we went, with plenty of free drinks offered!

We got to Boscombe Down in the evening, I had a headache and was feeling awful. From the station we had to struggle up the hill to Boscombe. As we did so a Flight Sergeant and a Sergeant were also walking up the hill. The F/Sgt said, 'You're struggling a bit sonny, aren't you? Where are you going?' I told him 'Up to the camp' and he replied 'I know that. Which unit?' I said 'BAT&DU.' He said 'Oh, give me your kitbag then,' and picked it up and carried it for me. He turned out to be an armourer on the squadron. That was an example of the camaraderie on the unit. This 'new' unit had to be formed very quickly and was largely comprised of returnees from France. They were damn good blokes.

A mate of mine had a choker-necked tunic stitched down the back with white string and a pair of boots with no sign of a heel on them at all. He had worn those off coming across France. He wouldn't go to the stores and replace them! When these chaps did come back they were all in a sorry state but still had their kitbags. I can remember them on the square at Boscombe. We said to each other, 'These lot are for us. Look at the poor devils,' and we had a whip round and bought them some fags. We took these fags on to the square for them. One of our returning chaps opened his kitbag and said, 'Here, you have one or two!' Their kitbags were full of fags! They'd dumped all their kit in the docks when they were waiting to leave France and filled their kitbags with the NAAFI wagon's stock of fags!

I was at Boscombe Down from the end of June 1940 to February 1941. I went to Wyton on the second detachment, where I stayed until the end of July 1941. At Boscombe and Wyton we used to assist with little things (like the moving of aerials) which were not really our job but were not worth sending away to have done. We also used to move instruments around as well. It was a very 'muck-in' sort of effort.

The Armstrong Whitworth Whitleys of 'B' Flight did not seem to do a lot, although we on the Anson ('A') Flight didn't have a lot to do with them. I remember the Whitley boys adopting a rather superior attitude, owing to the fact that they had 'proper' aircraft, or so they said. In reality, we were all rather proud of these monsters, as they added to the air of mystery surrounding the unit. A Whitley flew us up to Wyton in February 1941 to relieve the ground crew lads who had been on the first 'A' Flight detachment there and were going back to Boscombe. We all got in one Whitley. I was in the co-pilot's seat (they were all fitted with dual control at the time). Johnny Bull took us; he was a marvellous bloke. I can't imagine him standing anything from anybody. On the way it snowed and ice was hitting the side of the aircraft and I remember thinking, 'God, what's that? and Johnny Bull saying, 'It's only ice. Don't worry!' Halfway there he disappeared after setting it on automatic pilot and said, 'Look after it, shan't be a minute' and went up the back to relieve himself.

Wyton was chosen for the beam flying because the beams came through East Anglia and it was easier for them to be picked up in that area. There were two squadrons, 15 and 40, at Wyton, apart from us. They had Blenheims and then they changed to Vickers Wellingtons. Later No.15 changed to Short Stirlings. I remember standing in front of the hangar and seeing the first Stirling arrive. He couldn't get the undercart down and had to land on his belly. It was a perfect landing. If I'm not mistaken it didn't even bend the props because the ground was so muddy.

The detachment from 'A' Flight, at Wyton, was very small; we had three Avro Ansons and one Vickers Wellington. I should think there would not have been more than 25 men, ground staff and aircrew. Wyton was a filthy place. Lovely buildings but no concrete. When a kite landed in the winter months it literally disappeared in a great spray of mud. With the Anson you would pull open the bomb doors (they were on elastic) and you would find a square of mud like a big clay brick and you had to force it out – it had just filled the bomb bay and gone solid. Of course, we never used the bomb bays so nobody ever looked in them.

We as groundcrews had a very good relationship with the aircrews. It was a marvellous Squadron for that when it was formed. When we had been there about a week and had got settled into the hangar and got to know our jobs we began to get to know them. There was F/Lt Bufton, he was the CO. F/O Vic Willis (he had joined as a boy and was awarded a flying scholarship at Cranwell) would often come down to the hangar and ask, 'Everything alright this morning?' when you were trying to start the engine (this took some doing when the oil was thick; the Ansons were hand starters). On one occasion he came to me and said, 'What are you going to do if it starts?' and I said 'Cheer!' and he said 'What, apart from that?' I told him I was going to do nothing else except warm it up and sign the (Form) 700. He suggested we put warmed up oil into the engine by using a five gallon drum of oil heated over a fire. I told him I didn't think it would work. There was also George Grant, Bobby Sage and Fernbank. I would say that Bobby Sage was the most gentlemanly man I ever met in the RAF. He was a marvellous man. He never shouted. Everything that came to him he dealt with. If you had a problem he would be the first to see it.

At Wyton we were a compact little unit. We had a Nissen hut and a dispersal area at the top of the aerodrome towards the St Ives road and we had just one end of a hangar in the middle of the hangar complex – two offices, a stores and a crew room. We weren't allowed to park kites in the hangar for any reason other than mechanical failure or for inspection. Our machines were parked out on the top dispersal and we had a Nissen hut with a piece of oil drum nailed to the door because it said '109' on it (that was the Director of Technical Development number of the oil). All our stuff was kept in the hut and we did most of the work up there. Anybody (and I do mean anybody!) wandering about those kites would have had their heads chopped off.

We were encouraged to fly with the aircraft we looked after if we wanted. I flew up to North Weald, Hendon, Watchfield, Radlett. I even swam in the swimming pool at Aldenham Lodge and took part in the swimming gala there. We had a damn good time there: they were nice people. Radlett aerodrome was dotted with second hand cars awaiting disposal. When there was an air raid warning the people from the factory used to push them all over the 'drome to prevent anyone landing.

I was friendly with a Special Wireless Operator at Wyton named Sgt Johnson. On the morning of 10th May 1941 they went on a 'recce' which lasted from 10am to 11.30am. When they returned we waved the kite in and he beckoned to me and said quietly, 'It's Nottingham [my home town] or Derby tonight! What are you going to do about it?' I said, 'Well, there's nothing I can do about it Johnnie. If I rang up my father or mother they would think I was mad, not knowing what we are doing. We'll just have to hope for the best.' He said, 'I was hoping you were going to say that, but keep your mouth shut about it.'

At Wyton, on particularly dark nights, we ground crews found great difficulty in keeping the aircraft to the hardened taxi tracks. We eventually devised a method of stationing spare 'bods' at regular distances apart, waving blue torches. The airman directly in front of the taxying aircraft would take his path from them. We became quite proficient after a while, regularly parking them right over the pan picket points.

On arrival, the crews would get out of the kite, get their kit together, a little pick-up would arrive and take them down to the hangar. They would then 'de-kit' in the crew room where they had lockers. The Special Wireless Operator, Observer and the pilot would go into the CO's office on the other side of the corridor and then ring Radlett and report. None of us were allowed into the corridor whilst they were in there. It wasn't guarded. We were just told not to go in there and to put up with the consequences if we did! Anyway, I don't know what we would have done if we had got the information. It was all in 'gobbledegook' and a 'scrambler' 'phone was used.

Hal Bufton was another gentleman. He was Flight Commander and was second-in-command to Wing Commander R S Blucke, whom we used to call 'Mr X'. We called him that because you would rarely see him and the buzz would go around the hangar, 'Mr X' is here!' and you would all get busy. This strange figure would amble through the hangar nodding his head at each of us in turn. That would be the last time we would see him for another month!

Bufton was a strange person to us in a lot of ways. He used to disappear at weekends. Gradually a story came out. He had come to Boscombe Down from 9 Squadron at Honington (Wellingtons). We all knew that he was definitely 'cheesed off' by the posting. He had been taken off 'ops' and given this job, which he didn't like. Of course, in those days it hadn't got going. He had been through the course at Boscombe and had been a very good pupil (as had Robert Sage) and that is why he had been selected. Bufton was shot down over France in a 9 Squadron Wellington. He evaded through Spain. What was he doing in that aircraft when he was attached to 109 Squadron? Nobody at Boscombe Down knew anything about it. Was he going on 'ops' with 9 Squadron or, was he doing what they sometimes did in those days, and take a kite full of equipment and float around France, Belgium and Holland plotting where the flak posts were? Where they got a lot of flak they would come back and report the locations. Hal Bufton also did the experimentation for 'Oboe' and was a Group Captain at the end of the war. He went to Canada after the war and died a few years ago.

I lost a good pal on that flak locating job. His name was W/O 'Tich' Allinson. He used to be Fernbank's observer but he was flying with another crew and their Wellington got shot down in 1941. He was posted missing. I discovered later that two bodies, one of which was 'Tich', were found in the 1950s at the bottom of a ditch in Holland. The original story was that he had been shot down over the Humber and not found. The rest of the crew were buried in a churchyard in Holland.

The first thing that was done in the morning was to go and get the barometric pressure for the day and adjust the altimeter. One moonlit night at Boscombe Down, in September 1940, an experienced instructor, Sgt Munro, was up in Anson R9815 doing 'circuits and bumps' training with another pilot, when there was a gathering circle of mist in the valley at Boscombe. The main runway ran along the valley with the main hangars up on the hill. The pilot came in to land, ignored his altimeter, and landed on top of the fog. All but two of the crew were killed in the crash: one was Sgt D F Allen, later awarded the George Medal for his part in the retrieval of crew members.

Georgie Grant and his mates sometimes went on a summer evening jaunt. They would come down to dispersal in a pick-up, about four of them. All armed with .22s! They would start a kite up and they would lift the central and back windows and screw them up. Then they would take position. Grant would fly along the edge of the dispersal area about six inches off the deck and they would be potting rabbits! He'd 'rev' up, get a bit of speed up, and as soon as the aircraft floated forward he would throttle back so that he could creep up on them without making a noise!

I remember Eric Rostron – 'Lofty' as we called him. He had a nasty habit of settling himself in his turret, loading the gun, pointing it to the ground on the port side and firing a quick burst. The ground crew, who were assisting air crew to enter the door on the starboard side, were not very amused. Still, I suppose it kept the laundry busy.

At the beginning of August 1941 I went back to Boscombe Down again and the following month I remember catching a chap when I was on dispersal guard there. You got a lot of civilians at Boscombe and I saw this 'civvie' on our dispersal and wondered what he was up to. I got hold of another bloke who was also on guard and we crept up on him like Red Indians. He seemed to be leaning on a kite and then he moved off to another one. We told him to stick his hands in the air and he started blustering about what he was going to get done to us. He said, 'I've got permission to be here and this is my special pass,' and started to put his hand into his inside pocket to get it out. My mate told his to get his hand out of his pocket! Anyway, we marched him down to the Officers' Mess and told Bufton what we had seen. It transpired he was official and had been testing security. What he did was tie little bits of coloured wool to the engine cowling and then he would say later, 'I've blown that one up, and that one,' and so on.

We had spot kit inspections. I never knew anyone to be caught with a camera. It was the last place on earth you would have taken one.

One Saturday afternoon at Boscombe in the autumn of 1941 I was in charge of the duty crew (two airmen) in the dispersal shed. They asked if they could go for a cup of tea. I said they could as long as they brought me one back. Normally not a soul would come along but as soon as they had gone a Squadron Leader arrived. He asked me my name and what I was doing so I told him and he said, indicating an Anson, 'Do you need your assistants to start one of these damn things up?' I said, 'No, you wiggle the throttle and I'll wind it up.' So we got it going and I asked him to sign the 700, which he did. Then he said, 'What are you going to do now?' and I replied, 'Wait until you come back!' He told me to lock the door and go with him on what he said was a local beam test run. I complied with the greatest of pleasure. The next thing I knew we were over Salisbury with that darn great spire. He said to me 'What's that?' and I replied 'Salisbury Cathedral'. We flew twice round it. We waved to a bloke who was sitting in a trapdoor halfway up it replacing slates or doing something to it. I thought he must be mad. No doubt he thought we were! Then the pilot asked me how to get back to Boscombe Down (he was supposed to be flying on a beam!). I thought that I wouldn't criticise so I said I would show him when we got to it. When we got back over the Amesbury road I said, 'That's the road there. Follow that and it will take us into Amesbury and Boscombe Down is on your right.' On the way back we passed over Old Sarum where there were aircraft all over the place. My pilot decided we would visit so he did a quick circuit and we nipped in. When we landed he said, 'Keep it running, I shan't be a minute.' I thought he'd gone to the loo. When we got back to Boscombe I asked him if I should record our trip to Old Sarum in the 700. He told me that wasn't necessary, he had only gone in there to look at the Daily Routine Orders to see where he was!

At Boscombe Down kites were parked all over the place. They were nothing to do with us as we were only 'lodgers'. We had a couple of Sergeants posted to us from Flying Training Schools where they had been flying Airspeed Oxfords. One of the them was taken up in an Anson. Later he was told to take his mate up for a bit of experience. They flew around for a bit (in R9813, see table on page 69), then came back into land. They came in at a hell of a lick between two Spitfires and wrote them both off!

On the Oxford, the brake was on the spectacle grip and you would just push your thumb on it and work right hand rudder, right hand brake. On the Anson it was a handbrake on the throttle box. If you wanted starboard brake, you pushed starboard rudder and then applied the handbrake. Of course, by the time the pilot had got into trouble he didn't know where to go for the brake. He was stripped to LAC and the last I saw of him he was washing dishes in the airmen's cookhouse.

Another unusual thing about the Anson was that it didn't have a BTH compressor air pump. You pumped up the storage tank before you took off and kept an eye on it. Anything you used was gone forever, you didn't get that back again, and the first thing you did if you landed at a strange aerodrome was to find the duty crew and get them to pump it up for you. We had a lot of trouble with the lack of these pumps from people who were unused to Ansons.

When we became 109 Squadron, on 10th December 1940, we were allocated our own kites as ground crew. The squadron letters were 'HS-'; I painted the first letters for the squadron on mine, it was 'HS-K' on R9814. We also had to paint them black underneath when they first came to us because they were either in Coastal Command colours or yellow. They had already been to Swanage, I think, to have their equipment put in.

When we started using the aircraft all sorts of places were discovered where they didn't want the equipment put. It was, 'Come with me, bring the drill, screwdriver or whatever and shift that and put it over there.' We did get to know quite a bit of what was going on, but not officially. I was friendly with 'Johnnie' Johnson and he told me quite a bit of stuff. Anyone getting into one of our aircraft wouldn't have noticed anything unusual. Instead of one desk being filled with the old TR11 for the wireless operator and the other one being empty, it would be filled with equipment too but it was only ordinary like Hallicrafters sets and things like that. Unless you were a 'gen kiddie' on radio you wouldn't have known what they were.

A way was worked out to bomb the Cherbourg knickebein transmitter. It was a *method of bombing within the blind spot so they'd hit it. They didn't find out until afterwards that this damn thing was portable. It was in a caravan and the Germans could shift it. I remember the first night it was bombed. A Whitley was used. When the crew came back they said that as they turned away from the target and started back they started rubbing their hands and saying, 'That's put it out!' but the damn thing was switched on again before they'd come over the coast. They couldn't understand it.*

I had a motorbike at Wyton for four months and nobody knew I had it there. One day the SPs came snooping around and found out about it. I was told to report to the Station Warrant Officer (SWO). I was told this when I was working at dispersal and had muddy gum boots on – it was a terribly muddy station – and was given strict instructions to report to him immediately, without changing. So off I went. SHQ had a long corridor, the floor of which you could see your face in! The SWO's office was at the other end of the entrance I had to use. I walked all the way down and knocked at his office and told him why I had come. 'Oh, you are the bloke are you. What unit are you in?' I told him 109 Squadron whereupon he threw his hands up in the air and said, 'I can't do anything with you lot. Take the station over.' I looked at him in amazement and he said, 'Just a minute before you go,' and went to the door and looked out into the corridor. 'I thought so. Par for the course. I could follow you right back to dispersal where you have come from, couldn't I? Well, don't stand there. Go and get me a bumper.' As I went along the corridor there were two blokes sitting in a cupboard which contained cleaning materials. As I went by, I said, 'the SWO wants you,' and off they went. I dived out of the door and, as I did so, I heard him shouting at them. I disappeared and never saw him again. [20]

[20]
Interview and notes given to the author by Bill Baguley, 14th June 1996.

Aircraft Used by No.80 (Signals) Wing [21]

[21]
Data taken verbatim from Air Historical Branch aircraft record cards. Entries in italics are from other sources.

Armstrong Whitworth Whitley Vs (used by BATDU at Boscombe Down 1940-1)

P4943   *Allocated BATDU 1.7.40; 20MU 5.7.40; 58 Sqn, failed to return from Hamburg 7.11.40.*

P4944   *Allocated BATDU 1.7.40; 20MU 5.7.40; 10 OTU, failed to return from Bremen 25.6.42.*

P5019   *Allocated BADU 1.7.40; A&AEE July 1940, Cat.B 20.7.40 (SS Cars Ltd), assumed returned to BADU; 27MU 25.7.41; to various OTUs until struck off charge (soc) 26.4.45.*

Avro Anson Is (used by BATDU or 1473 Flight or 109 Squadron)

L7967   *Allocated Boscombe Down 10.10.39; to Martin Hearn Ltd 25.8.40; transferred to the RCAF 12.3.41.*

L9155   *Allocated Boscombe Down 5.7.40; 109 Sqn 21.1.41, Cat.B MR (major repair) 2.6.42; 5 AOS; Soc 16.8.44.*

R3313   *Allocated BATDU 5.7.40; 109 Sqn 21.1.41; S.A.S (servicing and storage ?) Martin Hearn Ltd 9.8.41; 16 OTU. Soc 25.10.45.*

R9812   *Allocated BATDU (new from A V Roe) 23.7.40; 109 Sqn 21.1.41, coded 'HS-F'; 1473 Flt 10.7.42; 19 OTU 23.2.44; transferred to France 28.6.46.*

R9813   *Allocated BATDU 23.7.40; 109 Sqn 21.1.41; 'PSO' (presumed struck off ?); Flying accident (FA Cat.E) at Boscombe Down 24.7.41, hitting Spitfire II P8036 and Spitfire V R7337; Soc 29.7.41*

R9814   *Allocated BATDU 23.7.40; 109 Sqn 21.1.41, coded 'HS-K'; Cat.B MR 2.6.42; RIW (repair in works) Martin Hearn Ltd; 6 PAFU; 12 PAFUs. Soc 22.8.45.*

R9815   *Allocated BATDU 23.7.40; Flying Accident (Training) - crashed at Boscombe Down while landing in fog at night, 5.9.40.*

W1708   *Allocated* 109 Sqn 2.2.41; *Flying Accident* (Training) - *crashed* in *the* sea *off Lyme Regis, 27.8.41.*

W1766   *Allocated* 109 Sqn 3.9.41; 1473 Flt 10.7.42; Cat.B 20.4.43; 4 (O)AFU. Soc 12.3.45.

W1891   *Allocated to A&AEE 20.12.40; 109 Sqn 21.1.41; 1473 Flt 10.7.42; 22MU 15.7.43; to Free French forces and transferred to France 9.1.45.*

W1903   *Allocated* 109 Sqn 14.8.41; 1473 Flt 10.7.42; 515 Sqn 28.2.44, *crashed in Holland 3.5.45.*

W1904   *Allocated* 109 Sqn 9.8.41; 1473 Flt 10.7.42; 24 OTU 28.2.44, Soc 3.9.47.

Vickers Wellington ICs (used by 109 Squadron)

T2513   *Allocated WIDU (109 Sqn) 4.1.41; 109 Sqn 7.3.42 after major repair on site; 26 OTU 26.7.42; Soc 16.3.44.*

T2552   *Allocated WIDU 4.1.41; crashed when flaps retracted during landing approach to Oakington, 21.11.41, F/Lt B Hennessy and crew all killed; three buried in Cambridge City Cemetery; Soc 21.11.41, total wreck.*

T2556   *Allocated WIDU 4.1.41; S.A.S. (servicing and storage ?) 29.3.41 ref 'casualty sheet'; 45MU 28.5.41; 11 OTU. Crashed 15.10.41.*

T2558   *Allocated WIDU (109 Sqn) 1.2.41; 29 OTU 25.7.42; 14 OTU; Crashed 17.2.43.*

T2565   *Allocated WIDU 1.2.41, abandoned near Pontiuy, France 5.11.41; Soc 25.11.41 Cat.E(m). See Chapter Eight.*

T2884   *Presentation aircraft, named 'FIJI'. Allocated WIDU (109 Sqn) 4.1.41; ; 11 OTU 20.7.42; crashed 26.9.43.*

T2916   *Allocated WIDU (109 Sqn) 2.2.41, RIW (repair in works) 13.6.42 Sealand (30MU?); 48MU 30.1.43; 105 OTU. Struck off charge 1.6.44.*

Anson R9812 was delivered new from Avro to the BATDU/WIDU and was used by them and their successors, 109 Sqn & 1473 Flt. This photograph was probably taken at Boscombe Down, around 1940. It is not known quite when it carried the code 'G', though it is believed to have carried the code letters 'HS-F' when with 109 Squadron. *Late Paddy Porter collection.*

Chapter Seven

SPECIAL
WIRELESS OPERATORS

The train proved to be
one that stopped at all stations,
so there was plenty of time to
think about the possible meaning of BATDU

John Harvey[1] had enjoyed the hobby of amateur radio before the Second World War, and with many like-minded individuals his expertise was used for the war effort. One of the six original Special Wireless Operators (SWOs) in the air arm of 80 Wing, he joined the special unit ten days after Flight Lieutenant Hal Bufton and Corporal Dennis Mackey had found the *Knickebein* beam. Harvey completed 156 special duty flights; the other SWOs were equally active. He explained how he was recruited:

The first six of us were amateur radio operators and were selected, apparently, by Flight Lieutenant (later Group Captain) Rowley Scott-Farnie, also a keen amateur radio man, who had joined RAF Signals Intelligence at the outbreak of war. I am not sure how I came to be chosen, but at the Wireless School at Yatesbury an airman named Duthie came to me saying that the Secretary of the Radio Society of Great Britain, John Clarricoats, had asked him to collect the names of amateur radio operators prepared to volunteer for 'special duties'. I gave my name. Many of the others who also did so soon afterwards 'left' the RAF. Only after the war did I learn that they went into SOE (Special Operations Executive) – as civilians.

Recruitment and Training

The pre-war radio enthusiast currently employed as a RAF wireless operator walked past the chattering teleprinter at Tangmere in July 1940. He idly glanced at the message being transmitted. Cursory examination quickly changed into personal interest, Aircraftsman Harvey, it related, was being posted to BATDU at Boscombe Down. Boscombe Down was on the map, near Salisbury in Wiltshire, but what was BATDU? He asked around, nobody seemed to know.

He settled down to his wireless operating, but not for long. He was to be transferred immediately. Told to ignore the usual formality of clearing himself at the various departments of his RAF station, he quickly packed his kit. A van which had been standing by whisked him away to the local railway station to entrain for Salisbury. Speed, it seemed, was essential.

Meeting a sergeant wireless operator/air gunner also travelling to the same unit, at Salisbury railway station, failed to enlighten him. His travelling companion also knew nothing about the posting. A very puzzled airman arrived at Boscombe Down. The usual procedure at the guardroom, a sort of reverse of the clearance chit system, was also cancelled. He was told to report

[1]
Flight Lieutenant
J C Harvey, RAFVR
(Retd), who
provided most of
the information for
this chapter.

immediately to a Corporal Mackey of the Blind Approach Training and Development Unit. The meaning of the letters BATDU was now solved but why the rush to join a training unit?

He soon found out. Mackey took the new recruit well away from any buildings and people into an open space clearly to avoid being overheard, and briefly explained the job to be done, 'The Germans are using radio beams to guide their bombers to the target and we have to find out all we can about them, and try counter-measures,' he told him. Quickly Harvey learnt what that entailed for the special crews.

Introduction to the recruit's new job was immediate. 'I understand that you are an amateur radio operator. Have you ever used a Hallicrafters S.27 receiver?' asked Mackey. Harvey replied 'No'. The reply brought succinct advice and orders: 'Well, you have about one hour to learn how to use it. Here is the instruction manual. You will be flying in about two hours, so that will give you time to learn about the set. You had better get some fresh batteries from the electricians for the mains voltage vibrator converter for the S.27. When you have done that we will look at the installation of the equipment in that Anson over there.'

Thus he found himself immediately operational. Suitably fed, (production of written authority in the Airmen's Mess had provided an early tea, 'My first introduction of the special treatment for BATDU personnel') he arrived, clad in flying suit, fur-lined pigskin flying boots plus parachute harness at the Avro Anson. A look of amazement on the pilot's face greeted him, 'Why are you wearing that parachute harness, boy, don't you think I can fly this aircraft properly?' This attitude prevailed. The parachutes and harnesses were usually left in a heap by the door of the Anson. It was not surprising that the harnesses were not worn in the limited space available. They were, according to Harvey, a definite hindrance to movement while fitting the special wireless set in its position on the navigation table. Later, when seconded to a bomber squadron, Harvey was questioned about not wearing the harness and facetiously observed that he would wait until the aircraft was three feet off the ground and would then step out! 'It did not take long to learn the foolishness of such an attitude,' he later observed.

The navigator worked with his maps and equipment on his lap, sitting in the right-hand seat next to the pilot. As soon as they were airborne the new SWO was addressed by the pilot. He did not believe in wasting words, 'Just tell me where you want me to go, lad', he said, as they journeyed into the night. The new man's induction had begun.

In the November after joining the unit, an incident occurred which particularly highlighted the difficulties of navigation on these flights. Airborne, the pilot handed over the flying of the aircraft and left his seat. He had a go at tuning the beam receiver to see how the SWO was performing, but was required to return to the controls when the port engine 'died' and the Anson could not maintain a straight course. Extra equipment and one more crew member meant that the aircraft could not retain height on one engine.

The pilot decided to head for Wyton, which was nearer, rather than Boscombe Down. Instructions were given to contact this airfield, the priority procedure being used. Later the signal was upgraded to 'SOS' as the situation worsened. After a while the pilot asked the navigator, 'How far to go Nav?' The navigator was unable to tell him immediately. The request was not an easy matter for the navigator, even over England, because chasing the beams required very many changes of course, and all the changes when keeping in the beam were so quick that the navigator did not have a chance to record all the directions, so that after a three hour patrol out of sight of the ground some wireless assistance was often needed.

'Ask for the aerodrome lights,' ordered the pilot. As the aircraft dropped lower there was still no sign of them from the aircraft. Wyton direction-finding ground station, which had orders to give priority to radio counter-measures (RCM) aircraft, told them they were 'near'. Suddenly the airfield came into sight, 'a blaze of landing lights and a searchlight' John Harvey gratefully recalls. The aircraft landed on one engine, stalling momentarily in the final approach, the sudden loss of height causing the 12 volt accumulator used for the special wireless equipment to rise from the floor and land heavily and painfully on the SWO's knees.

An air of mystery was added to the night's events by the ground crew being unable to find anything wrong with the defective engine which started immediately. Various opinions were offered for its malfunction. Maybe the magneto switches to the engine had been accidentally switched off when the pilot left his seat - perhaps caught by the flyer's helmet.

Operational Activities

SWO's slept in the small BATDU crew room at Wyton when on duty. The overnight stand-by crew had to be ready in about 30 minutes and it was the SWO's responsibility to alert them when the message came through to get going and investigate beams.

Once airborne, conditions for the SWO were far from ideal. He worked in cramped confines with poor lighting on his table, plus the frequency meter pointer in the equipment he used vibrating with the aircraft making an accurate reading very difficult. Frequent changes in the aircraft's position (usually 180° turns) also complicated his work. There was a general wireless silence whenever possible, and the crews relied on picking up the Boscombe Down or Wyton beams on the special receiver to get back to base.

Everything was done on a 'need to know' basis. The main spur to the crew's enthusiasm was to predict the target, but at first only the pilot and SWO knew what the job was. To find the beam and then predict the Luftwaffe target for the coming night was the objective and in the early days when the beams were switched on early in the afternoon the prediction could be made with some confidence, but later the 'spoofing' (false beams) laid on by the enemy made prediction more difficult.

Knowing the effect their accuracy could have on Britain's defences gave the crews a sense of involvement and they always worried about the accuracy of their predictions. They were able to check up unofficially. In the Squadron Ops Room there was a wireless receiver. At about 10pm every evening the name of the city being attacked would be announced by Lord 'Haw-Haw' (the New York-born German propagandist, William Joyce, who was executed for treason after the war), on Radio Hamburg, and the radio would be tuned in to check the accuracy of their predictions. Although the unit's work was classified 'most secret' and beams were not supposed to be even heard by those not involved in the listening, it was not long before everyone knew what the object of the exercise was. The early evening flights despatched to the expected target area as the raid was developing did not return until about midnight or later, and there was, apparently, no official notification to the unit of the city under attack. There was also more work to be done during the raid to assess the efficiency of the jamming.

The crews witnessed at close range the havoc wrought by the Luftwaffe on the British cities:

We must have seen every one of the cities under attack and burning. One night there was a very large fire area in Liverpool which could still be seen when our aircraft was over Boscombe Down (in Wiltshire) some two hundred miles away. We once saw a raider shot down, near Salisbury. A burst of tracer in the dark, then a fire growing in the aircraft which gradually fell to the earth, causing one of our number to say, 'Poor bastards!' Gravity was the common enemy.

The relatively easy monitoring of the beams at the beginning of *Knickebein* did not last long; the Germans employed counter-measures against the RAF's own efforts:

The Luftwaffe expected that we would be listening to their beam transmissions, and possibly forecasting the target for that night because our jamming had started. Beam frequencies were changed and some 'spoof' transmissions sent out. There was also evidence that beam aerials were being swung while transmitting. The signals became confused - dots, dashes, and equi-signals were being heard all over the place. The SWO's log book would quickly fill up with pages of frequencies, dots, dashes, as he tried to keep up with all the incoming signals. This led to a serious failure to note that the modulation frequency (1,500 cycles per second) had been changed to 2,000. The jamming continued on 1,500, but the enemy equipment had been fitted with filters which effectively cut out the jamming and the enemy crew continued to listen to the beam on 2,000 cycles per second.

The 500 cycles per second change in the note 'should have been easily noticed' Harvey believes, but 'the SWO's had become fixated to listening to the relative strengths of the dots and the dashes' as this indicated whether the RCM aircraft was approaching the beam, (and, therefore, getting into a position to identify the target), or flying away from the beam. In the latter case it was the responsibility of the SWO to decide the point at which it was necessary to turn on to a reciprocal course and not lose valuable time. After telling the pilot to turn round he would be concentrating even harder on the relative signal strengths of dots and dashes to see whether he had made the correct decision. Therefore it came about that the change in the modulation frequency (the musical note of the beam) went unnoticed for several days – with tragic consequences to Coventry on the night of 14th/15th November 1940. The beam jamming, which was generally successful, continued on the old modulation note, but the enemy aircraft had been fitted with a sharp filter to remove the jamming signal, while the new modulation frequency came through clearly.

Six SWOs had all missed the change. This was an example of how tight security and a general reluctance to encourage discussions about the job and the different guidance systems led to unforeseen problems:

If there had been better communication and briefing of the SWOs, and the discussion of possible counter-measures the modulation frequency change could have been expected and spotted immediately. The SWOs were not qualified radio engineers but they had the experience and initiative that go with amateur radio operating, and they could have made a greater contribution if they had been given more chance to be useful. There was some professional divide between the civilian scientists with honorary RAF commissions and the first batch of wireless operators chosen for the special duties.

All of the air arm pilots were experts in Standard Beam Approach (SBA) flying. They used the local (home base) beams regularly for landing, both during the day, even in fine weather, (for practice), and at night to avoid the use of airfield lights which might attract an enemy intruder, an all too frequent occurrence in East Anglia, a short flight from the Luftwaffe bases in Holland. Although the Lorenz receiver equipment was only intended to have a range maximum of five miles, one crew found that the Hallicrafters receiver used to intercept the beams could pick up the home station from 100 miles away at an altitude of 10,000ft. This was a great advantage after a number of alterations in course while chasing the enemy beams. By listening to see whether they were in the dot or the dash sector of the home beam they knew which way to fly their aircraft and thus return home to base.

There were occasional difficulties. SWOs had a card with the SBA frequencies of various airfields in case a diversion was necessary. Changes in frequencies and new stations were notified from the Air Ministry but sometimes there was a few days delay in the notification. This caused embarrassment to one crew. Returning to Boscombe Down in bad weather from the Gatwick area south of London the beam was picked up on the Hallicrafters. They flew along it until the signal cut out, the usual indication that the aircraft was over the transmitter of its parent field, and the pilot landed without contacting flying control for landing lights to be switched on. This was the normal procedure at Boscombe Down where the controller could easily recognise the sound made by the Anson's engines. When the aircraft came to a stop the crew found themselves confronted by an armed officer re-inforced by an armoured car. He demanded an explanation, for the airfield was not Boscombe Down but Cranfield, which is located between Bedford and Milton Keynes! Subsequent enquiries revealed that the SBA at Cranfield had recently had its frequency changed to that of Boscombe Down. The date was the 15th May 1941, five days after Rudolf Hess, Adolf Hitler's Deputy, had made his peace-seeking flight to Scotland:

An unexpected and unidentified aircraft orbiting the airfield and then landing without calling flying control may have led to the expectation that the next Nazi to arrive was Hitler himself!

The experience cast some doubt on the wisdom of 'following the beam home' without breaking wireless telegraphy (W/T) silence. Normally the SBA beam was aligned into the prevailing, westerly, wind so there was not a variation in direction which could be used to identify a particular airfield. It was decided that the best way of position finding was to use the direction finding (D/F) equipment on the airfield beacons.

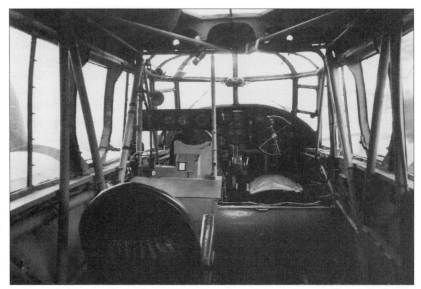

Interior of an
Avro Anson I.
Note the navigator's
table on the left
which was used by
the Special Wireless
Operator seeking
enemy beams.
*Author's photograph
courtesy of the
Imperial War
Museum, Duxford.*

There were often hair-raising moments which bore witness to the confusion of war. The special crews flew near to the enemy aircraft, although much lower, when investigating the beams and that meant that sometimes they were mistaken for them by the British defences. Mistakes were a fact of life. On an investigative flight over Calais the pilot of an Anson ordered his gunner to fire at enemy searchlights that were causing them trouble. He did so and the pilot dived away with the SWO still measuring his frequencies. They then made for Dover where there were more searchlights – this time British. On seeing them the Anson's gunner opened fire on them thinking he was back over Calais. He quickly learnt of his error. The Dover anti-aircraft (AA) guns returned fire on the RCM aircraft, throwing it over to one side. One warning shot was enough and the Anson immediately went back over the Channel – 'Never a healthy place, the Royal Navy used to shoot at any aircraft, regardless of recognition signals.' This time, however, the aircraft made it back to Boscombe Down.

On another occasion one Anson was flying at the usual height of 10,000ft investigating beams lined up on the Midlands when the pilot was told by the rear gunner that a Bristol Beaufighter was on their tail. Told to switch on the recognition signals the SWO put his right hand out into the darkness to find the switch. It wasn't there! Mindful of the four 20mm cannons of the Beaufighter – he had, apparently, previously worked in one – he quickly passed on the information that he was unable to switch on the lights and the pilot took immediate evading action. There was no further contact with the Beaufighter. The whole incident was over in 30 seconds, illustrating how a simple thing like a switch not being in the standard position could lead to disaster.

Problems of identification abounded. One night, London was the target and an Anson from Wyton was over the north east of the city close to the Thames Estuary, when an enemy aircraft was seen approaching, caught in searchlights with plenty of flak bursting around it. The Anson's gunner gave it a quick burst – the enemy aircraft was probably surprised at receiving it from the vicinity of the beam – and it made off. The Anson was now caught in the searchlights. Thus trapped it received unwelcome attention in full measure from the AA batteries guarding the capital. The gunners found the Anson, with a speed of 110 knots, an easy target. Two sets of Very lights were fired in quick succession from the aircraft in an attempt to identify itself – unfortunately they were the wrong colours for that particular day. The resourceful pilot took advantage of the Anson's ability to lose height very quickly, throttled back causing the aircraft to drop suddenly. Then the aircraft quickly left the scene!

Barrage balloons were a constant airborne hazard and the cables were often at the back of the crews mind when flying low in cloud. Indeed, RCM aircraft had been lost. Early in the beam investigation period an Anson from Wyton had collided with a barrage balloon killing all the crew including one of the original six SWOs, Henry Biggs. The flight had been ordered to take place at 1,500ft to see if beam signals could be picked up at low level. The night following the tragedy a similar flight was ordered which, fortunately, passed without untoward incident.

On another occasion a Wellington crew returning to Boscombe Down after a night sortie into Wales was given the interesting information that, according to the Observer Corps, they had flown right through the Cardiff balloon barrage! There were many occasions during the winter of 1940-41, with the enemy air activity against the UK at its peak, that 80 Wing aircraft flew through balloon barrages. The Midlands, Southampton, Bristol, Cardiff, and London balloon defences were always potential hazards when icing forced the aircraft to descend to low levels. John Harvey recalled the danger:

On one occasion, on the outskirts of Southampton, I was looking through the side windows of the Anson when I saw a balloon cable go by in broken cloud. 'Squeakers', low powered short range transmitters, were fitted to the balloons to give a squeaking warning on the standard radio frequencies. The only trouble was to know which way to go to get out of the balloon barrage when the signal was heard. Up was the best direction, but an Anson's rate of climb was not particularly fast.

The special crews became used to operating in poor weather. 'We'll have to get below the icing layer,' the pilot of an investigating Anson informed his crew, on one occasion, 'it's building up fast.' It was the late summer of 1940 and they were searching for beams coming from eastern France and had been in cloud for two hours. The engines were throttled back and the Anson lost height slowly until at 3,000ft the crew began looking for the ground. Then the whiteness of the cloud began to grow dark as the aircraft came down to the cloud base. Suddenly, ground appeared through wisps of cloud – not below, but alongside as some rocks went by close to the wing tip. They had come down into the Pennine mountains, always a hazard for aircraft blown westwards from the Vale of York and below 3,000ft.

Blessed with good fortune the aircraft had descended into one of the deep valleys. They still had problems. Coming out of the cloud they saw the head of the valley in front of them. There was no choice but to turn the aircraft round sharply in the narrow valley and this was possible with the very manoeuvrable Anson. The skill of the pilot took the crew to safety by keeping low in the valley and following it out until the observer, who had plenty of flying experience in the north of England, was able to recognise a town which he knew, and the pilot steered a course back to Wyton.

Bad weather affected most of the UK towards the end of 1940 and was particularly bad in the south. The investigating aircraft, more often than not Ansons, were in continuous cloud from take-off to landing. Sometimes at Boscombe Down the crews got lost on the grass airfield which had no metalled runways or a perimeter track to guide them. On one occasion there was a delay of 45 minutes after landing before the pilot managed to find his way to the dispersal where BATDU aircraft were parked and then to the crew room to make the report.

Pilots were skilled at landing on the beam and could manage most weather conditions and the unit lost only one aircraft in 1940 because of bad weather. However ice at altitude was a constant problem – it could form as low as 5,000ft during the winter. Another potential hazard was Beacon Hill (668ft above sea level), several miles to the north of Boscombe Down, which was close to the approach line for beam landings at the airfield.

There was always eager anticipation to feel the contact of the aircraft wheels on the ground, which occasionally occurred before the crew could see the ground when the fog was thick. The airfield landing strip lights, a powerful visual aid, would not be switched on if enemy aircraft were in the area, but Harvey remembered:

This lighting strip at Boscombe Down was sensational when it did come on, red, white and blue, in sequence along its length. We were returning from checking up on the blackout of the local town, Salisbury, when I saw it illuminated for the first time. I felt it could be seen from France. It was a great blaze of light after an hour of looking into the blackness for blackout infringements.

He also remembered the invasion scare in 1940:

...at night over East Anglia one could see numerous winking lights. Were they from enemy agents passing messages? There was some talk of shooting at them... but this was never done. No satisfactory reason was ever given for the lights. Certainly the area was feeling the jitters because of the expected invasion.

The secrecy surrounding the beam investigation work frequently manifested itself in complicated ways. Sometimes it caused extra danger to the crews. At Wyton, one SWO, having received instructions to ensure the duty aircraft was to be sent up, ran through the married quarters (at the time accommodating the WAAFs) to get to the officers' mess to rouse the pilot. He was arrested and kept in the guardroom for being in the WAAFs' quarters. Unable to state his business beyond the bounds of the privileged few he was kept incarcerated thus despite his protestations. The ordered flight did not take place from Wyton and an alternative aircraft took off from Boscombe Down. When the pilot of this SWO's aircraft found where he was lodged, his release became immediate. Senior officers were very angry about the incident and the telephone wires 'hummed'. After the incident no BATDU personnel were ever questioned or detained.

Early in August 1940, during the afternoon, one SWO on airborne patrol was told 'Search 63 Mc/s this time.' He tuned in the set between 60 and 65 megacycles expecting the usual dots and dashes. Nothing. The Luftwaffe must be trying another frequency, he thought, and tried elsewhere. Again he was unsuccessful. After about a quarter of an hour he wondered if the set was working. Hearing the usual 'hiss' and other background noise he decided to try an old favourite, 31.5 Mc/s, to check further, receiving the signal on this frequency loud and clear. 'No joy on 63 Mc/s, Skipper, but plenty on 31.5 Mc/s,' he reported to the pilot. 'You idiot – don't you know 63 Mc/s *means* 31.5 Mc/s?' was the irritable response, 'Check on that to see if we are heading to or from the beam.' This was done but there had been a considerable delay. Epitomising the old saying that 'The Road to Hell is paved with good intentions' the cause of the error was simple:

A decision had been made somewhere to double all frequencies mentioned in telephone conversations between the unit and Fighter Command for security reasons, to avoid mentioning beam frequencies. The pilot had been informed of this from HQ and knew about the arrangement, but the first time it was used no one told the SWOs about the change – an example of how security can fail by being too good.

Investigating aircraft were sometimes closely examined by other RAF aircraft not privy to the confidential function of the special flight. On one occasion an Armstrong Whitworth Whitley flying over the Channel with a Telecommunications Research Establishment (TRE) radio engineer on board, acting as a target for radar tests was 'buzzed' by a Hawker Hurricane. Were they enemy intruders from a German base in France? Rumours abounded of the Luftwaffe using captured RAF aeroplanes after the fall of France. Fortunately the Hurricane departed satisfied, without incident. Because of the need for secrecy the RCM unit's aircraft movements were not generally notified, so it was unlikely that the fighter pilot had been told to look out for a Whitley.

There were regular flights to the air firing range in Lyme Bay, off the Dorset Coast. The target, a smoke emitting float, was dropped and the pilot of the attacking Anson dived downwards firing the fixed forward firing Browning gun. As they passed, the air gunner made his contribution. There was no automatic cut out to prevent his turret-mounted gun from firing into the tail and this did happen to an aircraft from Wyton. The gun was locked in the 'rest' position when for some unknown reason it started to fire and the whole pan of ammunition was pumped into the aircraft's tail. Fortunately this aircraft made it back to base but an aircraft was lost in one of these exercises, and perhaps, this was the cause. Or maybe the aircraft just dived into the sea. It was difficult to judge altitude when flying over the sea. Anyway, it was 'just another 'plane vanished without trace – five telegrams to the next-of-kin.'

The SWO's job was not confined to listening to his wireless set! As there were not enough of the Hallicrafters receivers used for listening out for the beams to be fitted into all the aircraft they were forced, from time to time, to bundle the equipment in a replacement aircraft at short notice making electrical connections while the aircraft was climbing, sometimes working by torch light in the dark. Harvey remembered one such occasion when a faulty Anson required him:

Encumbered by flying kit to unscrew and disconnect the electrical circuits of the set and lug the gear across to another Anson. By the time I had got to it and transferred the gear the crew were all waiting to go. 'Get a move on, we should be at 10,000ft by now,' grunted the pilot. I had experienced some of this sort of thing before so I had in my pockets the necessary torch, screwdrivers, pliers, and pieces of wire ready, and the wiring was done while the aircraft was taking off and climbing, knowing that the pilot was impatiently waiting for signals before he could decide which way to go for the centre of the beam.

The SWO's extra duties sometimes extended beyond functioning as a porter/mechanic. Being of lowly rank, one of his jobs was to crank the Anson's engines (this aircraft did not have a starter motor) when ground crew were not available:

The job needed strong arms and sufficient height because the cranking had to be done at head height for a short person. The effort and the blast of the slipstream when the engine started made the job less than attractive – definitely one for a specialist in the mechanics of aeroplanes! We were expected to do all sorts of odd jobs ... but consoled ourselves with the thought that we did at least know what job the crew was really doing, while the rest of the crew, apart from the pilot, were supposed to be in ignorance for reasons of security.

Life on the station for the SWOs was hectic. They did not mix much with the rest of the personnel of the airfield and therefore took any opportunity to get off camp which presented itself, either in the air or on land. John Harvey was keen on flying and took the opportunity to indulge in any 'unofficial' flights that came along. He was often to be found in the gun turret, or helping to navigate for practice:

There was a sense of elation at just being in the aircraft and it was not difficult to find a place on an aircraft making an air test or communication flight.

Devotion to air activities did not go down well with his Signals Officer; he was never about when equipment changes and repairs were required. The flying was more fun than lugging equipment about or installing it or taking it out! He took every opportunity to increase his knowledge of flying.

Sometimes, however, 'The fun element was unexpectedly lacking.' Quickly taking advantage of an offer to go up in a Whitley late in the winter of 1940, he found himself in the front turret of the aircraft flying over Liverpool, at 20,000ft, twice the usual beam investigating height. It was bitterly cold. Ice crystals were building up all round his oxygen mask and microphone set as the Whitley staggered up to its maximum height. One of his legs became cold and then went numb; it warmed up but the condition transferred to the other lower limb. To add to his discomfort there was a continuous jet of ice cold air 'it was –40°F' coming through the openings of the turret.

An inquisitive Supermarine Spitfire arriving on the scene to see what this particular aeroplane was doing over Liverpool did little for his peace of mind. The volunteer air gunner had an urge to 'give it a squirt of Vickers gun ammo up its tail as a kind of redirected aggression,' but controlled the impulse, and the Spitfire left the scene.

Great relief was forthcoming when the Whitley dropped to a lower altitude in the process of landing, 'The warm air coming through the cracks in the turret made everything feel so warm relative to the temperature of the previous two hours. It was difficult to believe that it still was around freezing point.'

Land-based pursuits could also be hazardous. An offer from his air gunner to 'nip down to Bournemouth from Boscombe Down for a few drinks on the back of his highly-prized motor-bike' posed, on the face of it, the possibility of an interesting experience. Once, during the journey, when the rider was slowing down to take a bend, Harvey looked round his side and saw that the speedometer was registering 80mph, 'The 35 miles to Bournemouth was soon over. On the way back one's feelings were more carefree!'

If John Harvey had ever doubted the part played by luck in war he had it emphasised dramatically and tragically in the late summer of 1940. A signals expert, Flight Lieutenant Allway, came down from 80 Wing HQ to find out for himself the difficulties encountered by the SWOs. Harvey showed him how to operate the equipment and was disappointed when this officer said he could cope on his own and the SWO would not be needed for the flight. Returning from a visit to the local pub he was told the aircraft had crashed on landing at a fog-enshrouded Boscombe Down. All the crew, except the air gunner, who made a valiant attempt to rescue the occupants of the aircraft (he later was awarded the BEM), were killed.

Once the information regarding the beams was obtained the main object was to return to the base as soon as possible and make a report. With Boscombe Down in the middle of the area through which the director beams for the Midlands passed many of the investigations lasted only thirty minutes to one hour. One pilot (who later became a master-bomber in the Pathfinder Force) had mastered the technique of getting an Anson down to earth quickly by imitating the descent of a 'falling leaf', a sight which always drew an audience and was reckoned to be of sufficient interest to cause the stand-by crews to leave the card table in the crew room and come outside to watch.

In February 1941, engine trouble in a Whitley found it diverted to Abingdon. As they landed they were followed in by an enemy aircraft which dropped a stick of bombs on the airfield, killing one man. They were not the most popular people to arrive. Settled in to temporary accommodation for the night they found they were at an airfield which housed an Operational Training Unit. Extending their imaginations to the ultimate they regaled the trainee air crews with great tales of 'derring do'. They had just managed to get back from Berlin despite *flak* damage and the rear gunner was seen negotiating the sale of his 'lucky' flying jacket.

The special crews seemed to have a knack of drawing attention to themselves on the ground, perhaps it was the reaction to the secrecy of their work. In the winter of 1940 in the Boscombe Down crew room, the fire was not co-operating in spreading warmth about the place and was nearly dead. Simple. Put some aircraft 'dope' in the top of the cylindrical stove to encourage it; some was obtained from the hangar next door to the crew room and placed into it. Nothing happened for a few seconds. Then an explosion blew off the top of the stove and ejected coke 'like an erupting volcano!' The official enquiry was confined to ascertaining why one man's parachute (value

£70) had come to be rendered useless for further operations by fire – some of the hot coke cinders had landed on it.

One moonlit night, early in 1941, a Junkers Ju 88 bomber found Boscombe Down and dropped several bombs near the hangars, returning shortly after to dispose of the rest of the load. One 50kg bomb landed on the tarmac between two hangars causing slight damage, but another landed in the soil just outside the crew room. The soil absorbed the force of the explosion and the wooden hut survived. The SWO on duty went outside to take a look, and fell into the crater!

Catering in the Sergeant's mess at Boscombe Down was of high quality. The mess caterer having useful contacts with local farmers, chicken was often on the Sunday Menu. The news of this 'haute cuisine' spread to other stations. Strange aircraft appeared during the day and landed with engine trouble, fuel shortage and other excuses. The visiting crew always seemed to delay their departure until they had had a good dinner. There were, of course, some genuine cases. The greatest surprise one morning was a Wellington which had been in an air collision with a Bristol Blenheim over the Channel. The port tailplane had been destroyed entirely and the port wing curved gracefully upwards to a 30° angle at the tip. That crew had been definitely entitled to a good meal when they made their forced-landing.

Chapter Eight

PLEASE TO REMEMBER

Please to remember the Fifth of November,
Gunpowder Treason and Plot.
We know no reason why gunpowder treason
Should ever be forgot.
(Traditional since 17th century)

It is hardly likely that childhood memories of bonfires and fireworks parties figured prominently in the minds of the crew members of 109 Squadron Wellington IC T2565, as it soared, on 5th November 1941, over a blacked-out Salisbury Plain, into the dark unknown of the night. Their wartime activities had taught them to live uneasily with pyrotechnics of a greater, more frightening, intensity. This night's flight from Boscombe Down to enemy occupied Europe was yet another routine aerial investigation of Luftwaffe radio and radar beams.

To reach their targets in Germany, RAF bombers had to fly through a great defensive belt of searchlights and radar stations which worked in conjunction with the Luftwaffe night fighters. This was the so-called Kammhuber Line, named after General Josef Kammhuber, commander of the Luftwaffe night fighter force. It stretched from Norway in the north, through western Germany, Holland, Belgium and eastern France to the Swiss frontier. RAF aircrews had found it effective and accurate and a source of constant trouble. Investigative flights, carrying volunteer radar specialists from TRE, were ordered to be carried out.[1] Such was Wellington T2565's mission.

Nearly two hours after take-off things started to go wrong with the aircraft. The oil pressure of the starboard engine of the aircraft dropped. Pumping oil to the engine from the reserve tank did not remedy the fault. The pressure gauge fell to zero; sometime afterwards the propeller came off. Some fuel, radio equipment, and guns were jettisoned but the aircraft still could not maintain height. Just after 2030 hours, with the aircraft at 5,000ft, the Captain ordered the crew to bale out.[2] Norman Mackenzie, who as a Sergeant, was Second Pilot of the aircraft, clearly remembered the night:

All the wartime engines had their own way of going wrong. This night the oil pressure of the starboard engine failed. We tried to pump more oil in but could not restore the pressure. We did the obvious and tried to 'feather' the engine but were unsuccessful. It went on turning. It was a radial engine (the cylinders were round in a circle). Between the cylinders and the propeller was the reduction gear used to prevent the propeller going round too fast. Without lubrication the reduction gear overheated and expanded until its teeth cut through the casing causing the propeller to fly off. That type of Wellington did not have a good single engine performance. Normally on a bombing operation we could have released the bombs to make the aircraft lighter but we had extra radio equipment on board which we couldn't jettison.[3]

[1]
Most Secret War,
R V Jones, (Coronet Edition, 1979,)
pp.339-340.

[2]
AI.1(k)
correspondence,
E.40/1942, dated
20th March 1942.

[3]
Norman Mackenzie
in conversation
with the author
21st September 1993.

Its crew having departed, the Wellington carried on for several kilometres before crashing, to the east, near a farm 'Le Chene Sec' on the outskirts of the town of St Aubin d'Aubigne. The farmer's wife, standing in the doorway of the farmhouse making butter, was terrified to hear the sound of the decelerating Wellington passing low over the house. Shortly afterwards she was no doubt greatly relieved to find it had landed about 200-300 yards away from the family home on open, damp, land. On impact it burst into flames, the fire being fuelled by cartridges and oxygen bottles inside the aircraft. Finally, it exploded.

In due course German soldiers attended and guarded the wreckage for a fortnight, during which period a German general came and took photographs (for what purpose it is not known). Then the wreckage of the Wellington was removed. The soldiers taking it away left behind a small piece of padding, probably from a gun position, which was later given to Norman Mackenzie.[4]

[4] Henri Toutirais, the farmer, (who as a 16 year old in 1941 was living with his parents at the farm) in conversation with Norman and Ted Mackenzie, 14th September1984. He gave the piece of padding to Norman Mackenzie.

Parachuting brought the parting of the ways for the crew. Flying Officer Bull (pilot); Pilot Officer Grisman (navigator); Flight Sergeant Statham (rear gunner); Flight Sergeant Gannon (wireless operator); Sergeant Sheffield (mid-upper gunner); and Pilot Officer Cundall (a TRE 'boffin'), were all eventually captured by the Germans. Norman Mackenzie (second pilot) successfully evaded to Spain. (See Chapter Nine.)

Howard Cundall, the volunteer TRE radio and radar expert flying in the aircraft, remained at large in the enemy occupied territory for almost a fortnight. During this period he met an Englishwoman who lived in the area where he landed. She advised him to make for the coast and try and get a boat. Wearing the uniform of an RAF officer, hopefully for protection in the type of situation in which he now found himself, he was eventually captured near Mont St Michel on the Brittany coast gamely trying to propel a rowing boat, to which he had attached a makeshift sail, to England. 'The Germans were not pleased,' he told Norman Mackenzie after the war. 'They hung up the boat owner by his thumbs with piano wire for a few hours, presumably to discourage other boat owners from allowing their boats to disappear in similar fashion.' [5]

[5] Op cit [3].

Cundall knew a great deal concerning British radar and the Germans, had they been aware of it, had made quite a capture. But with the second pilot not figuring in their count they thought they had the entire crew in captivity. Thus followed almost four years as a prisoner of war (PoW) during which time he built a radio transmitter in his prison camp:

[6] MI9, Escape and Evasion, 1939-45, M R D Foot and J M Langley (Bodley Head Press, 1979) pp.114-5.

He (Cundall) *clearly knew a lot about wireless, and eventually became the secret wireless maintenance officer in Stalag Luft 3 at Sagan, and built a transmitter, or rather collected the parts for it; but the camp history states categorically that 'the transmitter was never assembled for use'.*

It has been suggested he sent useful intelligence data concerning German night fighter defences gleaned from captured aircrews back to England. The view has since been offered that information which was undoubtedly passed to London by Cundall from his prison camp was sent by other means than radio, such as coded letters.[6] Cundall was awarded, as a Flight Lieutenant, the AFC, in the 1942 New Year's Honour's List,[7] and was mentioned

[7] PRO AIR 26/580. No 80 (Signals) Wing Operational Record Book.

in despatches in 1947. A keen sailor, he was drowned in a post-war yachting accident in 1974.[8]

Flight Sergeant W G Statham, the rear gunner, was a man of some ingenuity, and seems to have given the German security forces plenty to think about during his captivity. On one occasion he changed identities with a soldier and was sent to Rottbach from which he escaped on 2nd June 1942. He was only at liberty for a day. In September of the same year, he and a companion escaped from their work at Gleinwitz. When detained at Kattowitz they managed to convince the police that they were Greek civilians and were allowed to proceed, only to be arrested near Cracow. During the next two and a half years Statham escaped on five occasions, his liberty varying from a few hours to six days. Twice he reached the Czech border. During the Allied advance he escaped from a marching column and met American forces 12 days later. He was awarded the BEM in 1946.[9]

Sadly, for two crew members their lives would end tragically in an act of callous, outrageous, illegality.

Two and a half years after the November night when he had given the order to the crew of the Wellington to bale out, the pilot, Flying Officer Lester 'Johnny' Bull, had become a leading tunneller in his PoW camp. Like many of the occupants of Stalag Luft III at Sagan, in Silesia, (in what was then the eastern part of Germany) he was fed up with his captivity and was contributing to an ambitious mass escape plan. After working enthusiastically on the tunnel code-named *Harry,* which he hoped would take him and many of his fellow PoWs to freedom, the time came for the escape. His friend and navigator from that November night, Pilot Officer Jack Grisman, who entered the RAF as a Boy Entrant and had achieved his ambition of becoming aircrew, was also in the camp and shared in the experience.

On 23rd March 1944, in the mid-evening, men packed into Hut 104. A mood of heady anticipation prevailed. Two hundred airmen disguised, carrying false documents and with food to sustain them on their journey assembled for last minute instructions. The tunnel, over 300ft long and two feet square, under the stove in the hut, was opened – power unknowingly donated by the Germans, lit the way. Small trolleys would convey the men to the end of the tunnel where a ladder went up to the surface.

At the top of the ladder 'Johnny' Bull worked hastily, but with difficulty, to remove the wooden cover placed over the hole. It was frozen. After he had eventually loosened it he started working on the earth and grass above. It was not long before he had made a hole and he cautiously poked his head above the snow-covered ground into the bitterly cold night. His morale plummeted. The tunnel had exited in the wrong place! Instead of being inside the cover of the wood they were out in the open in full view of a guard's post with its probing searchlight. He quickly returned down the tunnel and broke the news to the others. A quick and brief discussion between Bull and Squadron Leader Roger Bushell, the escape leader, produced a solution. A rope secured to the top of the ladder would be stretched to a spot just inside the wood where the controller, screened by a fence erected by the camp authorities and having a clear view of the guards, could signal the 'all clear' by two tugs on the rope.

[8]
Obituary,
Daily Telegraph,
15th June 1974.

[9]
Extract from
The Aeroplane, 20th
December 1946.

The delay in starting the escape, in addition to the severe weather – there was six inches of snow on the ground – and an air raid which cut off the electricity in the tunnel, plus two falls of earth, created serious problems for the escapers. However the escape went ahead as it was feared the tunnel would be discovered. Bull, having seen some 20 escapers on their way, handed over control of the rope and left to take his chance. Grisman followed later. The luck of the escapers was varied:

The tunnel was discovered after 76 PoWs had escaped. Four more were caught near the tunnel. The early discovery was due to an air raid alarm; the lights were put out and the guards doubled. The exit from the tunnel was found by the guards who had been sent to patrol while the air raid was on.[10]

[10] PRO AIR 40/2313.

One by one the Sagan escapees were rounded up and a fortnight after the escape of the 76 only three were still free. There followed, judged even by the superficial morality of war, a heinous crime. At various times and in differing places 50 of the men were shot, later being cremated in an effort to dispose of the evidence. According to information given later by a survivor, Flight Lieutenant Tonder, to an investigating team from the Special Investigation Branch of the RAF, Bull and three others were caught on foot when trying to cross the mountains on the Czechoslovakian border on 25th March and taken to Reichenberg (now Liberec). After arrest they were interrogated 'in quite a civil manner' by two Gestapo agents. The four airmen left at 0400 on 29th March 1944 and were said to have been taken back to Sagan. Urns were received at Sagan in due course and these showed them to have been cremated on 29th March 1944 at Brux, which is 50 miles west of Reichenberg.[11]

[11] Ibid.

Some 30 miles to the north, at Görlitz, Jack Grisman suffered a similar fate:

None of the other prisoners saw this party (of which Grisman was a member) leave on 6th April. The urns later received back at the Stalag showed that they were cremated at Breslau (about 95 miles east of Görlitz) on a date unspecified ... Grisman had been told 'his wife would never see him again'.[12]

[12] Ibid.

According to Wing Commander Wilfred Bowes, who headed the RAF Investigation, Bernard Baatz, Chief of Gestapo at Reichenberg signed the cremation order in respect of 'Johnny' Bull on the day previous to which he was shot and it was he who gave the order for Bull's execution.[13] Baatz was later tried and imprisoned for his war crimes including the death of 'Johnny' Bull. Grisman's murderer was never prosecuted.

[13] Minute dated 26th January 1949 in PRO AIR 40/2313.

Chapter Nine

LONG WAY HOME

I went through a cloud on the way down.
There was a jarring bump and I was sitting in this big field.
It was in the middle of the country and
there wasn't a soul to be seen, or a sound to be heard.[1]

Thus Sergeant Norman Mackenzie, second pilot of the abandoned Vickers Wellington IC T2565 (see Chapter Eight), narrowly missing landing in a nearby canal, arrived in enemy occupied Brittany in northern France. It was a cold moonlit night. As he parachuted down his mind dwelt on a Europe overrun with German soldiers; of the possibility of capture. Dumping his parachute behind a bush in a nearby dry ditch he wondered what to do next.

The first decision to make was which way to travel. North towards the Channel he had earlier flown over, or in the opposite direction? He decided to make for Spain, via the Unoccupied Zone of France. In the bright moonlight he checked his escape kit: a detailed map of France printed on silk; 2,000 Francs; a file; some chocolate and an orange. The map told him the nearest part of the Unoccupied Zone was roughly south east of where he had landed. Satisfied with his check of the inventory, he walked along a farm track until he reached a main road which, he noted, ran east-west. Carefully, hopefully, he headed into a journey that was to last four months, taking him through an unforgettable catalogue of nerve-racking experiences.

He walked along the road and a few minutes later passed a kilometre post which indicated he was near Hédé. Looking again at his map, he saw that the nearest part of Unoccupied France was just beyond Tours to the south east. That, he decided, was the direction to take.

Assuming that there might be German soldiers in Guipel, the first village he came to, Mackenzie did a detour. Later he became bolder and entered a smaller village, La Rivière. 'Getting very brave you see!' he later observed, with a chuckle. In the village a notice signed by General Stulpnagel, the Commanding General of the Area, was displayed, forbidding anyone to assist Allied escapers on pain of death. As an inducement to hand them over, a reward of 10,000-15,000 Francs for each Allied serviceman was offered to the civil population by the German authorities.

At Montreuil-sur-Ille he reached the railway line and followed it south. Somewhere between Chevaigné and Betton, overcome by fatigue, the Englishman laid down to sleep beside the railway embankment with bushes concealing him. It was light when he awoke and cold, being November. From his hiding place he observed considerable activity along a nearby road and, presuming it was caused by German military vehicles, decided to remain hidden for most of the daylight hours.

[1]
Norman Mackenzie, in conversation with the author, various dates in 1992-93. Most of the information in this chapter was provided by him unless an alternative source is stated.

At the bottom of the embankment was a brook or ditch. During the afternoon a man came along exercising an Alsatian dog. It must have smelt Mackenzie for it began to bark loudly. The wary airman was grateful the intervening ditch provided a barrier between himself and the noisy, troublesome, animal. Eventually both dog and owner departed, the dog's owner perhaps assuming that it had been barking at a rabbit.

Norman Mackenzie at the central Gunnery School, Warmwell, Dorset, August 1940.
N Mackenzie

With no real plan except to head south east, Mackenzie continued his trek. As dusk arrived, seeking shelter for the night, he knocked at a farmhouse door. He told the lady who answered of his plight but she shook her head and closed the door. Undaunted, he tried his luck at the next farm. The woman who answered his knock this time asked 'Quel Pays?' ('What country are you from?'). Mackenzie thought she said 'Quel Payez?' ('How much can you pay me?') and produced his money. This she declined and the mix-up was clarified when he told her he was 'Anglais'. She invited him in, providing him with a welcome meal of stew and calvados (a spirit made from cider). There were two children in the family. At great risk this fearless family allowed him to sleep in a big double-bed, sharing it with the two children, on condition that he left early in the morning. This he did.

Deciding that the German presence would be strong in a town the size of Rennes, Mackenzie skirted around its north east side travelling cross-country. He met one or two farmers. One gave him a shiny black anorak to cover up his stripes and the upper part of his uniform. Gratefully accepting this, he gave his benefactor a white sweater and cigarette lighter in return. A long conversation ensued. Care should be taken crossing the Fougères-Rennes road (the N12). It was well used by German Army traffic. Travelling by train would be safer.

Heeding the advice Mackenzie walked to Corps-Nuds, the nearest station. The railway was a little before the village and there was a farm there. Knocking on the door he asked once more for shelter. The farmer readily gave him a bale of straw and showed him to the cowshed. Another young man, not British, was also sleeping there. Language proved a barrier and there was no conversation between the two men. Mackenzie quickly settled down being disturbed briefly by a wandering cow which licked his face. The farmer re-tethered the animal and the tired airman was able to resume his desperately needed rest.

Next morning he walked to Corps-Nuds railway station, his knowledge that this was enemy occupied territory being emphatically re-inforced by the large number of German soldiers around. He wanted to go to Angers.

The lady in the ticket office, perhaps realising her customer was not French, told him in great detail that the railway did not go to Angers; he would have to take the train to Segré and then proceed by bus. Having bought his ticket he stood on the platform surrounded by German troops, hoping he would not be noticed.

The train arrived and he got in. As he stretched up his leg onto the step of the train from the low, ground level, platform a moment of fleeting panic gripped him as he realised he was still wearing his muddy flying boots. As he lifted himself up, they showed up shiny and black, where his trousers had rubbed them as he walked along. Fortunately nobody noticed and he got in, greatly relieved there were no Germans in his compartment although there were in the adjoining ones. In Châteaubriand, where he had to change trains, there was a wait of 40 minutes. Feeling very prominent on the station he spent most of the time in the 'Gents'.

The journey to Segré was uneventful. On his arrival he was a little unnerved to find the place alive with Germans. It seemed likely there was an army depot in the neighbourhood and that the soldiers were travelling to, or from, leave, there were so many. Nervous about waiting outside the station for the bus Mackenzie started to walk along the road. The bus came along, he waved it down, and when it stopped, he got in and asked for Angers. Due to lack of normal fuel the single-deck bus was propelled by gas made from burning charcoal. All the seats were taken. The standing passengers were packed in tight; the evading flyer joined them.

At Angers Mackenzie realised that, after two to three days in the open, he looked like a tramp and purchased a razor and shaving soap. A change of diet would also be welcome. He had had a little stew from the people he had met at the beginning of his journey, chocolate provided by the RAF, and the whole of the countryside seemed to be littered with windfall apples which he had lived upon. Now, ready for a change, he bought grapes in the street market in the town centre.

The next place to aim for was Tours. He began walking in that direction. As it was getting towards evening he knocked at another farm near the village of St Barthélémy d'Anjou, his fourth appeal for help since parachuting from the Wellington. This action heralded a change in his circumstances which would help tremendously his journey back to Britain.

The farmer, Monsieur Belloeil, did not take him in but instead asked the airman to accompany him back along the road a little way to 'La Romanerie', a large 18th century house on the edge of the village, the home of the Chatenay family, who were active in the French Resistance (see 'The Chatenays' at the end of the chapter).

The short journey to the mansion was Gallic in the extreme. Belloeil had just sold his horse and had, presumably, received a good price, for he had been celebrating in Bacchanalian fashion. With his four small children in train, the tipsy agriculturist entered the courtyard at the rear of the mansion with Mackenzie. Seeking Madame Chatenay he roared, 'Madam, Madam, I have an Englishman for you!' He was promptly silenced by an angry Victor Chatenay, who told him if the Germans arrested him he would make sure, 'the horse selling chap came along too!'

Suitably chastised, Belloeil passed on the reprimand down the line to his children saying he would kill the first one of them to utter a word! Next morning the local priest called on the Chatenays and told Victor he was aware that the English airman was in the house. He added that the whole village knew. Nobody breathed a word.[2]

Mackenzie had walked by the house earlier but, thinking it safer to accost a farmer rather than an unknown, richer man, had passed on to the farm. For the second time during his journey his experience had run counter to the advice given to aircrews who found themselves in enemy occupied territory.[3] The first was when he shared the bed with the two young children (it was thought they might talk at school or to their friends about their 'lodger' and give him away). Now he had veered away from the large house because rich families were thought to be unreliable. His treatment at 'La Romanerie' was an exception to this second rule. The Chatenays were hospitable and made a fuss of the flyer. They gave him food, then some time later, he thankfully sank into a bed (used after the war by a tall Frenchman of world renown – see 'The Chatenays') and quickly fell asleep. His hosts also knew what was required in the way of other practical help, having previously helped another airman to escape to Switzerland.[4]

Giving Mackenzie fresh clothes, identity and ration cards in the name of Maurice Normand it was agreed he should join up with the eldest son of the family, Michel, who wanted to reach England to enter the Free French forces. The advantage of having a native as a partner was not lost on the evading airman who was full of praise for him, 'He guided me and was very helpful'.

After the 'calm, friendly, kind and cheerful'[5] Englishman had been with the family for five days both were driven in a little van by Charles Poirel and Marc Deforges to Tours, on the River Loire, which was some five to ten miles from the Unoccupied Zone of France. Fortunately on this night security in the town was slack. The bridge across the river was unguarded.

After being dropped off on the north side, they walked across it, and spent the night in an hotel. They also went to the cinema where Mackenzie observed, with silent mirth, that the Germans had to keep the lights up when the newsreel (liberally interlaced with German propaganda) came on, as the audience were inclined to deliver their opinion as to its truthfulness in forceful fashion!

The Chatenays knew a man who drove a furniture pantechnicon and early the next day the two evaders met him. They climbed into his van and hid amongst the furniture just before he started on a journey towards Unoccupied France.

The line of demarcation was between Tours and Loches. When the van approached the frontier it was stopped by a German sentry. He told the driver to open the back door. The evaders hiding in the van were apprehensive and anxious for the inspection to be completed quickly so that they could be on their way. 'That's the only time in my life that my knees have knocked!' remembered Mackenzie. After what seemed an interminable amount of time the sentry expressed his satisfaction and the van was allowed across the border.

Buoyant in spirit at leaving the German-controlled 'Occupied France', the

[2] F C 'Ted' Mackenzie, a brother of Norman Mackenzie, inspected hotels on the Continent for the RAC. Letter to his family, after a conversation with Victor Chatenay at 'La Romanerie' 15th June 1967.

[3] *Secret Sunday* by Donald Darling, pp.69-70. (William Kimber, 1975).

[4] Obituary, Air Commodore P A Gilchrist DFC RCAF (Retd), *Daily Telegraph*, 11th September 1990.

[5] *Mon Journal du Temps du Malheur*, by Victor Chatenay, (Editions du Courrier de l'Ouest,1967)

travellers could not afford to drop their guard. There were many Vichy security forces acting in the Unoccupied Zone each functioning with varying degrees of efficiency and support for the powerful, all-conquering, German war machine. Particularly cunning and competent were the sadistic, detested *Milice*, who drew many of their recruits from the criminals in French Society, they:

... were Frenchmen who lived and worked in their home towns and villages, and used their local knowledge expertly... While the ordinary police might be friendly or at least neutral...the 'Miliciens' were sharp, suspicious characters wholeheartedly devoted to the bad cause and only too fully informed.[6]

Clearly the two men would still have to proceed with the utmost caution. Travelling on to Loches they left the lorry and caught a bus to Châteauroux, on the main railway line to Toulouse in the south. There were no problems. With their ration cards the two men were able to get a meal on the train. At Toulouse they spent another night in an hotel.

Being in Unoccupied France telegrams could be sent, via Switzerland, to England. Mackenzie took the opportunity to reassure his family back home, sending one to his sister:

Voyage se pour suite bien suis en bonne sante. Love Normand. (Journey is going OK. Am in good health. Love Norman). Sent on the 15th November, shortly after midday, it was delivered to his sister's home in south London five hours later, a remarkable achievement in wartime Britain. (See Figures 12, 13 and 14)

That same day Mackenzie and Michel caught the train to Perpignan:

Not, perhaps the best of places from which to run a trans-Pyreneean hiking agency. It is the nearest of the Pyreneean crossing zones into Spain and, therefore, much under observation even in times of peace.[7] as Donald Darling, diplomat and expert on the Iberian Peninsula, later wrote. As Agent *Sunday* he masterminded much of the organisation for these crossings.

Back at 'La Romanerie' they had discussed how to get across the border. The Chatenays had heard of a garage proprietor, Michel Parayre in Perpignan who could arrange it. On arrival in the town they found an hotel and booked in. The next day Michel went to see Parayre. He agreed to make the necessary arrangements but said the weather was bad in the mountains and therefore it wasn't possible to go immediately. They had to wait three weeks. Some time later, in Spain, Mackenzie spoke to an evader who had attempted to cross with another organisation at this time and his party had had to turn back with severe frostbite. It was apparent that Mackenzie and Michel had been given the correct information.

Parayre, code-named *Parker*, figures prominently in 'escape' literature and his recruitment is described by Nubar Gulbenkian, who carried out the negotiations, in his autobiography. Gulbenkian, a pro-British, wealthy, businessman, worked for British Intelligence. An Armenian neutral and therefore with freedom of movement, he arranged to meet *Parker* at a cafe in Perpignan and set up the taking of British servicemen across the border into Spain. The British would pay £40 per officer and £20 for other ranks, payment would be made according to results, and the money would be kept in

[6]
SOE in France by M R D Foot, p.120, (HMSO 1966)

[7] Op cit [3], p.27.

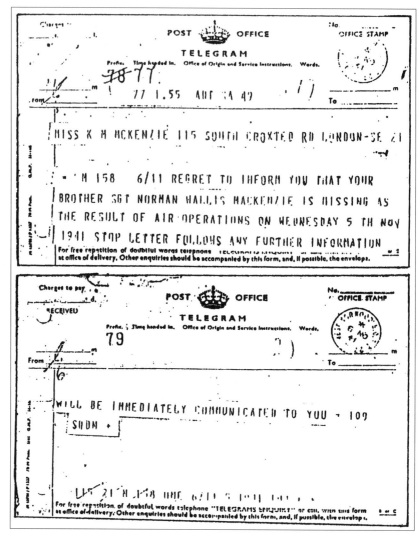

Fig.12
Telegram:
Norman Mackenzie
'Missing'.

England and paid to parker when peace returned. Evaders and escapers would attend *Parker*'s garage and he would pass them to smugglers and guides who could take them to Spain. Negotiations took 20 minutes. 'It was none of my business,' he writes, 'how much he had to pay to the men who did the work of smuggling the escapees across the frontier... He understood what was required of him and agreed to carry out his part of the bargain.'[8]

It was now that the money began to run out. Michel had given all of their money, 40,000 Francs (well above the 'going rate' it seems) for the border crossing. He had an aunt in Montpellier so he went there in an effort to obtain funds. Gaston Teisserenci obliged:

He was ready to help Michel who only asked for 2,000 Francs but Monsieur Teisserenci gave him more and was surprised to be re-imbursed several months later by an English emissary ringing at his door.[9]

[8]
Pantaraxia, by
Nubar Gulbenkian,
pp.200-201,
(Hutchinson,1965).

[9] Op cit [5].

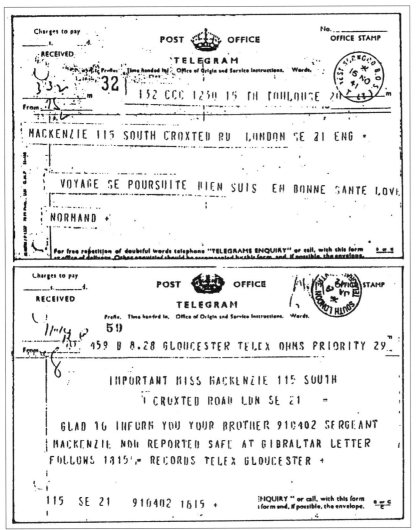

Fig.13
Telegram:
Norman Mackenzie
'Alive and Well'.

Fig.14
Telegram:
Norman Mackenzie
'Safe at Gibraltar'

Perpignan is about ten miles from the coast and a tram runs from there to the beach. Visiting the seaside one day, the two travellers walked along the beach and wondered whether rescue by sea was possible. However nothing came of it. They were unaware at the time that, indeed, people had been evacuated from this very spot. As a further antidote to their boredom they occasionally visited a bar in the centre of Perpignan. As the days ticked slowly by, the two began to wonder if Parayre would ever send them on. Other routes to Spain were considered. For instance, there was the cross-border railway at Bourg-Madame, and the Principality of Andorra might have possibilities. However, eventually, the day came when instructions were given to them to take the evening train to Banyuls and follow a man out of the station. It was dark by the time they arrived there. They found the man – then lost him! The frustrated pair booked into a nearby hotel.

The next morning two French detectives arrived at the desk to inspect the books. Mackenzie fortunately saw them arrive and told Michel. The latter went down to see them and the officers were satisfied with his story. Pleased to be conveying the good news to his companion he rushed back to what was, apparently, an empty hotel room. However when he closed the door he saw that Mackenzie had been hiding behind it.

On 10th December 1941, almost five weeks after Mackenzie had baled out from the Wellington, the two men met the guide who told them to meet him at two o'clock in the afternoon at the exit from Banyuls. This they did and joined a party of about 15 people, a mixed bunch, who neither gave nor sought information about their fellow travellers. Clearly they were all nervous. The group started along a quiet road with no traffic on it. After about three miles the guide turned off the road and started leading them over the hills. They climbed along a track to La Martine and travelled along the Coll del Tourn.

The climb up the hill was fatiguing; it was about 1,500ft high but this was the most exertion they had. The guide climbed with the agility, skill and energy of a mountain goat and the party was hard pressed to keep up with him. It was here that Mackenzie's shoes, given to him back at La Romanerie by the Chatenays, became the worse for wear and one of the soles started to come off. Fortunately he still had a piece of his parachute cord with him with which he bound up the shoe.

Then, almost before they realised it, they were in Spain, crossing over by frontier post No 593 at Puig-del-Tourn. It was still necessary to proceed with caution as the Spanish Government interned any Allied escapers or evaders captured. They started walking down the hillside through vineyards; in the dark the branches kept slapping against their faces.

Eventually they neared the railway station at Vilajuiga, on the main line to Barcelona. Relaxing in a vineyard they waited for the first train. As the time for this drew near the party made their way to the station where a new guide took over. He was a Spanish policeman and knew what was required:

Many sent over the Pyrenees were met at the railway station at Vilajuiga... by a plain clothes policeman named Eliseo Melis who, passing them off as Spanish political prisoners, took them without trouble or interference to the terminal station, thence by underground train to our Barcelona Consulate.[10]

[10] Op cit [3], p.35.

Reaching Barcelona without incident Melis took them to a cafe where they ate a roll and drank a welcome cup of coffee. Then the party split up into their different nationalities. Mackenzie and Michel went to the British Consulate, Paseo de Gracia 33, and were lodged at the flat of a chauffeur who worked there. They were cautioned by him not to make too much noise, 'as Franco people live upstairs!'

A week later a car arrived, driven probably by Agent *Monday* (another diplomat, Sir Michael Cresswell, who drove his own Sunbeam Talbot thousands of miles in Spain to assist evaders).[11] He took Mackenzie, Michel and two other passengers to the British Embassy in Madrid.

[11] Ibid pp.56-57.

On their arrival they were put in a semi-basement with 20 or more other servicemen, Army as well as RAF, anxious to return to Britain. Here, about eight weeks after he had baled out, Norman Mackenzie wallowed in the luxury of a bath. Bread was rationed, a small loaf each day, and the waiting group was required to look after itself to some extent. Breakfast was sent down from the Embassy kitchen but the waiting men made their own tea. The town was 'out of bounds' – there had been trouble previously. Some of the time was spent packing up parcels for the Internment Camp at Miranda del Ebro which the officers delivered.

Mackenzie and Michel stayed in the Embassy for the fortnight covering the Christmas and New Year period. On Christmas Day they had tea with the Ambassador, Sir Samuel Hoare, and his wife. Sir Samuel must have been overcome by festive spirit, for he had always been less than enthusiastic about diplomats aiding evaders. Eventually, Hoare was relieved of this particular group of 'embarrassments'. 'We left on a train, with a crate of oranges for food, for La Linea, the Spanish border town next to Gibraltar. We were collected there and taken to 'Gib' by road. There we had a long wait for a boat back to Britain,' Mackenzie recalled.

On 4th March 1942, Mackenzie and Michel sailed for Britain on the Polish ship the *Sobieski*, which in happier times had been a passenger liner operating between Gydnia and New York. The ship, which had only been commissioned shortly before the war, was considered fast enough to avoid U-boat attack. Therefore it sailed unescorted.

In between taking his turn at manning one of the Hotchkiss guns he celebrated his return by imbibing in the only drink available on the ship, Spanish Sherry, 'It was probably not the best, I had several headaches,' he recounted with feeling! The *Sobieski* docked at Greenock, in Scotland, on 10th March 1942, Norman Mackenzie's birthday. Four months of high adventure were over. (See Figure 15.)

Norman Mackenzie was mentioned in despatches for making this journey. Three months after docking at Greenock, having transferred to Bomber Command, he found himself, after a raid on Essen, with the rest of his crew, in a dinghy in the North Sea. They were picked up by air-sea rescue and taken to Gorleston, on the Norfolk coast. He possesses a *Daily Mail* photograph recording the event. Described as an 'exceptional' pilot by one CO, he transferred to the RAF Pathfinders when they were formed in August, 1942, and flew with them until January 1943 when he joined 627 Squadron flying de Havilland Mosquitos. In April 1944 the squadron was detached on loan to 5 Group for low level marking. Their work was recognised in June 1944 when, after commenting on the improved accuracy of the bombing operations for the month, tribute was paid to 'the pilots of 627 Squadron who have gone in low to mark the target and have not allowed their aim to be spoilt by the light *flak* defences. Their accuracy has been consistently of a high order, far exceeding that of any other system of marking so far tried.' [12]

[12]
No 5 Group RAF, News,
30th June 1944.

Flying a Mosquito, he filmed the raid on the U-boat pens at Brest, and, on one occasion, casually pointed out to the present writer the huge bomb, released from a bomber at higher altitude, passing uncomfortably close to his own aircraft! He finished the war with the rank of Squadron Leader and was awarded the DFC and Bar. Towards the end of 1944, 'Perhaps I was time-expired' he muses, he answered a call for pilots to fly for British Overseas

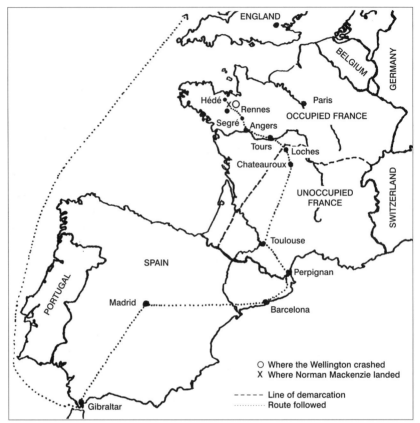

Fig.15
Mackenzie's
Progress.

Airways Corporation, which he did for some time, moving later to the Dutch national airline KLM, for whom he was to do most of his civil flying. When he retired, in 1968, he had completed a total of 21,000 hours in his flying career. Norman is a member of the RAF Escaping Society and regularly attends their functions.

The Chatenay Family

People who undertook wartime clandestine operations in occupied Europe did so at great personal risk. In a book about the SOE written some 20 years after the war, one writer describes, concisely and accurately, the atmosphere in which agents were required to operate. These conditions could be extended to anyone, working anywhere, in the Resistance:

We live in a free society, removed by some distance in time and space from the immediate urgencies of war, occupation, and repression. It is easy for us to forget what life was actually like for SOE agents in occupied territory, or even for the ordinary inhabitants of France… Every step in their everyday existence might be reported, considered, commented on by one secret police force or another… if they were men of anywhere near military age, they were in constant danger of being sent off east in a forced labour convoy. Moreover they were contending with enemies of exceptional savagery.[13]

[13] Op cit [6], p.115.

The Chatenays were a truly remarkable family, passionately keen to help the Allied cause. Victor Chatenay, who had an interest in the firm which made Cointreau liqueur, was described, in the evening of his life as, 'a very small, very thin, very alert, delightful old boy with a fine sense of humour.' When he was young, he said, he asked God to give him a life that would not be dull. His prayer was answered positively. During the Second World War he gathered intelligence for the British which was usually flown back to England by the RAF in a Westland Lysander. On one occasion, whilst at 'La Romanerie', he was warned of an impending visit by the Gestapo and fled. The Germans were angry at missing him and, after searching the house, left two fire bombs in the roof which set fire to the house but apparently burnt only the roof. The house lay derelict for a year.

Later, when the Gestapo tried to arrest him in the middle of Paris, he fled and was shot in the leg but was able to make his getaway into the Metro. After that incident the Gestapo were never far behind him and the SOE arranged for him to be flown to England in 1943.

At the end of the war he became Mayor of Angers. The main road from the town to Paris is named after him. He was a great friend and political ally of General de Gaulle, who stayed at his home on a couple of occasions. Chatenay proudly displayed at his home a portrait with a signed, personal message from the General written thereon. He wrote about his 1939-45 war experiences for the information of his children, and was later persuaded to publish them 'leaving out the most bitter passages.' He was clearly a man of some reputation. Norman Mackenzie's brother, Ted, seeking directions to 'La Romanerie' some 20 years after the war's end, was greeted by the person he was asking with, 'Oh yes, Monsieur Chatenay of the Resistance!' Ted wrote of having left his company 'feeling exalted'.

Barbara Chatenay, (*née* Stirling), British by birth, was also a lively character, and Norman Mackenzie is ever grateful for all the help she gave him. She was a First Aid Nursing Yeomanry (FANY) ambulance driver at the front in the First World War, where she met her husband. He was in the French Army. After being wounded in the trenches he was placed in charge of her unit. He later observed - with a twinkle in his eye - what a lucky chap he was to be chosen out of the whole of the French Army to be responsible for this large force of beautiful women! Arrested (for the second time) in January 1944, she was imprisoned in Ravensbrück concentration camp until the end of April 1945. She knew she was free, 'When I was helped into the bus by a Swedish officer!' Whilst in the camp she met a Madame Cremer whose son married the Chatenay's only daughter, Anne-Marie. Madame Chatenay died in March 1966, after 'a short but painful illness'

In addition to the eldest son, Michel, who accompanied Norman Mackenzie on his journey, another son, Jacques, escaped to Britain in 1942, via Spain, and joined the Special Air Service (SAS). He parachuted into Brittany on the night of 5th/6th June 1944, (D-Day, when the Allied invasion of Nazi occupied Europe began) and was killed fighting in his native land two months later. The third son, Louis-Pierre, also crossed the Pyrenees, but became a prisoner of the Spanish. He was subsequently released and arrived in England in October 1943. He became a liaison officer with the American

Forces. The youngest son, Toni, aged 17, was arrested in Paris by the Germans the day before he was to be flown to England. He was placed in Buchenwald concentration camp for a short time before being transferred to Schönebeck. He survived the war. The youngest child, Anne Marie, was flown, at the age of 14, to England in August 1944, where she was re-united with her father.

'La Romanerie' is no longer owned by the Chatenay Family and is now 'a smart restaurant and place for gatherings such as wedding receptions' set in the middle of an industrial area.

Chapter Ten

ANTI-JAMMING UNIT

… and the jammer would always win
because the enemy could blast our
aerials with watts per metre …
Len Pittendrigh

Like so much activity in Britain in the early days of the Second World War, the development of radar equipment took place hastily, and the equipment itself was often assembled in emergency situations:

The design and production of radar equipment in this country had in the first instance to meet a sudden emergency and for this reason all available effort had to be spent on producing the maximum amount of equipment in the minimum possible time … The danger of enemy interference was realised, but at such short notice anti-jamming systems could not be incorporated.[1]

[1] PRO AIR 41/46, p.52.

Therefore, whilst it was realised that there was always the danger of such interference with the British radar channels little could be done initially to combat the threat. Stop-gap methods only could be employed to try to keep the channels open, and it seemed to those working on the problem that whatever equipment was designed was always one step behind the enemy.

It soon became clear as the problem increased that a long term policy of research would be necessary to counteract this. This meant that the operational demands on the Anti-Jamming Section at the Telecommunications Research Establishment (TRE) to produce equipment would have to be substantially reduced to enable it to carry out in-depth research work in its laboratory. It was eventually decided to set up a special Anti-Jamming (AJ) Unit to carry out the day-to-day field work, thus allowing the research organisations (including the Admiralty Signals Establishment which liaised closely with TRE) to tackle the general problem of either producing radar circuits that would be immune from jamming, or a universal AJ device that would handle all sorts of jamming.[2] The new unit came into operation in March 1943:

[2] Ibid.

To investigate and develop 'First Aid' anti-jamming measures for the purpose of countering without delay any jamming attack that the enemy may suddenly produce…[3]

[3] PRO AIR 26/281.

Accommodated in 'The Houseboat' in Watling Street, Radlett, premises which had formerly been occupied by a failed night club in pre-war days and latterly by Handley Page Aircraft Company, the unit was commanded by Wing Commander A M Rodgers working under the administrative umbrella of 80 Wing, although he was never involved in the AJ Unit's technical activities. Apart from its service personnel the unit comprised an intelligence cell, a body of scientific officers headed by Ray Calvert and a small workshop/laboratory. It absorbed the already established 'J' Watch, ('J' denoted enemy jamming of coastal radar bases) which had come to life late in 1942 at TRE under the command of Squadron Leader Len Pittendrigh where, he remembered, 'a motley collection of airmen worked in a lab under Dr Jay and others making up AJ electronic devices'. He described its origins:

'J' Watch arose from the ashes of a shambolic dash of two German Navy capital ships ('Scharnhorst' and 'Gneisnau') from Brest to the Baltic Sea early one morning in February 1942, when all the CH (Chain Home RDF) and CHL (Chain Home Low-Flying) stations around the south and south east coasts of Britain had been blanked out for the first time, by powerful jamming transmissions from the opposite French coastline between Cherbourg and Calais. The jamming gave radar displays where the whole face was either totally distorted (CH) or was like a 'full moon' (CHL)

This resulted in TRE, at Great Malvern, HQ for the scientific work connected with RDF (Radio Direction Finding), later known by the American word 'radar', being given the task of overcoming the technical counter-measures and of locating the sites of the jammers and dropping fireworks thereon. I took command of this outfit and we established three coastal monitoring stations at Dover Hill (Kent), Holland Haven, near Walton-on-the-Naze, Essex, and at Ringstead (Dorset), plus employing 'lodgers' at main Chain RDF Stations as operations required. After a few months the unit was transferred from Malvern to 80 Wing HQ at Radlett where it became Central 'J' Watch, remaining there until a month or so before D-Day.

My command included two WAAF Officers, Margaret Dukes, a mathematics honours graduate and Mary Christy, commercial artist and map expert. No words of mine can express the ability, perseverance, tact and hard work shown by these two outstanding officers. We were backed up by RAF NCOs and airmen, and WAAFs employed on clerical duties. There was also a USAAF Officer, Captain Jack Giles, who had been detached for liaison duties between US Intelligence and ourselves. We also keep in constant touch with the Air Intelligence [AI4] at the Air Ministry in Whitehall ... My own duties had tasks quite outside Radlett with visits to the three monitoring sites each of which had its own officer in charge. I had no contact or knowledge of 'other ranks' beyond 'J' Watch.

We took over a requisitioned roadhouse on the main road to St Albans wherein two TRE scientific personnel had established a laboratory-cum-workshop. Ray Calvert, a Senior Principal Scientific Officer, was a brilliant scientist whose name lives on in the firm of RACAL. The second Principal Scientific Officer was Bob Light. He designed and built the first panoramic receiver. This gave CRT (Cathode Ray Tube) display over a wide frequency band of any frequency transmitting any signal. Thus the 'J' Watchers would look at their separate search equipment, without otherwise swinging their tuning controls continuously and, as could happen, miss something worthy of our attention.[4]

[4]
Len Pittendrigh
letter to the author,
8th November 1992.

The coastal AJ sites collected the data and the Central 'J' Watch Radlett, as it was now known, daily reported the previous day's events 'for a selected distribution only.' The AJ unit never became involved with other 80 Wing activities. The first few months brought an inevitable spate of teething troubles due to shortage of trained personnel, material and equipment and a great deal of special equipment had to be provided by the unit itself.

Leisure for the personnel was difficult. 'There was no such thing as being off duty,' Len Pittendrigh recalled, 'and life was dictated by events as they

'The Houseboat',
Radlett, in 1992,
formerly HQ of
Central 'J' Watch.
Author

occurred. This applied to any small unit. Spare time was spent in the Officers Mess playing darts, bridge, snooker, reading and generally chatting and refreshing ourselves at the bar.' There was a 'very occasional romp to adjacent Boreham Wood of film making fame' and on one such visit he 'encountered the girl of my post-war planning.' He married in March 1944 and still proudly owns a crystal silver mounted biscuit barrel, a present given to him and his bride by the officers of 80 Wing.

Squadron Leader Pittendrigh sometimes tried to lighten the load of his subordinates by an injection of humour. 'It was not,' he remembers, 'in our nature to take war seriously.' Artwork was produced 'to boost the morale of my troops by seeing a funny side to our efforts by gentle exaggeration and misrepresenting.'[5] (For examples of this art work see Figures 16 and 17.)

The former unit commander summarises the function of 'J' Watch which was two-fold:

1 *To pick up and analyse all technical data required by the scientists who would try and devise anti-jamming circuits and other devices.*
2 *To provide Air Intelligence with information regarding the location of the enemy jamming sites in order that they could be destroyed when considered necessary.*

The 'J' Watch at Radlett, and at Dunkirk (Kent) also built, and later manned for D-Day and elsewhere abroad, Mobile 'J' Watches for jamming enemy radar. These were used with the advancing Allied troops, and were operated with considerable success. One NCO from the unit, Sergeant Mason, was decorated for his actions during the 'Battle of the Bulge'. Len Pittendrigh thought the jamming to be a qualified success:

'J' Watching convinced me and my staff that elaborate and well conceived AJ devices were a waste of time and effort at operational stations for this reason ... To read any signal whatsoever the wanted signal had to be read over the jamming signal ... and the jammer would always win because the enemy could blast our aerials with watts per metre into receivers sensitive to microwatts per metre.[6]

The Air Historical Branch's history of 80 Wing claims a good deal of success for the unit which often materialised as a by-product of the anti-jamming

[5]
Op cit [4],
11th December 1992.

[6]
Op cit [4],
5th August 1993.

work. 'Although' it records, 'It must be admitted that the results obtained were quite inconsistent with the amount of work involved ... much valuable information was obtained even from the negative results.' Understanding of counter-measures used against jamming broadened with the experience gained bringing about a sound AJ technique strategy. Apparatus improved in efficiency, and the upgrading of the special skills of personnel by allowing them to acquire practical knowledge under jamming conditions contributed greatly to their training. 'It was the knowledge gained from this subsidiary work', the History observes, 'and in the correlation of the work done with other services and research establishments involved in jamming, that the AJ Unit served a very useful purpose.'[7]

[7] Op cit [1], p.54.

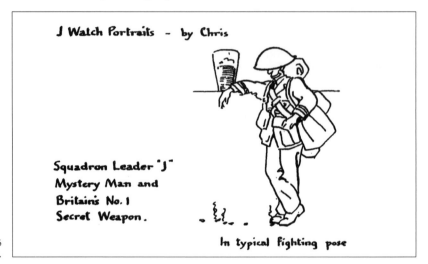

Fig.16
'J'Watch - Cartoon.

Fig.17
'J'Watch - Shield.

'J' Watch cartoon and shield reproduced with the permission of Sqn Ldr LWD Pittendrigh RAFVR, Officer Commanding 'J' Watch, 1942-1944.

Chapter Eleven

COLLECTING BOMBS

Don't worry about me.
I've got me tin 'at on!

Decoys in battle must be as old as warfare itself but although the date of their initial use against aerial bombardment is not known, the following story must relate to one of the first. The first bombs dropped on a town were from a Zeppelin on Great Yarmouth in Norfolk in 1915. In an excellent chronicle of life on the 'Home Front' in the First World War an Essex parson, the Reverend Andrew Clark, records that dummy fires were used in the following year outside Ipswich in Suffolk:

Saturday 26th August 1916
Notes of the Zeppelin raid of the Thursday night ... Outside Ipswich is a heath. When the Ipswich folk heard that Zeppelins were coming, they plunged the town into total darkness. Then some went out on the common and lit a bonfire here and there to look (as seen from a great height) like the flare of big works. They also put up a few acetylene-gas lamps on bushes here and there, to look like lamps at street corners. They lit a lot of squibs to attract attention. Then they went back to Ipswich and waited. Presently a Zeppelin passed right over Ipswich, hovered over the illuminated common, and dropped a ton-load of bombs about it. Then, having got rid of their cargo, turned and went back seaward, to report in Germany that it had destroyed a great town.[1]

The perilous position in which Great Britain found itself in the summer of 1940 urgently required a broad defence strategy for the nation to survive. Many plans were made. Some were quickly discarded as unworkable; others survived. Among the latter was the protection of key areas in this country by using 'decoy' fires (later code-named *Starfish*) to divert night raiding enemy bombers from their genuine targets in this country.

There are conflicting accounts about who actually made the first suggestion about the use of these decoys. Bob Morrow, who wrote an article on 'Decoy Cities' for the *Scots Magazine* received information from an Edinburgh writer, Forbes Macgregor, stating he had made detailed suggestions to the Air Ministry in 1938. This is confirmed in another letter to Mr Morrow from one of Mr Macgregor's friends who says he discussed the matter with Macgregor in that year. All Macgregor received was a brief acknowledgement that his letter had been passed to the Home Office.

He heard no more and, in 1954, wrote to the Home Office seeking only, as he put it, 'a phrase of thanks'. He was curtly informed that the idea had

[1]
Echoes of the Great War. The Diary of Reverend Andrew Clark 1914-19, James Munson (Ed), (OUP, 1985), p.153.

already been under consideration in 1938. Mr Morrow has seen original copies of the correspondence and is of the opinion that 'plans identical to Mr Macgregor's were put into effect in every last detail in 1941.'[2]

[2]
Article
'Decoy Cities' in
Scots Magazine,
January 1989, by
Bob Morrow, and
correspondence
received by
Mr Morrow and
sent to the Author.

The idea seems to have originated, 'officially' in a letter[3] from HQ Coastal Command in July 1940, to Colonel (later Sir) John Turner, the former Royal Engineer and pre-war Director of Works at the Air Ministry. There had been four raids on a Coastal Command station at Bircham Newton, near Kings Lynn in Norfolk, and:

In order that the enemy should not be depressed at his lack of success, fires were made. This was done by putting a large quantity of branches and dried ferns into a pit or bomb crater with two wing tip flares wired up to the night dug-out. The fires could then be started when incendiaries were dropped. In addition oil fires have been prepared for future attacks.

[3]
PRO AIR 2/3212.
Letter dated
9th July 1940 from
Commander-in-
Chief, Coastal
Command to the
Air Ministry.

Early in the War, Colonel Turner, 'a retired officer of drive and initiative'[4] had been given responsibility for building dummy airfields and other deceptions (other than camouflage). The building of 'decoy' fires was seen as an extension to this. Based at Sound City Films, Shepperton, he used in full the expertise of the film industry's technicians to design these deceptions. By 1st November 1940 Colonel Turner was able to inform the Chief of Air Staff, Lord Portal, that:

[4] PRO AIR 2/2878.

A great deal has been done in the dummy fire line. Twenty seven have been constructed to guard large Air Force stations such as depots, training establishments etc. Many more will be constructed (some have already been started) in our big Civil Decoy Scheme.[5]

[5] PRO AIR 8/317.

A change of tactics was also taking place. Until then the decoy fire had been used as a 'secondary' decoy. It was not supposed to be lit until the parent target was under attack, the idea being that the station under attack should put out the fires as quickly as possible, light the decoy, thus transferring attacks to it. Now Colonel Turner reported:

I am adopting the decoy fire as a direct decoy... I have selected five sites and expect to select a good many more around London as close in as possible with the idea of using them, under the control of 11 Group Fighter Command, as direct decoys. This means that when 11 Group know the line of attack on any particular night they will be lit and, it is hoped, bombs will be dropped on the decoys instead of London... No 11 Group is very enthusiastic. You may take it then, therefore, that dummy fires have been very much taken up and there will be increasing numbers in action each month.[6]

[6] Ibid.

Using RAF personnel to preserve secrecy and allow him to act freely, Colonel Turner's organisation was removed from the RAF chain of command. Known simply, to all who came into contact with it, as 'Colonel Turner's Department' it sometimes confused those in authority who only knew how to operate using service procedure. The personal experience of a *Starfish* site member, described in the next chapter, highlights this. There were initial difficulties but these were overcome. In the beginning the Air Staff ordered trenches to be dug on suitable experimental sites and filled with oil 'until something better could be evolved'. These were of little value. The oil fires cracked the soil; oil seeped through it into ponds and streams causing pollution. 'A chorus of protest at once arose from farmers and others, which continued long after this hasty type had been abandoned.'[7]

[7]
PRO AIR 41/3
AHB Decoys and
Deceptions.

Clearly further research was necessary, and the inventiveness of the film men at Shepperton produced three different types of fires, one burning diesel, another paraffin, and the third using scrap wood and sawdust. A combination of all three provided realistic variations in flame and smoke:

On each site two quite separate groups of these three types were located to provide two large fires each of some 30 tons of inflammable material, for lighting on two successive nights… Each 30 ton fire burned for four hours and was electrically lit from a shelter some 800 yards away.[8]

They could be 'Full' (diesel oil), 'Medium' (paraffin), or 'Short' (baskets of scrap wood), depending on the size and type of fire it was decided to imitate.[9] Later, dummy electric lighting ('QLs') used to simulate railway marshalling yards, factories and other key targets was added to some sites.

The Ministry of Home Security supplied a list of the most important towns and a hunt for suitable sites began.[10] They were built, in the first instance, around Coventry itself, and other Midland and Northern industrial cities. By the end of December, 18 sites were in place.

Timing was a prime factor in the lighting of the fires and operational control for setting them alight was vested in 80 Wing HQ who 'were considered to be best able to correlate all the various factors governing the choice of the best site to bring into action and also the optimum moment for lighting the fire.'[11]

A member of Colonel Turner's staff, known as Fire Control Officer, was attached to the Operations Room at Radlett, which also maintained close liaison with Fighter Command and the Ministry for Home Security. (Later much was left to the discretion of the NCO in charge of the site as was the case in the sites covering London and Southampton prior to D-Day, in June 1944.)[12]

After the disastrous night raid on Coventry on 14th November 1940, it was decided that 'Decoy lights, however well designed, were of little value when the German Air Force could see its target town in flames… Only large 'decoy' fires lasting several hours, could expect to draw off this new form of attack.'

Sites were speedily constructed. At the end of March 1941, 108 had been erected, rising to 155 in July. In 1943 the total had reached 235, although many in the interim had been closed down as the fortunes of war improved and they were no longer found to be operationally necessary. The average site, was about 10-15 acres in area and had to be within a few miles of the target and more than 800 yards from the nearest house.[13] The personnel at each site, particularly at the beginning, consisted of a Sergeant in charge, three corporals, two electricians (Leading Aircraftmen), two drivers, and 16 General Duties aircraftmen.

The role played by *Starfish* site 43B in a raid on Norwich on the night 8/9th May 1942 indicates how the system worked.

The extract overleaf,[14] (Compiled from the Operations Officer's Diary; *Starfish* Control's Diary; Meacon Control Log; VHF Logs; charts and jamming logs at 80 Wing HQ) shows the co-operation necessary, particularly between the radio counter-measures (RCM) and *Starfish* sections, and how essential good communications were:

[8] Ibid.

[9] PRO AIR 41/46. Air Historical Branch History of No 80 (Signals) Wing.

[10] Op cit [7].

[11] Ibid.

[12] PRO AIR 26/583.

[13] Ibid.

[14] PRO AIR 41/46. Air Historical Branch History of No.80 (Signals) Wing, App.5.

2331 Home Security reports via Liaison Officer, Fighter Command, a fire
25 miles south west of Norwich. This is the remains of one started
by enemy action during the last raid. *Starfish* Controller (No 80 Wing
HQ) is advised, and he is contacting Norwich local *Starfish* Control
for further details.

2331 Scientific Analyst (in Operations Room, at Radlett,) advises that a
complete set of *Ruffians* are active and laid in the Norwich Area.
Fighter Command and Air Ministry (Director of Ground Control)
advised.

2359 *Starfish* Control concentrating liaison with sites in Norfolk.

0018 Four enemy aircraft left enemy coast near Dutch Isles, flying north
west as far as the latitude of Norwich then turn west.

0020 67.25 Mc/s *Ruffian* beam active from Boulogne. Controller orders
BROMIDES to jam 67.25 and 74.5 Mc/s. Receiving Room, Radlett
advised. Final analysis by Scientific Intelligence indicates beams laid
on Norwich area.

0040 First enemy aircraft crosses Norfolk coast. All jammers radiating.

0043 *Starfish* Controller in contact with Norwich gets report that flares
have been dropped about three miles south east of the City just
south of *Starfish* site 43B at Bramerton.

0050 Aircraft now concentrating on Norwich

0057 Norwich reports to *Starfish* Controller that there are flares and fires
to the south of the City. Also high explosive (HE) bombs dropped.
Instructs local *Starfish* Control to set off a 'Short' *Starfish* at 43B Site
at Bramerton. About six enemy aircraft approaching from the east

0106 Norwich report to *Starfish* Control that Bramerton 'Short' *Starfish*
was set off at 0102. No report of any more fires. Flares and bombs
dropped south of Norwich. Will advise if 43B is attacked.

0110 There are now ten enemy aircraft approaching Norwich from the
east and north east,

0118 There are now ten enemy aircraft over Norwich and nine more
coming in.

0120 Investigative flights report jamming effective.

0125 *Starfish* Controller cannot raise Norwich local *Starfish* Control.

0140 *Starfish* local Control at Norwich now contacted on tie-line (direct
land lines in RAF/GPO network). Difficulty caused by Norwich
Exchange evacuating and forgetting to switch over to emergency
board. Norwich reports eight HE bombs and one unexploded bomb
'collected' within 800 yards of the 'Short' *Starfish* lit at 43B Site at
Bramerton. About 30 bombs dropped in the vicinity of Norwich –
mostly in the outskirts. A fire is reported at Stoke Holy Cross but
there are none in Norwich. The enemy aircraft appear to be
between Norwich and the coast but are wandering.

0148 There are still seven enemy aircraft near Norwich. The remainder
have gone home.

0155 There are now three enemy aircraft crossing coast on their way
home. There appears to have been 30 enemy aircraft involved in
tonight's raid.

0200 Table now clear.
0210 Cover re-allocated. *Bromides* switched off as *Ruffians* became
     inactive.

The effectiveness of the 'decoy fires' has caused much debate. The weather
had to be right. It was useless lighting a fire in open country in bright moonlight unless there was a ground mist, and the ignition had to co-incide
exactly with the build up of enemy air activity.

And there were failures. It seems likely that experienced Luftwaffe crews,
such as those of the *Kampfgruppe* (KGr) 100 'Pathfinders', were not easily
deceived, particularly in good weather. By May 1942, however, Colonel
Turner was claiming that enemy pilots 'were more easily taken in by the
decoys than their predecessors a year ago' urging that the *Starfish* should 'be
used more boldly' [15].

[15]
PRO AIR 2/4759.

Fig.18
Map of
Starfish Sites
mentioned in text.

Typical *Starfish* site, showing the layout of basket and boiler fires.
Crown Copyright /MoD

Boiler fire in action. A water flush has caused an explosive burst of flame. The oil and water tanks feeding the fire can be seen on the left.
Crown Copyright/MoD

Some reports should be treated with caution. One Junkers Ju 88 pilot 'recognised' dummy fires over London on 24th November 1940,[16] when, in fact, the first *Starfish* was lit over a week later, at Bristol.[17] Official Records admit, however, that 'There were many German prisoners of war who knew of the Richmond Park fire!'[18] This site was closed and moved, in May 1942, to Kenwood on Hampstead Heath in North London. In addition, a map found in a Heinkel He 111 brought down by night fighters near the White Horse at Westbury, in Wiltshire, on the night of the 16th-17th June 1941 had 'dummy fires' ringed with a red circle.[19]

Poor communications, difficulties in placing sites, and errors of judgement were not unknown. Lack of speedy transmission of information during a raid on Hull in May 1941, prevented effective use of the local *Starfish* sites and much damage was caused.[20] At Birmingham unavoidably long distances (10 to 14 miles) between sites and the centre of the target reduced efficiency.[21] In October 1941, a 'short' *Starfish* was lit at Manchester with the best of intentions, after a report was received that incendiary bombs were falling in the area. This turned out to be a false alarm thought to have been caused by 'sparking' set up by high-tension cables which were broken at the time and incorrectly assumed to have been the incendiaries.[22] There was always considerable danger in the vicinity of the sites. In April 1941, a bomb aimed at the site on Rainham Marshes, in Essex, fell on a nearby anti-aircraft emplacement and killed four soldiers.[23]

Weston airfield in Somerset was protected by a site at Bleadon. During a heavy raid on Weston on 2nd/3rd January 1941, when the site was ordered to activate, the ignition switches failed. One of the site members, AC2 Bright, rushed out and lit the *Starfish* apparatus by hand. The site was immediately attacked 'collecting' hundreds of incendiaries and HE bombs. Bright was later awarded the Military Medal for his courage.[24]

There were other successes. The first *Starfish* used on 2nd/3rd December 1940, during an attack on Bristol, 'collected' 66 HE bombs (claimed to be 75% of the total effort) on the two sites. On the night of 19th May 1941, 14 HE bombs dropped on the Bleadon site. Some cows were killed but neither Weston nor the airfield were damaged. Subsequent evidence from prisoners of war showed that although they knew of the 'decoys' their idea of the composition and location of the sites was often completely wrong.[25] In May 1941, the staff in the Operations Room at 80 Wing HQ preparing themselves for yet another raid were puzzled by the enemy's movements. John Whitehead, Controller on this night, remembered it well:

This time the foe seemed to be concentrating his efforts on an area some 25 miles due east of Nottingham. We could not understand why because there were no targets there. It was open countryside... They went home and their return was followed by a broadcast that Nottingham had been successfully attacked.[26]

In fact, they had attacked the Vale of Belvoir, with 230 HE bombs, one oil bomb, and five groups of incendiaries killing two chickens![27]

Perhaps the most successful was at Hayling Island, near Portsmouth, on 17th April 1941:

... all the indications pointed to Portsmouth being the target that night. The relevant authorities there were warned to go on standby, with a special request to the fire

[16]
The Diving Eagle. A Ju 88 Pilot's Story, Peter W Stahl, translated by Alex. Vanags-Baginskis. (William Kimber, London, 1984).

[17] Op cit [9].

[18] Op cit [12].

[19]
The First Pathfinders: Operational History of KGr100, 1939-41, Kenneth Wakefield. (William Kimber, London, 1981), p.180

[20]
Deception in World War II, Charles Cruickshank, (Oxford University Press, 1979,) p.10.

[21] Op cit [12].

[22]
PRO AIR 26/580.

[23]
The History of the 17th Light Anti-Aircraft Regt, RA, 1939-45, Lt Col H S Eeles OBE MC TD, (Courier Press, Tunbridge Wells, 1946).

[24]
Somerset at War 1939-45, Mac Hawkins, (Dovecourt Press 1988) p.107.

[25] Op cit [9].

[26]
Letter to the author from Wing Commander John Whitehead, RAF(Retd), 28th February 1993.

[27] Op cit [9].

Grid fire in action. The paraffin feed tank is on the extreme right. This fire provided a variation in flame colour, being very yellow.
Crown Copyright/MoD

Marshalling yard fitting (MQL) showing adjustable bracket, feed socket and shade.
Crown Copyright/MoD

people to get the initial fires out quickly and let us know when they had. The subse-quent operation went like clockwork – call-sign 'F4G' – KGr100 aircraft responding – aircraft spotted on radar – final warning to Portsmouth – KGr100 start fires and go home – following bombers spotted on radar – Fire Brigade report fires out – 'Starfish' ordered to light – bombs fell on 'Starfish' in large numbers! I telephone the man in charge of the 'Starfish' and ask him if he is alright, 'Yes, sir' he says, 'Don't worry about me. I've got me tin 'at on!'[28]

[28] Op cit [26].

The official figures were 170 HE bombs, 32 (out of 34) parachute mines, and approximately 5,000 incendiaries (90% of the attack) 'attracted' to the Site.[29]

[29] Op cit [22].

Sometimes nature lent a hand. At the beginning of a period during which Hull was being attacked at night with frequency a stray aircraft dropped its bombs at a point on the North Yorkshire Moors several miles inland west of Flamborough Head, starting up a peat fire which lasted for several weeks. This fire attracted several more attacks while it lasted. It was assumed in the Operations Room at Radlett that the erring aircraft had mistaken Flamborough Head for Spurn Head, at the head of the Humber Estuary.[30]

[30] Op cit [26].

Opinions have varied over the years concerning the efficiency of the *Starfish* sites in the defence of the UK. Were they as effective as has been claimed or costly time-consuming failures? Probably the official view sums up quite neatly their actual contribution and gives the most accurate appraisal:

It is difficult to assess with accuracy the number of bombs which fell on, or near, 'Starfish' sites. Nevertheless, the deception succeeded in materially reducing the weight of bombs falling on towns and cities in the UK.[31]

[31] Op cit [12].

Junkers Ju 88A-5 w/nr 3457 '4D+DL' of I/KG30 landed at RAF Lulsgate Bottom, Bristol, on 23rd July 1941, most probably as the result of 'meaconing'. The aircraft was allocated the British service serial number EE205 (as illustrated). It was evaluated by the Royal Aircraft Establishment and went on to join 1426 (Enemy Aircraft Flight). It was most likley scrapped in 1948. *Late Paddy Porter Collection.*

Chapter Twelve

IN THE FIELD

Safe in dangerous times
B B Smith

The operation of a *Starfish* site was always connected to enemy air activity. Some were blessed with a quiet life. One 'Erk' (RAF slang for Aircraftman) who was attached to 29 Site, at Arborfield in Berkshire, from March 1941 to December 1942, told the author:

We covered Reading, which was never attacked at night. Consequently we never went into action! …thus I have no heroics, no grim action, no excitement to record.

In their private world, the staff, he wrote, never heard news about other sites and were thankful to be away from RAF station routine. They mixed freely with the villagers and enjoyed 'civilian' standards of living. However, they took their job seriously and genuinely regarded the site as 'very hush-hush and not to be chattered about – although it transpired that the worthy villagers knew very well what we were up to!' Some found the tranquillity irksome:

Ultimately, it became just a trifle boring – safe in dangerous times – but for some of my restless colleagues, rather uneventful.[1]

[1]
Letter to Author
from B B Smith,
8th June 1992.

Other sites were busier. John Kent, an LAC electrician, and Alfred Simmonds, a driver, were attached to 43B Site at Bramerton, Norfolk – covering Norwich. They had a much livelier time. Closer to the East Coast of Britain, therefore well within range of enemy bombers, they were often in action. They present their stories.

We had no idea what we were in for!
John Kent

When the war came I wanted something in electrical or radio. I used to mess around with electrical things. They wanted me to be a Wireless Operator/Air Gunner (WOP/AG). The problem was I am left-handed. When still at school they tied my hand behind my back to stop me writing left-handed. However, I had a maths teacher who said if I wanted to do my work left handed I could do so. Consequently I had got to the point where I wrote right-handed and did figures left-handed. That became difficult when you did Morse. When I was on the rifle range at Blackpool I had nothing on my target from my five shots and the chap next to me had ten on his! I also had difficulty when drilling and saluting. I kept wondering which hand to use. Well, of course, this prevented me from becoming a WOP/AG so I had to learn something else.

First they were going to send me on something called 'Parachute and Cables'. The idea was you shot up a rocket with a parachute on it in the hope that it brought down the 'plane. The trouble was it brought it down on the people who were operating it!

When I went to Coltishall I didn't have an inkling what I was going into. We all went into this room; then they drove us out to Bramerton. Our HQ was a chicken shed in Cushion's Farm. The bloke in charge of the 'phone used to sit in the hallway of Mrs Cushion's house. At the beginning we had no idea what we were there for. First of all a whole load of chaps came down from Sound City Films to the site. They put up the original *Starfish* site. Only a *Starfish* – nothing else. Then they sent us to Sound City Films at Shepperton on a course. That was when we learnt what we were going to do.

When I went back to the site they wanted electricians for the job. The corporal in charge put me forward as he knew I was interested in that sort of thing. So I went to Dollis Hill, (GPO Engineering Branch), to learn about the relays. The course lasted for about a month and the people on it with me knew a little about electricity. When the contractors put up the site (see Figure19) I used to help them do the wiring. It was all done through Sound City Films.

We originally had a Nissen hut but we had to have somewhere for the generator when the 'QL' (dummy lights) came. That is the bit that is left there now. Our Nissen hut was beside it. They ran two wires up to a relaying system. We had a series of numbers like a telephone. You pressed the numbers you wanted, pulled the lever and up it went. The baskets were stuffed with reeds, anything.

Eventually they got us a telephone system that went to the Police HQ at City Hall, in Norwich, on a private line. [This was the local *Starfish* control.] They had the signal through from whoever it was. [No 80 Wing HQ at Radlett.] It certainly wasn't Coltishall. They would 'phone us every night with a code word. We had one night on and one night off. The GPO supplied all the relays and every fortnight we had to go into Norwich to change the batteries.

The 'QL' represented the lights in the marshalling yards at Trowse. One group were supposed to represent a locomotive. All that was really was four orange bulbs, one in each corner, shining into the middle which was supposed to be the cab of a train engine. That was placed on a separate line to the other lights. First of all you would have all your lights blazing when you were told you were going to have a raid. When you heard 'Jerry' coming over it would suddenly dim down and then go out. The idea was to give the impression you had suddenly slammed the door of the 'loco' firebox. You had to give the impression you had stoked up the fire and then suddenly slammed the lid and gone off. When all the lights went out we also had 'mistake' lights which were left on to give the impression of a 'chink of light in the roof'. They would stay on all the time until 'Jerry' decided he would drop his bombs. Once he had done this they told us what to fire. First of all we would 'fire' the first basket. Then we'd go on to fire the next one and so on.

We also set off boiler fires. They were fantastic things. Each had a long metal trough with two tanks, one filled with diesel and one with water.

There were two lavatory cisterns. Underneath were all the detonators and the coal and other fuel to heat it up. It got red hot. Once it was hot it burnt a cable through and down came the diesel. And as the diesel came down it caught fire and at the same time it pulled the cistern of water. And that flushed the water down and the water shot the diesel up into the air and so it kept on repeating. It was very effective. All the *Starfish* were controlled from one cable with a relaying box.

We never saw much of the officers. They came about once every six months. Every so often we had to change these detonators on the baskets. We had to fire off the old ones. The field was full of wires and we had to be careful so I used to 'fire off' six at a time.

One day the CO from Martlesham Heath came and said, 'You're wasting your time there, boy, fire the lot off at once.' I said it was a bit dodgy with all the wires about. There were 42 lines to the different things. The whole bloody lot went up and he said, 'What do we do now?' I said, 'I'll have to rewire it, I suppose. I've got a plan.' He gave me and the bloke helping me £5 each.

I originally lodged in a cottage by the river towards the edge of the wood; my billet had its windows blown out. The house opposite had large cracks in it so they couldn't live in it. The old dear who lived in it was chasing around after the officer asking him what he was going to do about it!

We asked an old chap who lived on the road to Norwich where one particular bomb had dropped. 'What bomb?' he asked. 'The bomb that fell in your garden.' I replied. Shouting, 'My bloody rhubarb!' he rushed off to look. Another time, old Cushion – the farmer, told one of our lads 'The doors have been blown off my bullock shed and the cows have all got shrapnel in them.' He received the reply, 'That's alright, guv'nor, you'll have tinned milk in the morning!' Cushion wasn't at all pleased.

Squire Blake, a solicitor in Norwich, told me, 'I knew you were no damn good when you came here!' He used to ride on a three-wheeled cycle the five miles to Norwich every day. I told him, 'It's no good moaning at me. I was sent here.' It was obvious that bombs were going to fall around the site when it was operating.

We were supposed to be the marshalling yards at Thorpe Station in Norwich. The first time we had a practice test they saw the smoke and flames at Colmans and sent a fire engine out from Norwich. It came tearing up the road to be told, 'It's alright. We don't need a fire engine. We know it's alight.'

Coltishall didn't know we existed except that we went in there for stores. They told us nothing about procedure. I never had a full kit all through the war and, other than the medical I had when I joined, I never had inoculations, injections, or saw the dentist, all the way through. I didn't finish recruit training at Blackpool because of the left hand/right hand business and they said they would put someone else in my place for 'passing out' at the end. The recruit training at this time of the war was ridiculous. We did try to march once from Stanley Park around the town for a 'Battle of Britain' parade but we lost the band (we couldn't hear it!) so we gave up and didn't bother to finish the parade.

Once the chaplain from Coltishall came to see us. He said we weren't paying into the RAF Benevolent Fund! We said we wouldn't get anything out of it. He got us to pay 6d a week. We asked for a wireless set. He sent a battery radio with no battery. We couldn't get any batteries so it stood there for most of the war, unused.

I wrote home regularly to my mother. Whenever I had a day off I used to go into Norwich so I thought I would post the letter there. I walked up to the Main Post Office and put my letter in.

There was an RAF Police sergeant standing there. He asked me if I was on leave and I said, 'No, I'm posted here.' Then he said, 'What are you doing posting a letter. Don't you know it's got to be censored?' I told him I was unaware of this. He asked where I was stationed and I replied, 'All I can tell you is we collect our stores from Coltishall.' We had been told early on by an officer that on no account were we to say where we came from.

Sometime later we got a letter from Coltishall telling me I was on a 'fizzer' [a disciplinary charge]. I had never had any problems before.

At Coltishall the station warrant officer marched me in front of the adjutant who was in front of a blooming great map. He said, 'Where's your site?' I said, 'I can't tell you, sir. If you want to know anything about the site you'll have to get in touch with Martlesham Heath. They'll tell you what you want to know.' I told him I wasn't allowed to say where I was stationed. He then said, 'Well, give me some idea of where you are then.' I said 'I can't.' He then said, 'Give me a rough idea,' so I drew a bloody great ring round Norwich and said, 'Somewhere there, sir!' 'Well, go back to your site,' he said, 'and try and post your letters in the village next time!'

They had no idea what we were doing. We wore uniforms, of course, but the buttons were never polished. We always said that was so they didn't show up in the dark! We had a lovely time. We used to go down 'The Brickmakers' every night when we were off. I don't think we ever left there before 2am to return to our billets.

One night we had a raid. George Say and me had experience of bombing from London but another fellow, a North Country boy, hadn't. When the shrapnel started flying about he got a bit 'windy'. So we told him to go inside and make a cup of tea. As he was doing this a piece of shrapnel shot through the door and hit the teapot. He came rushing out with his tin hat on saying that it was safer outside!

Our site was never boring. I was always building up the site and rewiring as I was the only electrician there for most of the time. Local opinion was that we were a dummy aerodrome for six Spitfires! I was on the site from 1941 until we closed it at the end of the war in 1945.

When 'VE' Day came we all went down 'The Brickies' and we stayed there for three days and nights. We never went back to our billets. We slept on the floor.

I was never officially an RAF electrician so when I went back to a 'proper' camp they didn't know what to do with me. The station warrant officer told me to, 'walk around the camp with a worried look and a piece of paper in my hand!' We had no official trade. We were 'Colonel Turner's Department'. We were just *Starfish* Operators, that's all.[2]

[2]
Interview given
to author
by John Kent,
7th September 1992.

All this decoy work originated from film making.
Alfred Simmonds

I was attached to Starfish 43B. We were just posted to the site. I was posted from Blackpool via Coltishall. We came from all over the place to make up the 24. Two of us were 'transport'; two electricians; a Sergeant in charge and a Corporal. We formed the nucleus. I was the lorry driver. I was the first to go out to 43B; it was a Saturday in January 1941: there was snow on the ground.

All this decoy work originated from the film making. All we dealt with came from Sound City Films. Colonel Turner was involved there. I met him about May 1941. I started to go down to Sound City Films to pick him up and I took him around the sites. I used to take my truck to Shepperton, leave it there and pick him up in his car and drive him around. He was a very nice gentleman but he never talked about the job. One time we were out on Burnham Marshes, near Maldon in Essex, there were only cart-tracks there. The fog came down and we got lost.

I knew we were under very strict secrecy, we were told that from the very start. They wouldn't release any of our chaps to go abroad, particularly in the early days. Several of them received postings but they weren't allowed to go. They thought the enemy might pick them up and find out about what we were doing.

We did most of the building; contractors brought all the heavy stuff in. Most of it was scaffolding (to hold the tanks). The fires were about four times the size of a tea chest. There were big squares all in hessian, and filled with burnable stuff. We soaked them all in creosote, about once a fortnight. There was an electric detonator under the middle of each. We also had big diesel tanks and troughs. There was a middle trough inside the one big trough. Underneath the big trough we fired the detonators. Water came down into the inner trough when it got right hot. This caused a series of explosions. Also we were supposed to be 'drawing off' for the marshalling yards at Trowse. We had lights which represented the yards. We had lights, firing material, plus electric detonators on the Site. (See Figure 19.)

We could control everything from the guardroom. It was 500-600 yards away. We also had an 8hp engine in there that we drew all the lights from. We had 'dimmers' and everything. We could bring them down from 'full on'. The art was bringing down the lights so that the enemy could see them going down. Another of my jobs was to go round the sites and keep them serviced with oil and petrol, and look after the small engines they had on the 'QL' sites. We were very successful with 43B. I think we only lit the fires twice but the lights were always working. Once you got the fire going you had to spread it and it had to be at the right time. It attracted many bombs but none directly onto the site.

Towards the end of our time there the staff was reduced to 12. We used the 'phone mostly but we also had a despatch rider. We were given a short-wave radio but it didn't work because we were in a dip. We did not know until after the war exactly what was done. I later saw a map showing where all the bombs had dropped around the site (within two miles). It was surprising. They ringed the site; it was called a 'spread'.[3]

[3]
Interview given to author by Alfred Simmonds, 8th July 1992.

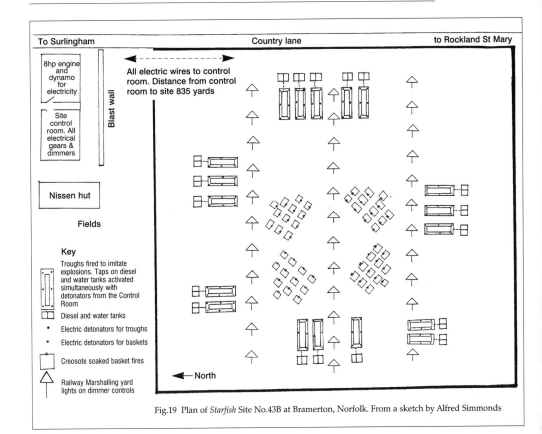

Fig.19 Plan of *Starfish* Site No.43B at Bramerton, Norfolk. From a sketch by Alfred Simmonds

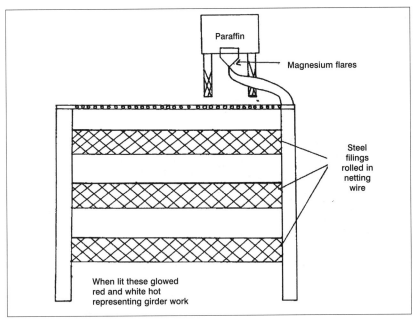

Fig.20
'Steel Girder' Fire.
From a sketch by
John Stevenson

No one had a clue why I was there
John Stevenson

John Stevenson left the coal mine where he was an electrical/mechanical engineer to join the RAF. He was stationed on a *Starfish* site at Condorrat, north east of Glasgow. After further training he went to Abbotsinch, a Royal Naval Air Station in the west of Scotland:

No one had a clue why I was there. I thought maybe it was something to do with Balloon Barrage work... then I went to Bishopsbrigg, near Glasgow. I was sitting in the NAAFI one day when an officer and sergeant came in and claimed me for 'Starfish' work. I went to Condorrat about five miles from my home. In a mossy area two miles outside the village the site was set up. I settled down to 'Starfish' duties. The staff consisted of one officer, one sergeant, three corporals, three electricians and six airmen. Each shift was manned by a Corporal, one electrician, and two airmen for general duties. We were 24 hours on duty and 48 hours off and were billeted in the village - needless to say I was home more often than at Condorrat!

The site was spread over about a mile square and was enclosed by a nine foot perimeter fence. It had six steel bunkers approximately 20ft long and 3ft high loaded with coal. The control bunker was about 400 yards from the main road and over half a mile from the *Starfish* site. Fixtures in the site included rolls of steel-turning scraps enclosed in circular rolls of mesh wire 2ft round and 15ft long stacked in rows of six on top of each other. (see Figure 20); boiler fires (see Figure 21); and basket fires (see Figure 22).

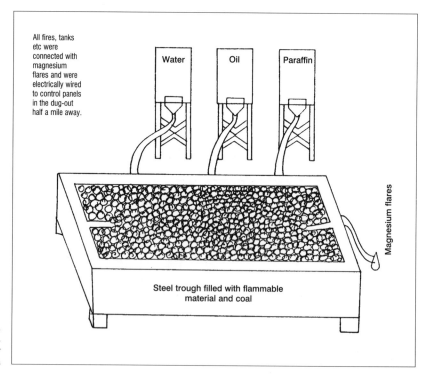

All fires, tanks etc were connected with magnesium flares and were electrically wired to control panels in the dug-out half a mile away.

Water

Oil

Paraffin

Magnesium flares

Steel trough filled with flammable material and coal

Fig.21 'Boiler' Fire. From a sketch by John Stevenson

The rolls of steel scraps would glow when hot representing steel girders; the boiler fires mimicked explosions and flare-ups; the basket fires represented ordinary fires. All were controlled from the command bunker shelter. On instructions being received from the RAF at Abbotsinch they would be ignited and, as Bob Morrow puts it in his article 'Decoy Cities' in *The Scots Magazine*, 'Within ten minutes theoretically, the whole site would be ablaze giving the impression of an industrial conflagration.'

John Stevenson described the effect of a *Starfish* site erupting into life, even if in this instance it was not for an 'operational' reason:

The theory was spot on. One night during a thunderstorm a bolt of lightning set the thing off, and in no time at all it looked for all the world like a raging factory fire, with the steel turnings glowing like girders would do in the real thing.[4]

The site was rebuilt by private contractors and whilst this was being done the staff were transferred to other duties. Stevenson was posted to a night fighter squadron and, four months later, was sent abroad for four years.

[4]
Article
'Decoy Cities'
by Bob Morrow,
The Scots Magazine,
January 1989.

Uneasy Bystanders

The site at Bramerton brought the perils of aerial bombing, usually confined to the urban areas of Britain, into the Norfolk countryside. where, even in wartime, the inhabitants usually lived quietly against a backcloth of rustic tranquillity.

Fred Vincent, a villager in Rockland St Mary, recalled wartime events generated by the closeness of the site:

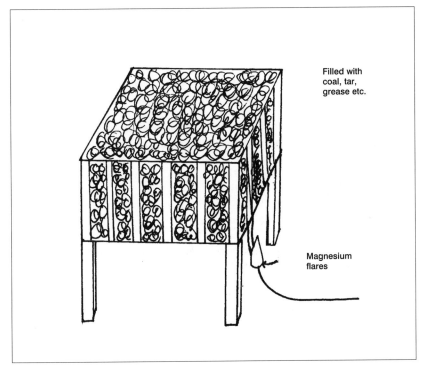

Filled with
coal, tar,
grease etc.

Magnesium
flares

Fig.22
'Brazier' or
'Basket' Fire.
From a sketch by
John Stevenson

One night after duck shooting 'Jerry' came over and dropped flares in the surrounding villages of Rockland St Mary, Ashby, Claxton, Bramerton and Surlingham. These villages were in the middle of the flares. It was so bright you could read a book by it. There was a 'dummy aerodrome' at Bramerton which was lit up at night to kid 'Jerry' it was Norwich.

In times of shortage he was obviously skilled at converting anything he found to serve some function in his life. When a land mine fell on Claxton Marshes, failing to explode, he acquired the parachute and its ropes. His girl friend made the parachute into panties and he used the nylon ropes for 'drawing' calves at birth. The casualties were not always human. Incendiaries dropped in a field at Ashby occupied by a flock of ewes set fire to many of them. The burning sheep were dispatched by the old shepherd's knife.[5]

[5]
Letter to Author
from Fred Vincent,
16th March 1992.

Daphne Brettingham spent her childhood in the same village as Fred Vincent. She was nine years old in 1941 when she heard that there was a 'dummy' airfield in the fields between Rockland St Mary and Bramerton – the next village west. All the villages in this area south east of Norwich close to the Broads were small, close-knit communities of a few hundred people:

We lived about a mile from the site. Rumours were rife about its function but no-one knew exactly what was there. This remained so for many years after the war. I knew where the site was because I was not allowed to ride my bike through the lanes to Bramerton and Surlingham any more. They were closed to the public.

The 'thrum' of aeroplane engines overhead was a familiar sound in Norfolk during the war years. Daphne remembers standing on the back step of her house with her father, after the air raid warning had sounded, listening for German aircraft. These were easily distinguished from Allied aircraft by the sound of their engines and:

Sometimes there were lights in the sky in the direction of 'Starfish' 43B. They would dim and we thought this was to black out the site for security purposes. One night we saw a bright glow coming from the site and we thought it had been hit by bombs. We did not have air raid shelters for the first few war years, probably because we were a rural area.

The peace of quiet village life was often shattered by anti-aircraft fire, the scream of bombs, dogfights overhead and shrapnel zinging into the roads and hedges. Bombs exploding on the marshes made a different sound – a more muffled thud – than when they dropped elsewhere. The presence of the site clearly attracted enemy activity:

One night a stick of bombs fell across the fields at the back of our house in a line from south-east to north-west directly towards the site. In a later raid incendiaries set fire to some nearby fields. On another occasion a delayed action land mine exploded near our house and my mother was blown off her feet into the house by the blast. Little damage was done to property in the village during the war as far as I can remember.

The brutality of war also impinged on childhood innocence:

[6]
Memories recorded
by Daphne
Brettingham
(the author's wife)
7th May 1994.

Once I saw a German aircraft caught in searchlights and shot down. It crashed at Ashby. The next day I went on my bike to see if I could get any aeroplane glass. This was made into rings, pendants, brooches etc. I saw an RAF man collecting something in a bag from the perimeter of the field. I said, 'Is there any aeroplane glass?' He replied, 'No, these are bits of the pilot.' I went home.[6]

A view of *Starfish* site 43B at Bramerton, Norfolk, in 1992. *Author*

As a result of his article in *The Scots Magazine* many people contacted Bob Morrow passing on unusual, interesting and, at times, hair-raising experiences,[7] concerning the *Starfish* sites which had been placed to the north of Glasgow in a bid to entice enemy raiders away from the heavily attacked docks. Below are some examples:

[7] Letters sent to Bob Morrow and loaned to the author, 26th August 1994.

Mrs G Gilchrist lived at High Craighton close to a site:
'During the war we had three RAF men billeted with us and five others who came to us for meals. We were paid 2/7d [12½p] a day to feed them and rations were very sparse. These men were manning the site on the hills behind us … When the German bombers came over the decoy was very successful and our property was the recipient of all sorts of shrapnel and incendiary bombs as it was not very far from the 'target'. My husband and I used to 'firewatch' with our ARP helmets on and the entrance to our house was protected by sandbags. The children were evacuated to an air raid shelter dug into the side of the hill, and which accommodated ten people.'

Mrs Elizabeth Reid lived at Renton, north-west of Dumbarton, in the Leven Valley:
'We were well aware of the 'mock airfield', as we regarded it, on the Kilpatrick Hills opposite us … I remember a night when the decoy proved its worth … we had terrific bombing, with waves of enemy planes droning over us and discharging their lethal cargoes on to what we were not sure until the 'all-clear' sounded. Then we emerged from our shelters, amazed to find an

almost intact village luridly lit by the dancing flames that leapt skywards along the whole length of the hill beyond us. It was a never-to-be-forgotten night and we breathed a prayer of thankfulness for our decoy, which had taken the full force of the raid, though we wondered how many casualties there were up there.

For weeks afterwards delayed action bombs were still exploding from time to time on the hillside. I remember on several occasions working at our kitchen window and seeing a bomb go up and jumping back to escape the blast that followed and fiercely thudded against the glass. Some windows were blown out but ours escaped although they were badly shaken.

I am not sure how we got to know of the decoy on the hill, but we often saw faint lights there and we certainly knew what it was all about... I know nothing of the other decoys ... but am firmly convinced that *our* one saved the Leven Valley from a similar fate to that of Clydebank.'

Rev Diana G Forman highlighted the danger of living near a site:
'I was a VAD [Voluntary Aid Detachment] in a camp reception station in Crosslet House, Dumbuck when the raids took place and because of decoy beacons on Dumbuck Hill immediately behind the house, we were serenaded the first night with incendiaries (one of which landed in our mess) and HE bombs.

Luckily our only casualty was our RAMC staff sergeant who was standing in the doorway when the bomb exploded and a piece of coping stone from the porch hit the front of his tin hat, the edge of it striking the bridge of his nose.

We coped with the fire in the mess by one VAD (myself) standing in the bath which was full of water and stirrup-pumping into a bucket in the passage, while another girl pumped from there to the seat of the fire which was in a leather armchair. I may say that my shoes never recovered (and in those days coupons were needed to buy new ones); the following day we were moved as every window in Crosslet House had been blown in.'

Agnes Hendry indicated how the effects of the lonely, often boring vigil which the staff of sites experienced, sometimes brought a breach in security:
'In the summer of 1941 I took my nephew who had been evacuated to Kirkintilloch for a walk in the Campsie area. As we sat by the roadside having a picnic lunch a man looked over the field gate beside us and started to chat. Eventually he said, "Would you like to see my shelter?" We followed him through the gate and across the field where he led us to an underground chamber.

'To our astonishment we were confronted with an impressively large switchboard which, he informed us, controlled the lighting up of the "Decoy City" which was laid out in the Blane Valley. Each switch had a name attached, "Argyle Street", "Sauchiehall Street" etc.

'When we left, my 12 year old nephew said to me solemnly, "We must never tell anyone what we saw today." As the essence of the exercise was secrecy one wonders how many more casual passers-by were invited to "see my shelter." '

Chapter Thirteen

OUTSTATIONS

But only a host of phantom listeners
That dwelt in the lone house then
Stood listening in the quiet of the moonlight
To that voice from the world of men
The Listeners, Walter de la Mare

If RAF Radlett was the nerve-centre of the operational activities of 80 Wing its large number of outstations were the highly sensitive nerve-ends; its eyes and ears. These small units, often situated in remote country districts and operating under strict security, led a detached existence from the conventional RAF stations. Personnel had little connection with service life generally and, except for the mobile units despatched to Europe after D-Day and certain large outstations formed in 1944 to try and counter V-2 rockets, were accommodated in civilian billets conveniently placed for work at each unit. Lasting friendships with local people often arose; sometimes these led to marriage.

The build-up from empty field to operational outstation was, particularly in the early history of 80 Wing, a complicated *ad hoc* affair. Installation improved as experience was gained.

The diversity of the locations brought problems. Outstations could be situated almost anywhere; in the low-lying farming country of East Anglia: perched on the Dover Cliffs and subjected to enemy cross-channel bombardment; in the depths of Surrey's commuter-land or remotely positioned high on the moors in the Peak District. Normally small RAF units relied on a nearby parent station for their administration, equipment and other services. This, for security reasons, was not acceptable in the case of 80 Wing outstations. A system capable of meeting all the administration and provisioning requirements for outstations which extended from the north of Scotland, through England, to the south of Wales was necessary.

Initially few sites were assigned their own officers, and to meet the technical requirements a large staff of visiting technical officers was maintained at the Radlett HQ whose responsibility was for the equipment at the outstations. At first they advised on installation of individual equipment eg, 'Meacons', *Aspirins*, and *Bromides*, and any important administrative decisions which were found to be necessary at what were really self-contained units. This was quickly found to be unsatisfactory for such a large area.

In April 1941 the work was de-centralised. Six 'areas' were formed – Northern (Marske, Yorkshire); Eastern (Braintree, Essex); Midland (Hagley, Warwickshire); South Eastern (Windlesham, Surrey); Southern (Ashmansworth, Hampshire); and South Western (Fairmile, Devon) each being responsible for the technical supervision and administration of the outstastations in its own region. A visiting mobile store looked after the clothing of personnel. Each area was under the command of an area officer (usually a Squadron Leader) with a senior NCO as deputy. They were responsible for visiting all outstations in their area. In the case of special equipment, advice and assistance was given by specialists from Radlett.

The siting, installation, and opening of new outstations still remained the duty of 80 Wing HQ and they would only be handed over to the area when fully established operationally.

The final development of the 'area' system brought about a complete de-centralisation of equipment and stores, each area HQ dealing directly with the appropriate maintenance unit, the exception being equipment peculiar to 80 Wing functions which was still provided through Radlett.[1] Thus order was brought into the administration and operating of the outstations. There had been a build up in efficiency; it had not always been so as personnel involved at the beginning readily testify.

[1]
PRO AIR 41/46,
Appendix 'M'.

Setting-Up a Site

Vic Flowers, a pre-war amateur radio enthusiast, who provided much of the information in this section, was a Civilian Wireless Reservist pressed quickly into service at the beginning of the war as a wireless operator. Evacuated with the British Expeditionary Force from France in June 1940 he arrived at RAF Yatesbury, dressed, 'with only what I stood up in.' Rekitted, he was told to report to 80 Wing, 'the nature of the duties involved not being disclosed.' Thus he arrived at Flimwell, near Hawkhurst in Kent, the first outstation.

It consisted, he found, of 'a few service vehicles and trailers in a large, recently requisitioned farmer's field on the outskirts of the small village.' Directly across the road from the entrance to the site was a General Post Office (GPO) Sub-Station which was later 'to perform a significant part in the location and operation of my new job.'

Closer examination of the field disclosed a number of places where underground cables had been terminated and, more obviously, some steel masts carrying aerial wires. It soon became obvious that 'the job' was still under development and undergoing a series of tests.

Initially, operational progress on the site proceeded very slowly and his duties consisted mainly of 'labouring and maintaining a 24 hour guard duty... the war seemed a long way away.' He was jerked back into the reality of the situation when, 'one morning a German bomber dropped a stick of bombs straddling the village, one of which landed on the site ten yards from the signals trailer.' Fortunately little damage was caused – only a broken window.

When it became clear that although Vic Flower's RAF trade was 'wireless operator' he also had knowledge and experience of radio techniques he became involved in the final development and setting up of the system which required careful liaison and exercise of discipline between the site at Flimwell and the Receiver Site at Hurst Green three miles to the south.

Like Flimwell this site was in a field close to the road. Equipment was housed in a wooden building 25ft by 12ft. Just visible over the sandbag protected blastwall were mounted three RAF direction-finding loop aerials each with a vertical wire supported by two telegraph pole masts. A partition separated the operator's room from the men employed on guard duties. In the operator's room a full length bench had been divided into three positions, each of which had a rack carrying a receiver and ancillary equipment.

Transport was non-existent apart from RAF pedal cycles. The only motor vehicle there was owned by the civilian technicians who were seconded from the Post Office Radio Research Department at Dollis Hill. Subsequently a Norton motorcycle combination (with a toolbox in place of a sidecar) with motorcyclist was added; later a new Hillman van was provided for use by the sergeant at Flimwell.

The Site developed:

As soon as the system was proved, the situation changed rapidly with the introduction of a strict service routine to take care of the influx of staff to both Sites. Flimwell received most attention with the addition of buildings to house more transmitters which were arriving from a variety of sources, all different and posing problems for the installers as they came with no technical information. The exception was a large STC transmitter, the M11, which was contained in two former 56-seater passenger coaches. One housed the transmitter and the other a diesel generator. This worked perfectly from the start.[2]

[2]
'Radio Counter-Measures – Meaconing', article by Vic Flowers in *QRV, The Journal of the RAF Amateur Radio Society*, Autumn 1993.

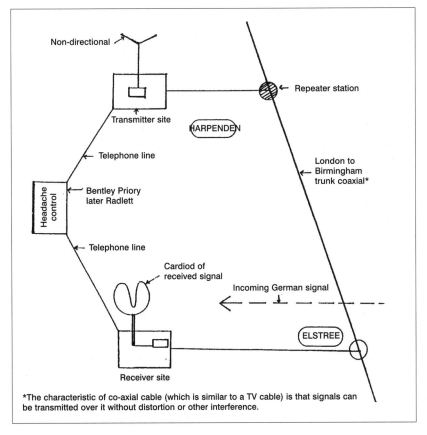

Non-directional

Repeater station

Transmitter site

HARPENDEN

Telephone line

London to Birmingham trunk coaxial*

Headache control

Bentley Priory later Radlett

Telephone line

Cardiod of received signal

Incoming German signal

ELSTREE

Receiver site

*The characteristic of co-axial cable (which is similar to a TV cable) is that signals can be transmitted over it without distortion or other interference.

Fig 23. Harpenden and Elstree sites.

The technical problems of setting up the early sites are described by Eric Palfreman who was a junior engineer at Dollis Hill from 1938-43 and worked on several:

The procedure was first to inspect and choose the site. Then we liaised with the local Telephone Section (for cabling) and then got the equipment installed and working before 'hand over' to the RAF team which was often 'officered' by ex-BBC Engineers.

The logistics for this were a bit haphazard in the extreme. The Harpenden site (See Figure 23) was one which could illustrate the difficulties. It was one of the first. There were very few transmitters available but we eventually got hold of an old BBC one. It had a lethal condenser which had to be discharged after transmitting. I used an old broom handle for this with a bar of copper at the end.

Initially, no huts were available for use but these were obtained by strong representation to the 'top man' at the time, Lord Beaverbrook (as he later became), Minister of Aircraft Production.

Sometimes it was necessary to spend the full 24 hours on the site, which, in view of our low wages at the time, was a Godsend. Accommodation was difficult. At East Stour in Dorset I had to sleep in the toilet of a garage. Also at that site we were bombed and E H Seaman and myself spent the night in a ditch. At Brotton (Yorkshire) and Fairmile (Devon) I stayed at local pubs where things were very different.

I mostly worked on my own with casual supervision ... sometimes the design was inadequate and local adjustments to components (obtained from local radio shops) had to be made. The 'stops' on the loop aerial rotator at Fairmile were made by the local blacksmith! The routing of the co-axial cable between Fairmile and Honiton had to be 'flexible' as the diggers needed to have access to pubs for their cider! [3]

[3]
Letter to author
from E Palfreman,
18th January 1994.

Equipment

The type and functions of equipment used by the Wing over the years of its existence varied between the smallish requisitioned diathermy sets employed in the early counter-measures against *Knickebein* to the giant US *Tuba* equipment it was intended to use much later in the war against German night fighters over Continental Europe.

Most of the radio manufacturers of the time seem to have participated in providing equipment. A variety of manufacturers' products on the same site was not uncommon. One site had four transmitters.[4] One Marconi; two STC (one was an M11, the same type installed in the liner *Queen Mary*: the other had been intended for use as one of the many satellite transmitters for BBC Television); the fourth was an RCA transmitter provided as part of the Lend-Lease – an Agreement, engineered by President Roosevelt, whereby the US assisted Britain with the accoutrements of war without actually, at this time, participating.

[4]
Letter to author
from G Rose,
4th December 1993.

Equipment provided to the Wing was sturdy and fulfilled the requirements although modification was often necessary. By April 1941 it could be reported that:

Many of our 'Meacon' transmitters have now been in operation for over 2,500 hours with relatively few breakdowns which reflects credit on installation, maintenance and supervision staffs.[5]

[5]
PRO AIR 26/580.

Sometimes the apparatus was plucked from unusual sources. Gerry Beaumont was, like Vic Flowers, a member of the Civilian Wireless Reserve and was called up just before the war started. He took part in the search for diathermy sets. A member of Emergency Fitting Party No 3 based at Market Weeton, near Driffield in Yorkshire, he and his colleagues scoured the country, under Flight Lieutenant Heald – he stayed in Heald's Hampstead flat for several weeks whilst they were working on the project – seeking out and collecting the sets. These were converted into power amplifiers which fed the signals into the aerials. The small transmitters which drove them were made at the Peto Scott factory in Stoke Newington in North London.[6]

[6]
Gerry Beaumont
in conversation
with the author,
19th July 1994.

No 80 Wing
Receiver Hut,
Elstree, Herts, 1940.
Left to right:
Ike Hatch, Geoff
Kent, Ken Fry,
Ian Johnstone.
R Lowson /
V Flowers

Elstree, 1940. The
Receiver Hut with
direction finding
aerials on the roof
and sandbag
protection for its
wall. R Lowson /
V Flowers

One transmitter at Harpenden in Hertfordshire had been taken from a US Navy destroyer sent to Britain under the Lease-Lend Agreement. It was:

... an old fashioned, ornate, effort, with curly bits of brass, very few meters, long handles instead of knobs ... We had to get it going, find out how to tune it (no handbook!), calibrate it and tabulate results. However we sorted it out and it was eventually used to assist our own aircraft.[7]

Elstree, the Receiver Site for Harpenden, nearest to the Radlett HQ of the Wing, was often used for trying out ingenious pieces of equipment and experimentation:

One piece we tried out was a very slow moving gramophone turntable with slotted moveable bits round the edge and a spring contact resting on them. The bits could be arranged so that when a signal from a signal generator was applied, a continuous signal and Morse call-sign was produced. This was fed to Harpenden and sent out via the US destroyer transmitter (see above). If the signal was interfered with the bits were re-arranged to 'scramble' the call-sign and warn our aircraft not to use it. Later a little instrument called a 'mutilator' was added which, when switched in, did the 'scrambling' automatically.[8]

Ralph Gabriel was chief engineer at the Rediffusion factory at Wandsworth in south-west London in 1940:

We were called upon in a very great rush to produce some transmitters for 'beam bending'. This we did by converting a number of 2kW audio frequency power amplifiers, which were going through the factory at the time, into radio transmitters; they were given the type number G12E. The 'E' stood for 'emergency' and the G12 was the type number of the audio amplifier which was converted. After the first rush we designed a new transmitter for the same purpose which, I think, was called G100.

We continued to make and install transmitters for 80 Wing for the rest of the war, including a very large one towards the end, which was intended to divert V-2 rockets, though we did not know if it ever actually went into service... Although we were fairly closely connected with the operation it was all very secret and we were never allowed to know anything about its successes or failures.[9]

A hint of irony was produced when the RAF Lorenz Blind Approach Transmitters were used, after modification by 80 Wing, for jamming, as this type of apparatus was originally used by the Luftwaffe for *Knickebein* transmissions.

When power was not connected to the mains – a frequent state of affairs on early sites – or there was a breakdown, diesel generators were used and it was essential that the staff at a site knew how to maintain and operate this equipment. This work could be strongly physical and labour intensive. There was also a problem with air locks when they ran out of fuel. Perched on Gibbett's Hill, a largish exposed site at Hindhead in Surrey, prone to cold winds, particularly in winter, Gordon Barrow remembered the drawbacks:

Having to start the big lorry-mounted Lister three-cylinder diesel-engined AC stand-by power units. It took two men on the starting handle, with the compression release valves open to get the fly-wheel turning, and a third to knock the compression lever on when we got a bit of speed up.[10]

Others found them equally hard to start and at times positively dangerous:

On a cold, frosty morning they were a menace. The starting handle was about four feet long, and one had to crank them up to get the necessary pressure. The kick-back was terrific, and caused several broken limbs I can tell you.[11]

[7] Letter to the author from R Lowson, 3rd June 1994.

[8] Ibid.

[9] Letters to the author from R Gabriel, 9th December 1993 and 18th December 1993.

[10] Letter to the author from G Barrow, 19th January 1994.

[11] Letter to the author from H J Skinner, 12th February 1993.

The wireless equipment itself was equally intimidating as a member of a site at Kimmeridge (Dorset) witnessed on one occasion:

'Mandrell' [jamming of German ground-based radar which controlled their night-fighters] *was now in operation to give the German radar a headache around the Cherbourg Peninsula opposite. We were told our equipment had been put together for the Dieppe Raid. It must have been done in a bit of a rush because the tuning knobs on our equipment made no contribution to its operation.*

An alternative way of tuning was found using a connecting piece, two upright tubes and a rod. The set was switched on for the instant response of an observer crouched over the power-pack below, under the bench.

If the valves in it came up white hot he uttered a formula like, 'Christ, switch off!' This prevented the thing going up in smoke and gave another chance for adjustments until the valves were a docile cherry red and the thing was tuned to the frequency suggested by a call from Radlett that day.

One day the chap under the bench was so alarmed at the state of the valves, he shoved his hand in and, straightening up with a severe electric shock almost dashed his brains out on the underside of the bench. We lived dangerously![12]

Routine work had to be carried out. Sets were 'run up' each evening on full 'dummy load' to test for operational efficiency when not in use; regular maintenance was required on the equipment, and work on the aerials was sometimes viewed with apprehension.

One man remembered having to lower one of the massive aerials at Mundesley in Norfolk which was successfully accomplished despite, 'Everyone expecting the thing to come crashing to the ground.'

Most outstation RAF personnel had great respect for the aerial riggers.

One could remember a BBC rigger at Alexandra Palace who, 'Could climb like a cat' and another, who witnessed the erection of aerials at Windlesham in Surrey still speaks with awe of the men who did it:

A gang of aerial riggers ... came, sometime in 1941 or 1942, and replaced our four sets of 70ft long aerial masts with 150ft ones. Each 150ft mast[13] *comprised six tubular sections, three of which they fastened together on the ground. My memory is not clear enough to be sure what happened next, but I imagine that they attached one end of this three-section*

[12]
Letter to the author from C Prior, 20th January 1993.

[13]
Perhaps this particular feat of 'derring-do' is put into perspective if one dwells upon the thought that Nelson's Column, in London's Trafalgar Square is something of the order of 170ft high.

Below: Alexandra Palace, North London, 1993. It was used for RCMs against *Y-Gerät. Author*

to a suitably hinged, firmly fixed base; about which they then hauled it into the vertical position and locked it there by suitable stay wires.

The next step was to combine two of the remaining three sections, and then to haul it up vertically... until the bottom was slightly above the top of the already erected three-section. Then came the tricky bit! One of the crew was hauled aloft in a bosun's chair, with the rather unenviable job of solidly connecting the bottom of the two-section on to the top of the three-section. Finally, a sixth section was sent up and the same luckless individual would have the further thankless task of connecting section six on to the top of section five.

Well, all the above operations were completed without a hitch on all the four pairs of masts at Windlesham, and most of us practically went down on our knees; not only to worship the obvious guts of the crew who had done the job, but also to thank Heaven that we ourselves had not been expected to take it on.

After the crew moved on we heard a rumour, never substantiated, that at another site, Templecombe, I think, a serious accident had happened to the occupant of the bosun's chair.[14]

[14]
Letter to the author
from C Lister,
10th February 1994.

Peter Bramham worked in the GEC Research Laboratories from 1942 onwards. Much of the work taking place was on equipment for radio counter-measures; he worked, for a time, on the ground-based part of *Grocer*, the ground installations of which were designed to give protection to returning RAF bombers. There were two sites for Ground *Grocer*, Dunwich near Southwold in Suffolk, and the other at Walmer in Kent. Here he described a visit to the latter:

The scanning receivers which we had put together were normally brought back to the Lab if they needed repair or adjustment. However on one occasion we were able to visit the site on Walmer golf course to deliver and re-adjust equipment... To go into a 'restricted area' you were supposed to have a special identity card – all I got was a letter from GEC saying that I was on work of national importance.

The receiver hut was under the shadow of a large parabolic reflector (what we call a 'dish' nowadays) which pointed out to sea. In the huts were racks containing equipment – a 'panoramic receiver' labelled 'AB26R' (AB26 was the Ministry of Aircraft

Production contract number) and a spare receiver, each with its power supply, and a panel for remote control of the transmitter. There was also a panel carrying a 'Variac' transformer for adjusting the mains voltage.

We waited for instructions from Radlett for the transmitter to be switched on... the frequency was set according to these telephone instructions. Later we saw spiky signals on top of the noise signal. These were, presumably, radar pulses.

In wartime, there was no briefing on projects such as 'Mandrel' and 'Grocer' – at least not at my level. You kept your ears open and your mouth shut, put two and two together and carried on from there. With 'Mandrel', the transmitters were in the aircraft taking part in the raid and with 'Grocer' relatively high-powered transmitters on the coast were used in an effort to protect our bombers from attack by enemy night fighters.[15]

Later in the war, 80 Wing personnel worked with US scientists as the European conflict moved towards its climax. One of them remembered life at the Sizewell outstation, located on an old coastguard station (now covered by the nuclear power station), on the Suffolk Coast:

The unit comprised of an experimental extremely short wave transmitter designed by American 'boffins' at Harvard University, (Dr Salisbury and his team), to be used in conjunction with 80 Wing personnel. Its object was radio counter-measures against enemy night fighters particularly in the Ruhr Valley. The site technical facilities were a transmitter caravan, and vans housing transformer unit, diesel generator etc, It was set up under the supervision of Dr Salisbury who was backed up by American construction and carpentry personnel. The three diesel generators were set up by the American manufacturer's representative. Apparently his firm had won the contract to supply, install, and maintain it for the whole time of the complete operation. He also introduced us to peanut butter and 'ringers', a game played with old horseshoes, which he endeavoured to play during every leisure period.[16]

[15]
Letter to the author
from P Bramham,
12th February 1994.

[16]
Letter to the author
from L G Dunbar,
6th February 1994.

Personnel outside
the GPO building
opposite entrance to
RAF Flimwell,
80 Wing, 1942-43.
Vic Flowers

'Salisbury's Circus', at Sizewell, Suffolk, in 1944. The RAF personnel were part of a US-led team from Harvard University under Dr Salisbury, who had built a giant jammer, code-named *Tuba*.
L Dunbar

This very extremely short wave transmitter was *Tuba*, high-powered equipment suitable for 'barrage' jamming. Whereas *Grocer* was low-powered and single-frequency jamming, TUBA was 300 times stronger and was to be used over the maximum barrage possible. As a large power input was needed it was located at Sizewell. Due to lack of enemy activity it was placed on 'care and maintenance' in December 1944, although a mobile *Tuba* had experimental tests and one unit was operational in February 1945 on waveband 330-450 Mc/s. In March 1945 all the equipment was dismantled and put in storage.[17]

[17] PRO AIR 41/46, part 2.

Dr Salisbury's team, a small, compact group of six Americans, 20 RAF personnel– plus the caravans, were nicknamed 'Salisbury's Circus'. All the technical motorised vans were manufactured in the US, placed in crates which looked like enclosed wooden garages, and shipped to Liverpool:

Our first task involved uncrating the equipment on the quayside at Liverpool, checking it, and ultimately transporting it to Sizewell. This took place during one of the coldest spells ever recorded on Merseyside up to that date and during our first coffee break we were unpleasantly surprised to find that the tariff included 'five shillings' [25p] deposit charge per mug. The dockers, it seems, were notorious crockery collectors!

The site was speedily completed and became a fully operational transmitting unit using, to quote Dr Salisbury, 'the latest "top hat" valve development to generate technical "mush" to mess up enemy night fighter oscilloscopes'.

Output from the transmitter (See Figure 24) was fed by an enclosed copper-lined conductive chamber, similar to a ventilation duct system, which increased in definite dimensions to join a purpose-made prefabricated netting antenna system also increasing in dimensions and lined up to the Ruhr Valley.[18]

[18] Op cit [16].

Post-War

There is an interesting sequel to the above story. Godfrey Frank, a young and inexperienced National Service Pilot Officer, found himself in 1947 in charge of the Ground Radio Counter-Measures Flight in Griston, a village on the edge of the airfield at RAF Watton, Norfolk. He found that he had inherited the Equipment Rump of 80 Wing and 100 Group. His 'parish', he remembers, consisted of three huge hangars, and a few huts:

The first hangar contained a very large number of assorted signals vehicles ... headed by two dozen huge American six-wheel convoy vehicles. The second hangar was piled high (much as one sees film of grain storage hangars on television now) with aerial mast 'cigar' sections, guy ropes and tethers. It was literally full of stuff, jumbled and up to the roof, and nothing else. The third hangar was full of 12ft high racks stuffed with condensers, resistors, valves and other component spares.

Shortly after he took over he received instructions that 'with the return of full accounting in the RAF' it was necessary for him to make a full inventory of all items held in his flight and to make a return of the lists within 21 days! He was surprised that he later obtained a Permanent Commission, 'after my somewhat trenchant reply pointed out that my doughty score of troops, even with my assistance, might take several years over the project.'

His flight was, he recalls, 'comprised of fairly independently-minded National Service airmen and a long way from the rest of RAF Watton during the working day.' Discipline was not helped by 'the fact that our principal day-to-day employment was to jack up each of the very many vehicles, and to turn its wheels, one quarter turn, every month. It did not rate highly in the popularity stakes as a worthwhile activity!'

His story becomes connected to the Dunbar experience recorded above:

The convoy vehicles in the hangar turned out to be two beautifully – and generously – equipped American-provided operational equipment compiled, I believe by the Massachusetts Institute of Technology, each convoy being an equipment called 'Tuba', a jammer of apparently high power. We once started to set one out, according to the manual, and it was like a gargantuan fairground! All the kit was spick and span, and each convoy had a beautifully lavishly equipped workshop vehicle with it. (I wonder where the lathes went?) [19]

Dollis Hill

No 80 Wing relied greatly on the co-operation of other organisations. A typical example of this was the support given by the Radio Branch of the then Post Office Engineering Research and Radio Departments[20] at Dollis Hill in North London. This was substantial and extensive – particularly in the Wing's infancy. The Radio Branch developed and produced – often hurriedly with little time for preparation, and not a little ingenuity – much of the necessary equipment for setting up operational stations; brought them to service readiness; and produced training material for the RAF personnel. Motivated by the priorities of war, the Post Office Engineers made a vital and major contribution to the Wing's activities.

Several of the Dollis Hill staff have written about these experiences. Professor Jim Merriman, one of the key figures, recalled the times:

[19]
Letter to the author from C G H Frank, 28th December 1993.

[20]
These were separate and distinct – even jealously so – with separate channels of report and control to Deputy Engineers-in-Chief.

Fig.24
Sketch Net Antenna for *Tuba* at Sizewell.
L.G.Dunbar.

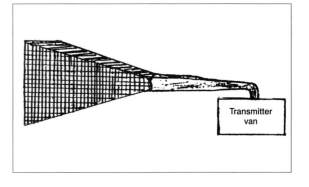

Transmitter van

In the early months of 1940 Harold Stanesby (another GPO Engineer colleague) and I began to speculate on ways in which we could manipulate the enemy's radio navigation systems without his knowledge... One idea was that whenever the enemy set up a radio beacon, we might be able to pick up and re-broadcast it on an identical radio frequency carrier and with identical modulation, but with completely confusing in-built location information.

The two GPO engineers initially identified two main problems. The first was 'to preserve absolute identicality since any distortion in the re-radiated signal not present in the original, would identify it as such and would nullify the objective.' It was also necessary to protect the receiving aerial from the re-radiated signal from the transmitter site. Therefore, it would be necessary to separate the transmitter and receiver sites by 3-5 miles 'and also introduce a small hill in between as well.'

This produced a third problem – how to bridge the gap of several miles:

Stanesby realised that the frequency of the emissions (150-600kHz) was within the capability of the then recently commissioned London to Birmingham co-axial cable.[21] *He saw that, if we could employ a section of that route, we could establish an operational system fairly quickly. Fortunately two tubes (there were four in total) of the cable were unequipped and the route of the cable was roughly in the right orientation, south-east to north-west.*

A receiving station was established on the roof of the Faraday Building (which was the Main Trunk Switching Centre of the GPO) in the City of London near St Pauls. The receiver was fed by a remotely controlled loop aerial, a vertical aerial, and a variable phase shifter. This fed a specially-built double super-heterodyne receiver[22] to re-constitute the signal. The first transmitter unit was located in a corner of a hastily requisitioned field some 13 miles away in rural Hertfordshire behind the Elstree Repeater Station.

A series of ground tests generated confidence, and showed that the technique of 'masking' at ground level had been mastered:

For several weeks we operated the system under the control of 80 Wing. We responded to mock 'target emissions' assigned by them, often at very short notice. Testing was often very confused since the airborne tests had to be controlled not only against the radio frequency emissions at that particular time but also, for the sake of the aircraft, with reference to the state of the balloon barrage which was both 'state of threat' and 'state of weather' dependent.

Whilst these early tests were being carried out, the Germans had advanced into Holland and Belgium and it had become obvious that they were increasingly dependent upon medium wave direction-finding equipment on land, sea and air operations. Scores of simply-coded MF radio beacons were being established both ahead of, and in the wake of, the German advances.

Listening posts were set up on the east coast to monitor these stations. For example, Professor Merriman has clear memories of spending nights in a direction finding (D/F) equipped van on the sea front at Frinton monitoring and logging these emissions. Fortunately the enemy used very simply-coded Morse identification signals emitted at a comfortably slow speed. It soon became clear that the threat was very real indeed.

As June approached it became obvious that these radio systems would be used in the developing aerial war against Britain:

[21] When this pre-war-installed cable was examined in 1980 it was found to have paper insulation, was lead sheathed and still in superb condition considering the long time it had been in the ground. Letter to the author from V Flowers, 23rd December 1993.

[22] The super-heterodyne is the most commonly used technique in radio reception. The incoming radio frequency is converted into a lower intermediate frequency by mixing it with a signal generated inside the receiver, called the 'local oscillator'. This intermediate frequency is easier to amplify and manipulate than the initial radio frequency.

Mumford therefore called a joint Air Ministry/Post Office meeting… and we decided to establish an experimental semi-mobile 'masking' unit and to make preparation for a major construction of several tens of such units if the pilot experimental system proved successful… We were to act as technical agents for the RAF's 80 Wing who were in operational command. We were to have responsibility for training and technical operations.

Albert (later Sir Albert) Mumford was head of the Radio and Research Branches at Dollis Hill and later became Engineer-in-Chief of the Post Office as indeed, subsequently, did Professor Merriman, who later still, became Board Member for Technology of the successor organisation, British Telecommunications. In 1940 the term 'Post Office' covered total responsibility for all forms of communications, telecommunications and broadcasting as well as the mail.

First it was necessary to see if the system would work. The Dollis Hill staff taking part were put into teams working under the overall control of Albert Mumford. Each team was responsible for a unit consisting of a pair of receiver and transmitter sites separated by a distance of five miles:

The site nearest the enemy would be the receiver with the aerials designed to reject the signals from the second site which was the transmitter. Signals were sent from the receiving site to the transmitter by overhead, suspended co-axial cable.

Professor Merriman thinks that, 'one of the minor miracles of the war' was that the development and manufacture of co-axial cable and other associated telecommunications equipment had, 'by accident come to a point of readiness at the right time.' This was due in no small part to the work of the former Post Office Radio Branch. 'It was also fortunate' he adds, that R F J 'Doc' Jarvis of that branch 'probably knew more about the radio frequency transmission capability of co-axial cables at that time than anyone else in Europe.' By his own efforts he had persuaded UK manufacturers to develop both lightweight, aerial and underground, protected, co-axial cable, 'He had in mind the possible extension of wire broadcasting into television broadcasting in the local telephone network.' Industry had already started pilot production of such cable and, 'we succeeded in commandeering a number of "frustrated" export orders in the Marconi works at Chelmsford.'

Flimwell, in Kent, was chosen for the first operational trial and with other colleagues, A N Christmas and E F Newley, (both would become prominent in Britain's post-war atomic weapons programme), 'Doc' Jarvis and Jim Merriman assembled the teams to manufacture and build it:

The double super-heterodyne receiving equipment was made in the Dollis Hill workshop, with long hours of overtime being worked, over a couple of weekends. Great support for the 'on-site' installation was forthcoming locally. Len Fagg of the Tunbridge Wells area of the Post Office Engineers, put all his resources at our disposal. Whatever we wanted was available almost before we had finished asking for it … it was an interesting phase in one's life. We had clearly defined objectives and almost unlimited power to command and control.

For a period of two to three months a significant proportion of the Radio Branch at Dollis Hill was committed to the 'Meacon' work, commandeering a considerable tranche of the workshop facilities and employing a large industrial back-up. By the end of October 1940, the operational teams had been set up and handed over to the RAF to operate 'Meacons' (or 'Mock beacons') at Elstree-Harpenden; Flimwell-Robertsbridge; Windlesham-Woking; Ditchling-Henfield; Eye-Diss; Scole-Harleston; Newbury-Henstridge; Ottery St Mary, Newton Abbot, Shepton Mallett and one in each of the Chatham and Southend areas. Professor Merriman recalled incidents from some of the sites:

At Flimwell we were bombed and shot up by two German Heinkels on the loose – fortunately without injury save to our dignity as we dived for cover... At Henfield, north of Brighton, we had the satisfaction of seeing a German bomber flying southwards into the anti-aircraft barrage obviously in the firm belief that he was heading northwards towards London. It was at 'The Swan' at Harleston, Norfolk, that a woman in near-hysterics ran into the breakfast room shouting 'There is a German in my back garden!'... The local policeman and an ARP warden took control of the situation. The German pilot had been shot down... having been totally disorientated by the confusion and failure of his navigation systems. Half-an-hour later he, too, was in 'The Swan' having hot coffee whilst awaiting formal capture.'

Sometimes the local population was unco-operative. Visiting the Woking site, in Surrey, Merriman and a colleague obtained rooms at 'a select hotel for country gentlefolk' but were 'bluntly and firmly refused re-admission in the early hours of the morning having got the "Meacon" on the air during a reasonably heavy air raid.'

On another occasion, driving back towards London with a colleague from the Scole site on the Suffolk/Norfolk border they were horrified to see the distant glow of ... *the first fire-bomb raids on the London docks and watched aghast from the Chelmsford to Brentwood road the mounting furnace flames against the night sky. We waited at the eastern end of the North Circular Road until an all-clear was given.*

As the Battle of Britain developed requiring extra resources, provisioning for the 'Meaconing' work became more difficult and 'there was much "raiding" of local suppliers for components.' There was also the problem of securing adequate power at the sites. The Dollis Hill engineers sometimes found (even when they had handed equipment over to the RAF) it was not properly looked after:

The generators were designed for continuous running and minimum maintenance, but not the sort of treatment that we experienced at the Shaftesbury site when, having handed over to the RAF, we had a shout for help two weeks later. There had been no maintenance whatever on the engine, not even a check of oil level. Under full load a 'connecting rod' had broken and been forced out of the engine casing to be found 50 yards away in a field.

But, it would appear, significant operational progress had been made in thwarting the effectiveness of enemy aerial navigation with these Dollis Hill efforts: *Unknown to us, during the latter weeks of our activities, our very success had forced the Germans to hasten the deployment of an alternative – 'Knickebein' – a navigation system of vastly improved accuracy against which R V Jones and Robert Cockburn developed counter-measures using the same principles as our meacons but about which, at that time, we knew nothing. It is possible that a cold, post-hoc, analysis of these operations would show that an excess of secrecy resulted in unnecessary re-invention.*

'Many warm friendships developed,' Professor Merriman remembered, 'some are still maintained.' He also recalls attending a post-war International Telecommunications meeting in Geneva where one of life's coincidences took place:

... I met my Bundespost *'opposite', and a friendship developed lasting until my retirement. It turned out that Ernst Dietrich (a good friend of many in the PO Engineering Department) had for a while been part of a team trying to unravel what we were doing to their navaids* [navigational aids] *and had eventually discovered how our interference with their navaids had been 'spoilt'.*

Professor Merriman summed up the work of the Dollis Hill teams as 'a little known story of the involvement of one small part of the Post Office in the war effort. It takes its own small place against the vast canvas and perspectives of the times.'[23]

[23]
From articles by Professor J H H Merriman in *RSS Newsletters* No 43 (July 1991); No 47 (July 1992), with some minor additions by Professor Merriman. The reader seeking greater technical detail should refer to these articles.

Jack Haworth was also in the team that went to Flimwell:

We worked all day and every day and it was with some surprise and pleasure that I heard Jimmy Hobbs announce on our first Saturday night that 'It's just past midnight, from now on it's Sunday and we get paid overtime!'

In addition to being shot at by German aircraft and running for cover they also had an unexploded bomb close to the receiving site. A member of the local 'Dad's Army' (Local Defence Volunteers – later the Home Guard) was detailed to mount an over-night guard on it. The following morning he failed to impress them as a candidate likely to rate a high score in an intelligence test by meeting them with a big grin and telling them he 'had moved the bomb – just for a joke – and was waiting to see the reaction of his commander and the local army officers!'

Jack Haworth was also full of praise for local support:

It was only necessary to telephone the area engineer, or his deputy, and I got all the help and stores items I required. I don't remember having to worry about records or paperwork. Considering 'There was a war on' it amazed me how quickly things got done – probably due to good staff work back at Dollis Hill.

He remembered how a site was built up:

With a bit of luck the first item to arrive on site would be a large pre-fabricated wooden hut which had to be erected. An RAF sergeant (a regular) would report for duty followed by a collection of airmen recruited from all walks of life. A local carpenter would make and fit a wooden bench and at the receiver site put three small platforms on the roof to support loop aerials. Equipment would arrive from Dollis Hill which we installed and tested.

At the transmitter site the RAF would erect the transmitting mast and aerials. Post Office staff from the local area would dig trenches, lay ducts and pull in cable. Sometimes staff were supplemented by soldiers from a nearby camp who would invariably dig a trench much wider than necessary.

In a short time the site was put together and then the Dollis Hill staff had to train the RAF men in the use of the equipment, 'which included staying up with them throughout the night when the system went into service.' Transport was a problem, 'We often had to walk'. At Flimwell one man borrowed a motor cycle combination. This was a linesman's vehicle fitted with a toolbox (a standard fitting in those days) instead of a sidecar. Occasionally it was possible to borrow a cycle, 'In Scotland, the area manager arranged for me to borrow a postman's "sit up and beg" cycle which was fine until the snow arrived!'

One minor setback occurred at Henfield, north of Brighton, when one of the lorries bringing the transmitter failed to arrive. It eventually turned up, 'and the driver – a typical cockney – explained he had been searching for us in *Enfield*, North London, instead of Henfield in Sussex.'

The enemy continued to prove unhelpful:

One Sunday morning at Ditchling, in Sussex, several German bombers came 'hedge-hopping'. They machine-gunned the village and then swooped over the site... I had a gang digging a cable trench and, as I dived for cover behind a stone wall, I noticed all of the gang had disappeared into the trench except one very large workman who was trying to get his stomach below ground level. In spite of all this, the link went operational in record time.

The little amount of off-duty time had its moments. Looking for accommodation in Eye, Suffolk, Haworth found 'digs' in a condemned abattoir. The next job took him to Braintree, Essex where:

... at the end of one very busy day the sergeant suggested that he and I should go into the town for a drink. There was a 'pea-souper' of a fog but in due course we saw a light under a door and on a signboard overhead we could just see 'The Sun'. We went in and ordered two beers but all we got was a very peculiar look from the 'barman' – we were in the Sun Insurance office!

Towards the end of 1940 Jack Haworth was in Scotland at Ayton, north of Berwick:

'It was December, we had lots of snow, and we joined the locals in celebrating Christmas and Hogmanay. Sometime during the celebrations Squadron Leader Barton-Chapple broke his arm. When we were ready to go operational he was in hospital at Edinburgh and the transmitting aerials, which he considered his speciality, were still lying on the ground. I read the erection instructions, collected all the airmen together and briefed them. Hardly daring to breathe I watched the masts slowly rise up, and then the aerials. We were ready.' [24]

[24]
From article by Jack Haworth in
RSS Newsletter No 46
(April 1992).

Robin Looser shed light on the back-up necessary in London:

At the Wembley Labs (an overflow from Dollis Hill) one lunch time we heard on the radio of the capitulation of France and then not long afterwards, we were launched into new activity which I seem to remember we called the 'German Beacon System'. Besides working on the production of tuner/amplifiers there was also the matter of joining up lengths of early polythene (or similar cable) to connect receiver and transmitter sites. I well remember spending a Saturday soldering joints connecting inner conductors and then forming the outer conductor from strands of solid tinned copper. The floor was covered with snaking cable but somehow it all got unravelled and coiled up and sent out.

A decision was made to run the cable in ducts as the joints in it were not robust enough to withstand manhandling in the field. Usually this gave little trouble but a problem arose on one occasion. At Ottery St Mary, Devon, the local gang started to draw in a new cable over existing ones. They broke for a cup of tea. When they returned:

They found the new cable impossible to move. It was soon realised that the heat gen-erated by friction had softened the rubber wax layer provided to protect lead-covered cables from corrosion in that area and that, on cooling, the old and new cables were welded together. When an empty duct was found all went well.[25]

He also remembered the effect of the V-1s on the civilian population:

... I was told to take an assistant and some equipment in a van to a small RAF station at Ditchling in Sussex ... on the way there we called for a meal at Lyons in Camberwell in South London and I well remember queuing up for service when suddenly the dreaded 'buzz' was heard. The manageress said, 'Oh, my God!' and disappeared. Looking around I could see only table tops with food on them – all the customers were under them. Very soon the engine cut out and the bomb landed and exploded – not very near us luckily – and everyone emerged and carried on as if nothing had hap-pened. When we reached Ditchling… the radio was quietly playing a tune of the time, 'Love is All' [26]

Monty Meatyard, found it was necessary to be fit and brave:

We took the transmitters from the 50 or so over-age American destroyers which had been transferred to the Royal Navy in exchange for the granting of air bases to the US in Newfoundland, Bermuda and the West Indies in autumn 1940. Our job was to adapt the units to the new power supplies and convert them to straightforward 1kW tunable amplifiers.

My most poignant memories are of having to manhandle a large number of these heavy, unwieldy units from the high tailboards of RAF lorries through two staggered doors into the lab and reversing the exercise after modification and testing. Also, of being conveyed at high speed and in almost total darkness (it was in the 'blackout', of course) through narrow Suffolk lanes in ten ton RAF trucks driven by intrepid RAF drivers.[27]

Tony Hastings helped to commission the Windlesham Site; he heard the church bells ring a false invasion scare, and 'we saw the light from the fires in the London docks 30 miles away'. Then he also worked on the ex-US destroyer transmitters:

We had about 60 of these things. They were mostly Marconi Marine transmitters, but we had a Rediffon 1kW – a lethal device! When it was wound up at the low-fre-quency end anything you got near, you drew sparks off. We had to modify them, of course. I should think they were manufactured in the 1920s. They were a 'Godsend' really and good enough for what we wanted them for. We couldn't get too many trans-mitters out of Marconi – a lot of people were after them at the time, (ie the other Services).

Christmas 1939 I found myself sat on top of the HQ Building (St Martin's le-Grand) with a transmitter. We were testing a radio compass at the time and I was up there with a Hallicrafters transmitter. It was perishing cold and the hut we were using was built for air raid precautions gas drill. There had been tear gas in there and if you stayed in the hut too long your eyes started running and you had to get out into the freezing cold for a few minutes to recover.

We tested a mobile unit for service in North Africa. The link between receiver and transmitter had to be radio rather than cable. These units were in big trucks, like an articulated lorry, the receiver in one and the transmitter in the other; aerials on the

[25]
From article by Robin Looser in
RSS Newsletter No 44 (October 1991).

[26]
Letter to the author from R Looser,
21st July 1994.

[27]
Letter to the author from L R Meatyard,
1st August 1994.

roofs. We made about four or five. They did the same job there as in the UK – 'Meaconing' and 'Jamming'. They were tested in a large field at Bricket Wood where 'mobile type' masts had been erected. A cottage in the field was used as the guard-room. Sten guns had just been issued to the guards and one of them let me have a go at firing one. A couple of days later one of the masts fell down and someone put the story around that I had shot it down!

Much later we were involved in the counter-measures against 'doodle-bugs'. We worked on a 'broad-band' thing, ie something that did not need tuning. Only about one in 20 had a radio. We got a panic call just after D-Day when they found these things.[28]

[28]
Interview with
Tony Hastings
by the author,
22nd July 1994.

Tom Kilvington remembers that all Radio Branch engineers who could be spared from other duties were 'brought into the picture' to superintend the installation, testing, and commissioning of equipment, and the training of RAF personnel in its operation. Security was tight. Not a member of the section of the Radio Branch which had started the meaconing work, he found that one section did not know what another section was doing 'except in case of need.'

Allocated for several weeks to Windlesham where the RAF contingent's CO was 'Stephens, a former BBC station engineer', like many others working on meaconing, he was unaware at the time what effect the scheme was having:

We had virtually no feedback as to the effectiveness of the 'Meacons'. The odd rumour turned up now and again to the effect that a German aircraft had landed at a British airfield way off its course and we all hoped it was due to our efforts. But it was not long before Medium Wave Beacons were abandoned by the Luftwaffe in favour of Very High Frequency systems as used for the Coventry and other similar raids.[29]

[29]
Letter to the author
from Tom Kilvington,
13th September 1994.

Chapter Fourteen

OUTSTATION LIFE

If we locked on to a German he was finished....
We just fed him to the fighters.
There is a story about a Dornier that threw out
its rubber raft over Croydon. I don't know how true that is!
H Manton

The tapestry of each outstation was created by the interweaving of the warp of common purpose with the weft of personal experience. Activities, observation and contacts made by the staff whether occupied with the task in hand, or in pursuit of leisure, created the atmosphere in which the outstation operated. A variety of incidents, sometimes quite bizarre, occurred. Some are anecdotally recorded below.

On Duty

Gordon Barrow (Heston Airport, London)
'I had no idea it was such a big operation... Our biggest fear was falling asleep and failing to shut down the transmitter at times previously decided by HQ. Everyone had to shut down so they could listen in to the enemy signals and the thought of us being the only transmitter on the air brought visions of "being shot at dawn!"'

Cecil Broadhurst (Ide Hill, Kent)
'I joined as an 18 year old. We were setting up a transmitter ... we were paid by money order, had a corporal in charge of us and an airman with a rifle to guard us... another wireless mechanic, along with the corporal ran the show for about three months until new arrivals increased our complement... At each site we were issued with special ration cards.'

Frank Churchill (Ditchling, Sussex)
'I learnt to read and send Morse whilst a scoutmaster in North London... In 1944 I was working against the V-1s at Ditchling. Some of them sent out radio signals for the Germans to use for direction finding for accuracy. Only about one in six of the V-1s sent out an automatic radio signal, but we picked it up and then "Meaconed" it by landline westwards towards Southampton, from whence the signal was sent out again by transmitter to 'spoof' (fool) the Germans as to their accuracy. As only a few carried a radio transmitter we, as listeners, really had a lot of wasted time, but it was very necessary in order to create as much confusion as possible.

We worked in wagons, camouflaged with netting, on daylight shifts mostly, as few of the V-1s came over after dark. We were sometimes able to listen to an approaching V-1 over the coast, plot it on our wall map, then walk outside the wagon trailing an extended lead for our earphones, hearing the signal from the V-1 and also be able to see the RAF fighters 'wing tipping' them which was the most successful way of destroying them.'

Philip Colehan (Mintlaw, Aberdeenshire)
'I was posted to Mintlaw in Aberdeenshire. It was 80 Wing's most northerly station. The weather could be extreme and one of the most unpopular jobs was to lower the aerials when there was a danger of them breaking under the weight of snow and ice.

In 1943 we used to provide 'homing' beacons for the US (Army) Air Force daylight bombing raids. They were known as *Splasher* beacons, and we used to 'key' the identification signal in Morse once every minute. Each day Radlett would telephone with transmitting instructions giving frequency, transmission times and the call-sign. One of our number did not know the phonetic alphabet very well. The instruction on this occasion was to use the call-sign 'Seven N-for-Nan Seven'. Our man wrote down and repeated, wrongly, 'Seven M-for-Man Seven'. The USAAF thought that this was a spurious beacon and did not use it for 'homing'. Our man was put on a disciplinary charge but fortunately he was a skilled, self-taught, radio mechanic. A few days after the incident he was on duty when some of our equipment failed. We had no spare and as the equipment was a sealed unit we were not allowed to open it up. To get a replacement would have taken 24 hours and so our man broke the seals, identified the fault and repaired it. Because of this he was reprimanded – and taken off the charge!

Another job we did at Mintlaw was to 'screen' a very powerful radio beacon in Northern Ireland which was used by pilots ferrying aircraft across the Atlantic. Because it could have been used by German pilots flying over the North Sea, we, and other No.80 Wing stations, used to re-radiate the beacon using a low field strength. This meant it could not be used for direction finding by the Luftwaffe.

In the summer of 1944 the flying-bombs (V-1s) were being used and V-2 rockets were expected. It was assumed that both of these weapons were controlled by electronic means and the 'boffins' prepared to take countermeasures. A small group of us were sent to Hawkhurst in Kent to erect, as a matter of extreme urgency, a group of aerials. These were made of wood, four-sided lattice type, approximately 100ft high. They were pre-fabricated, each piece was numbered and were bolted together like Meccano. About half the aerial was erected laid sideways on the ground, then we heaved it upright before climbing to finish the construction. It was high summer and we worked from early morning until dusk every day under the leadership of Flight Lieutenant Arnabaldi.

L G Dunbar (Longside, Aberdeenshire)
The main functions at Longside were to monitor the transmissions emanating from Norway, in particular Stavanger and Bergen, which, from time to time, transmitted, in Morse, call-signs 'SR' and 'BN' followed with continuous information to assist enemy aircraft in navigational direction. Our 'operators'

gave the wireless-mechanics a running commentary on many occasions of the fruitless requests from enemy aircraft for specific correct 'homing' details – this was unusual since full information was not often imparted.

Vic Flowers (Flimwell and Hurst Green, Kent)
'I felt quite at home arriving for the second time at Flimwell and Hurst Green. The sites were now in charge of a Pilot Officer and some of the administration duties previously done by airmen found to be suitably qualified had been taken over by NCOs. Even a small NAAFI was able to open for a time each day.

I was soon involved in a new system of 'Meaconing' which provided much 'job satisfaction' as it brought operators into a form of close contact with the enemy. The system, additional to the meaconing of static signals, operated exclusively on signals from German aircraft flying from bases in occupied territory... Much information was obtained from permanently monitoring the frequencies used by German airfield control towers who were testing the radios of the aircraft being prepared for a raid. From the call-signs used, details of the number of aircraft, type and squadron could be ascertained and advance warning given to our defences. The aircraft meaconing operator would 'phase out' (ie reject his own transmitted note) as near as possible and wait for a German aircraft to call his control and ask for a 'bearing': the ground station control would reply. The German aircraft would then send its call-sign and a series of 'A's in Morse for the control station to take a bearing. The aircraft meaconing operator would then meacon the transmissions from the aircraft so causing the German ground control to get an incorrect bearing... the aircraft meaconing operator would add to the confusion by allowing some of the enemy transmissions to proceed 'unmeaconed'.

The aircraft meaconing operators found that two hands were not sufficient to obtain a perfect meacon condition in the heat of the moment due to the number of operations involved. As a result the 'send' key normally on the bench was re-located on the knee with great success. Bob Lowson at Elstree developed this system and became a very skilled operator. When we were using *Aspirin* counter-measures against *Knickebein,* George Rose, a Leading Aircraftman in charge of a watch at Flimwell, could bring one of the STC 'TU4' transmitters used for this purpose on the air within half a minute of receiving the frequency.

At Flimwell, like every RAF operational site, it was necessary to provide security and checks at site entrances for the full 24 hours. The airmen employed on these duties had very little training in the use of firearms but each had been issued with a Lee Enfield rifle and a quantity of ammunition. There were several incidents involving the discharge of rifles either accidentally or mistakenly that could have led to fatal consequences. I was involved in one on a dark, foggy night when a guard fired several shots at what he thought was an intruder smoking a cigarette who had failed to answer his challenge. Fortunately I was able to establish to the satisfaction of the guard that the glowing cigarette was in fact a cracked insulator on one of the aerial mast guy ropes 'arcing' with the transmitter. The 'intruder' was a very convincing shadow.'

Peter Giles (Hurst Green: Scarborough, Yorks)
'Security demanded that guard duties were carried out. At Hurst Green, at least during the summer of 1941, the atmosphere was fairly relaxed. The guard on duty would patrol the field, which was right by the Tunbridge Wells to Hastings road, with his rifle slung, and keep an eye on the gate to admit authorised callers. One day fury descended upon us. A senior Army officer, a Brigadier I think, complained to HQ that, when passing our site in a staff-car carrying his pennant, "the proper compliment had not been paid by a sentry." From then on the guards were required to perform proper 'sentry-go' and only patrol the field at night.

Later I was posted to Scarborough to continue the watch against *Knickebein*. There were only four of us, in a ten feet by ten feet hut in the grounds of Scarborough Castle. We had 'Beveridge' aerials ('antennae' was an Americanism then coming into use along with their unpopular phonetic alphabet). The 'Beveridge' array consisted of four bare-copper stranded wire aerials each about 100ft long and only some eight feet from the ground. These were supported by wooden poles and attached to them by ceramic insulators… Well, clay-pigeon shooting was a popular pastime in the Castle grounds at this time!… One day, having gone over to the generator hut to charge batteries, I was trapped there while the guns blazed away. We lost a lot of insulators to shot-gun pellets!

In August 1944 I was posted to Hope Point, between Walmer and St Margaret's Bay in Kent. Early in September it seemed that the Germans were trying to get rid of their V-1s as the Allied armies advanced eastwards. What with their noise and that of our AA (anti-aircraft) guns there was 'Bedlam' at times. One day, towards St Margaret's Bay, an AA shell scored a 'near miss' on an approaching V-1, knocking it off its course. It partially corrected itself but height had been lost and the bomb flew straight into the cliff-face. Orange flame, black smoke and white chalk billowed up, followed seconds later by a thunder-clap!

Situated where we were, on a cliff top, with huts and aerials silhouetted against the evening sun (as seen from Cap Gris Nez) 'Jerry' may well have been curious. One evening in mid-September … there appeared a rash of what looked like little red sparks on the French Coast. After some seconds, explosions led us to think that ships in the Channel were being fired on. There were more 'sparks' and more explosions, this time shaking the ground. Vibration shook articles from the shelves and stopped the clock. Then shrapnel fell on the hut roof… one shell passed overhead and was heard to fall just inland. We were the target! Then all went quiet again.'

Ernie Hackney (Eastleigh, Hampshire)
'All I had to do was to listen in the afternoon, when the enemy were lining up their transmitters on 30 or 31.5 MHz and then tell Radlett if I heard dots or dashes. I was then instructed to switch my transmitter onto these frequencies using dots or dashes as required.'

Ken Humphries (Stockbridge, near Winchester)
'We were given arms instruction together with bayonet practice (a bale of

straw was the victim)… and were honoured – or so the 'powers that be' said – to be given the use of a Bren gun for a few days, together with sufficient ammunition for some of us to have a few bursts with the gun; we also had grenade throwing practice at Middle Wallop aerodrome. Later I was trained at Cosford as a PT (physical training) Leader and on return to Stockbridge I took PT lessons a couple of times a week, but received no extra pay.

As an AC2 Wireless Mechanic, a Group 1 Trade, pay was 4/3d (about 22p) a day; in November 1942 I was reclassified AC1 and received another 9d per day. In July 1944 I was promoted LAC (Leading Aircraftsman) whereupon my pay increased by one shilling (5p) a day.

As regards secrecy, everyone in the village purported to know "what was going on at the wireless station", but I don't think many people understood what was being achieved. We were once questioned by service policemen in Winchester about our unit… but we steadfastly refused to divulge the whereabouts of our site; we told them we were within bounds in Winchester. After a lengthy interrogation, the police commended us on maintaining our silence.'

Jack Len (Mundesley, Norfolk)
'I joined the RAF in July 1941… I was sent off on a Wireless Mechanic's course (the proverbial 'square peg' in the 'round hole' – perhaps someone noticed I matriculated with a 'credit' in physics! After three months in London doing a crash 'theory' course I was sent to Cranwell for 'practical' work.

In 1942 I went to Mundesley on the north coast of Norfolk. It was a bleak February day when I arrived. The railway station had a short platform at each side of a double track (much of the line was single track) and deserted except for one person in RAF uniform who had come to meet me. RAF Mundesley turned out to be just one field on the Cromer Road outside the village. In the field were five or six huts and a mass of tall wireless aerials. The first hut which was located near the gate served as guardroom, office and stores. The remainder were dotted about the field. Each housed a transmitter (or maybe two in some cases) – large pieces of equipment which today would resemble a domestic freezer. These transmitters were connected to the various aerials.'

Bob Lowson (Harpenden and Elstree, Herts)
'I had an amateur transmitting licence before the war and was very good at Morse which was why, in early 1940, I was kicked out of the RAF Radio School at Blackpool almost as soon as I got there and sent to 80 Wing at Radlett.

I was posted on to Harpenden and taught to handle the big transmitters used at the time to re-broadcast the German beacons. There were four transmitters and five huts (apart from the control hut in the trees); three were used for meaconing enemy beacons and the other for early experiments on meaconing aircraft… On one occasion the German Control Station 'FLR' gave an aircraft a position directly over us! He wasn't of course – we had meaconed him but that's where he thought he was!

During periods of concentrated German raids an all-night session of air-craft meaconing left one worn out and feeling like a 'wet rag'. For hours on end you couldn't relax; tense and keyed up on the equipment we were lost in a world of aircraft signals, ground stations requests for bearings or positions and making sure they got the 'wrong' ones. We would pick up a vulnerable 'plane and latch onto it until it ran out of fuel and was forced to land. It was a real battle between you, the German operator and the German control. It was very exhilarating when you won.

One night as NCO in charge of aircraft meaconing at Elstree I was tuning around the German aircraft frequencies looking for any activity when I heard a signal with a note like a 'buzz-saw' sending SOS. It was an RAF 'plane. It sent its position, said it was landing in the sea and vanished. I passed the information on to Radlett. Many years later I was talking to a Second World War pilot and mentioned the story to him. He asked me for further details and then said that at the very time of the above incident he had been flying a twin-engined aircraft back from a sortie over Holland and had been hit by *flak*. He lost height and was forced to land in the sea. His wireless operator had a damaged transmitter and could not tune it. He used his key in the hope that he was putting out a signal. They were not far from the English Coast and were picked up by an air-sea rescue launch. It could have been that 'plane I heard. I hope it was.'

H Manton (Mundesley, Norfolk)
'I was in the Civilian Radio Reserve because I worked at EMI. I went to Mundesley on 17th August 1941. Our site was right on the cliff edge. It was on rising ground; on the peak was a large radar station with great discs you could see 25 miles away. The Germans never touched them; they used them as landmarks.

We never knew at the time why we were doing things. We were just part of the system. Our satellite receiver station was at Edenthorpe, 5 miles away. We would re-broadcast in such a way that Edenthorpe could reject it, but nobody else could.

We used to get a marvellous reception of 'Lord Haw-Haw' from Hamburg. On one occasion we re-broadcast him. It was only after the war that I found out that Radio Hamburg was broadcasting coded weather information to the German bombers.

If we locked on to a German he was finished. The moment he touched his key – he'd be over the North Sea – we did exactly the same at Mundesley and they couldn't take a bearing. We just fed him to the fighters. There is a story about a Dornier that threw out its rubber raft over Croydon. I don't know how true that is!

When the Americans came we became a beacon station for them sending out coded transmissions for them to 'home' back in on.

Off nearby Happisburgh Sands was 'E-Boat Alley' where these fast moving German boats played havoc with the Allied convoys. There were land mines all over the place; we had a local farmer blown up near our site. Well, we got to know a couple of the local coast guards and they told us of a couple of places where you could get down to the sea without being blown up.

Sometimes, after a bad attack on one of the convoys, we would use one of the paths to the beach and pick any debris from sunken ships. We smoked Craven 'A' cigarettes for months... There was a railway at the back of the site and sometimes the train crews, who got to know us, used to throw out coal to us as they went by for our fire.

The whole area was stiff with troops. I was in charge of a night watch on one occasion. It was pitch dark. I was riding my bike along this country lane near the radar station (our site was about 200 yards from it at the top of the hill) to go on duty. I had about 10 minutes to get to the control hut, do my de-coding and get everything ready for the night's work. The next thing I knew a pair of arms came round me and I was lifted bodily off the bike. This was in 1942 and I thought they were Germans and that I had had it. I was wrong. I had been 'attacked' by two soldiers – with blackened faces – from a Highland Regiment who, presumably, were practising! They dragged me into a tent in a field. Sitting at a table was an Army major. When I found out, after I had recovered my breath, who they were I let them have it. The officer got upset but I persuaded him to telephone Radlett HQ on our private number on instant priority. This he did. I don't know what was said but he became very red-faced and let me go. They frightened the life out of me. Later, I got a 'ticking off' from Radlett for insulting an Army officer but was told, "Don't worry, you will be severely left alone in the future." I think they treated it as a bit of a joke at Radlett; I could hear someone laughing in the Ops Room there.

The young chaps on the site were conscripted and put through Yatesbury. They were just given the barest minimum of wireless knowledge. If anything went wrong they just sent for us. When they had a breakdown and couldn't find what was wrong I was often there during the day when I should have been in bed.

When the Americans came the transmitters never got cold. There was never enough hours in the day to put things right – you just had no time at all. As I said, we only knew our own part.

When you were on the air on a frosty, winter's night, when it was drier, you had to be careful if you touched a door handle or something like that. Everything was live. We were pumping out kilowatts and anything metal induced current. One horrible winter's night we had an electrical storm. We had these great 'ship' type aerials. I looked up to the top and saw it glowing blue and red and it was making a 'shooshing' noise. The next thing I knew there was a big 'arc' and the lot dropped on to the ground. We were in the middle of an operation!

Once when I was travelling home via Liverpool Street I chatted to an RAF navigator on the train. I told him that I was stationed at Mundesley. He said, "The radar station?" and I said "No" whereupon he said, "Oh, you must be one of the beam-benders then," and told me what we were doing!'

Arthur McAughtry (Mintlaw; Longside; Ringwood (Hants); Beachy Head)
'I went to Mintlaw, 40 miles north of Aberdeen, arriving there on 16th December 1941. As I recollect, operators did 12 hours shifts and, once on duty in the huts, locked themselves in. On one occasion we had an intruder

trying the doors of some of the huts. The guard challenged him and fired several shots but the person escaped by scaling a high wall onto a neighbouring estate. Much later we heard that a spy had been landed by submarine off the coast near our site and caught at Waverley Station in Edinburgh; it could have been our intruder.

At Longside we had a system where a pre-taped signal was transmitted on a different bearing to further confuse German aircrews, the incoming signal being transferred on to a sort of mechanical turntable and fed into the transmitter.

Later I was transferred to Ringwood, just outside Eastbourne. We were primarily searching between given frequencies in an attempt to locate V-1s – the assumption at the time being that these machines were directed on a beam. Any unusual signals on these frequencies were immediately telephoned through to Radlett. A beam would be picked up – a continuous note with a three figure combination of letters and figures which would be superimposed on the beam at intervals. Primitive means (by today's standards) were used to get a bearing on these signals – a rotating cardiod loop – and these would be transferred to Radlett. Other stations along the coast would do likewise to get a cross-bearing and identify the target.

It was commonplace to see the V-1s coming over in batches having got through the fighters and anti-aircraft at the coast. Some of these 'buzz-bombs' were so low the jet exhaust would be seen red hot and the Bofors guns would fire over 'open sights'. In the early days of the V-1s, some of them would be underslung below a Heinkel and released on the coast. I did, in fact, see this happen. Little bits of memories are still fresh. The mass of 'planes and gliders on their way to Arnhem; the sky was black with them. We got a magnificent view of this from the cliff-top at Beachy Head. Also the cross-Channel shells coming over from Cap Gris Nez – count 20 after the bang, then get your head down!'

George Morle (Beacon Hill, Wiltshire: Parliament Hill, London)
'I volunteered for the RAF in 1940. I was already a wireless operator but did a wireless course at Compton Bassett, in Wiltshire. After this I was posted to No.80 Wing. My first introduction to Radlett was the reception at HQ on arrival, a 'pep' talk on secrecy, followed by the clearance procedure after which I was transferred back to Wiltshire, to Beacon Hill, being taken there in a small van from Radlett. My billet was in Bulford, three miles away, and the van took me there. The billet was a cottage on the outskirts of the village. The local police sergeant told me later he had great difficulty persuading these folk to take me in... he hoped it would work out alright. Getting to the radio station at Beacon Hill would take nearly an hour being uphill all the way. I had my cycle sent from London but it was only useful for the ride down.

Beacon Hill is the high ground behind Bulford Army Camp; it was a site for the original beacon warning of the Armada 400 years ago... In 1941 it was enclosed with barbed wire and guarded by the Army. One side of the hill was covered by several mobile vans and two huts, each housed a transmitter. The vans were converted furniture vans which had previously been used along the south coast to try and locate the enemy beams. The site was a hive of activity... Post Office Engineers working with TRE (Telecommunications Research Establishment) personnel from Worth Matravers, Swanage, were installing equipment on a permanent basis, working up, as they said, "From bits of string to solid state!"... On the far side of the hill was another, smaller hut, the Receiver Hut ... my place of work. On the job training started immediately, (radio counter-measures against *Y-Gerät*).

The receiver hut was the heart of the job. It controlled the whole operation. The receivers were Hallicrafters S21 and there were two main positions along one side of the hut, each with a receiver and a control unit containing a cathode ray tube. TRE had fitted an antenna balance unit on the roof inside the hut, so that our own transmitter did not swamp us during transmission. The S21 receiver had a large dial, covering both the 30 MHz and 40 MHz band, and it could be difficult to get an accurate reading ... Eventually we were supplied with wavemeters to check our readings, but this took many months to happen.

When a German ground station came on the air (usually Cherbourg or Cassel in France) ... we would report the signal 'on' and order our own transmitter to power up to 'standby'... and awaited orders from Radlett. There would be flying time before the aircraft crossed the coast en route for the target. Meanwhile a beam station would come up on a different frequency. The signal was checked, the speed of the dashes counted and reported. If it was a big operation other stations would be logged in a similar way. Ground stations would call their aircraft giving us a lead to call signs to be used. If in our range these would be picked up on the wide band receiver on 47 MHz. When in the target area the ground station would transmit further signals which we re-radiated. This was also an indication that we would soon hear the 'drop-bombs' signal, which took the form of an exaggerated SOS sounding like three dashes followed by long dashes and three dashes. This was so distinctive and important that our reaction was immediate and we used our Morse keys to jam the signal. The excitement and tension is hard to explain. We would also receive either Morse or speech from the Germans, all logged from beginning to end.

The Army guards were friendly and got used to our odd hours of coming and going ... On quiet nights one of us went off duty about 2am. Many times I passed through the camp unchallenged but one night I was attacked by a guard. I shouted loudly and he backed off.

One of our chaps tried to keep fit by exercising to a gramophone record and, in summer, this was done in the open. One day a farmer was ploughing his field when the horse saw our man swinging his arms about – and bolted! The farmer was not amused.

As time passed the nature of the enemy signals changed. In addition to the normal stations we received a strange one which sent out a three tone signal in repetition like a beam signal. This we monitored, measured, counted, but to no avail. Eventually, after the famous commando raid on Bruneval on the French Coast, where a German radar station was dismantled and the equipment brought back to Britain, we lost our signal without explanation.

Raids on the cathedral cities (*Baedeker* Raids) gave us more operating opportunities. As a sequel to these I met, in 1986, a Luftwaffe wireless operator who was shot down on his second raid on Norwich in 1942. He was surprised to find that I had spent time listening and using his system. I am now his English friend and we exchange Christmas cards each year!

The night the German ships *Scharnhorst* and *Gneisnau* dashed up the Channel was one of our quietest nights, and there were no enemy signals. Our log was later queried by HQ. On another occasion we received a freak transmission which was subsequently established as having come from a Panzer Division on the Russian Front. I also learned the RAF used nearby Boscombe Down for research purposes; captured German aircraft were examined and tested there.

In about March 1943 I was posted to Parliament Hill, near Hampstead Heath just to the north of Central London. I became the Corporal in charge when Leslie Werscker (whom I knew from his days as a Corporal at TRE) was posted away as a Flight Sergeant on training duties.

London was completely different from the country life, although the nature of the job was much the same. The building on Parliament Hill was solid brick and concrete rather like an air-raid shelter, and the site was enclosed with barbed wire and guarded by RAF Regiment. Close by was a barrage balloon operated by WAAFs, and lower down the hill a large area housed anti-aircraft guns.

The site on Parliament Hill had been set up at the beginning of 1939. Trees were removed to clear the area. Hampstead society complained, but the project went ahead. The building was first used by the Post Office Research Station at Dollis Hill but was later taken over by the RAF. This part of the hill, sometimes known as Kite Hill, is noted for its panoramic view of London to the south. During the war, under the Defence Regulations, it was forbidden to fly kites, or sketch or draw the skyline of London from the spot. Crowds frequently came up the hill at weekends and holiday times and sometimes people asked the guard at our site, "What are the masts for?"

Among my responsibilities was defence of the Heath in case of invasion. In relation to this the local Home Guard were constantly trying to get us involved in small arms practice. This was held in a local pub, 'The Freemasons Arms', in itself a very attractive location, but we eventually pleaded "service needs", that it was interfering with our work, and we got out of it. We had rifles, ammunition, even hand grenades. Sealed orders were locked away until the need arose. Luckily it never did.

Later, after D-Day, I was sent to Europe. We left Tilbury for Ostend with snow on the ground, and eventually settled in the town of Uden in Holland and set up our station. We were to provide navigational aids to the USAAF and jam particular frequencies with a magnetic steel tape called *Jostle* which sent out multiple tones. We had a control station in the town square with a main generator which supplied the station, the local cinema and also, unknown to us, the local dentist. The latter fact was found out when we switched the generator off one day to save our oil only to receive a frantic plea from the dentist for the restoration of the electricity supply as he was in the middle of drilling the tooth of a patient! We made many friends amongst the Dutch people.'

Ken Myers (Ivybridge, Devon; Alexandra Palace; Harpenden, Herts; Up Somborne, Hants.; Flimwell, Kent)

'In Summer 1941 I was sent to Ivybridge, a jamming site, with instructions to report to the local police station. The police officer, quite rightly, was not forthcoming about the hush-hush activities taking place on Dartmoor above the village. My credentials were checked, a billet arranged, and I was conducted to the site, a mile away up on the moor. The route was via a wide stone and grassed banked track which emerged on to the open moor, then a climb up a well grazed path to the site which had a rudimentary fence to keep the ponies, cows and sheep out … there was a small hut used as the control and office, and, I think, this had an ex-hospital diathermy machine which had been converted as a transmitter for jamming on 30 Mc/s. There were two or more trailers housing transmitters with roof-mounted aerials. It was easy to lose one's way on the open moor in misty rain or dense darkness and the noise from the diesels was not a reliable guide, so after someone had wandered off for a while, a rope suspended between posts was provided. Animals looming in the darkness would give one a start. Incidentally the site was completely unguarded and I don't think we had any weapons.

Early in 1942 I went to Alexandra Palace. It was a change from the primitive to the refined! … We had the luxury of beds in the tower underneath the aerial mast; we didn't appreciate the vulnerability! The rooms, which presumably had been offices, included television receivers with miniscule screens. We enjoyed the facilities, a restaurant and badminton in the studios beneath the television halls. There was a huge bath in one of the dressing rooms, perhaps designed for a circus fat lady, but the supply of hot water was usually inadequate even for us of more modest dimensions.

After three months of luxury I went to Harpenden, north of St Albans in Hertfordshire. This 'jamming' and 'meaconing' site was located in a large field (at Kennels Farm, Kinsbourne Green) on the A6 (now A1081) road, a short distance from the entrance to Luton Hoo. In a copse was a small repeater station of the GPO for the London to Rugby co-axial cable link. The meaconing signal from the receiving station (Elstree), was relayed to our transmitters from this repeater. I think the site was supplied from the mains. There was a control hut with PBX telephone switchboard to each of the transmitters, enabling the receiving station to speak direct to the transmitter operator. Operating the control was quite a satisfying activity requiring one to be on the alert as the meaconing frequencies changed. Some huts had a 1kW exposed element electric fire which when laid on its back could be used to heat up a tin of soup, and if one was patient could also be used to roast a potato in its jacket. The operating personnel all seemed to have some sort of technical background and were a good class of chap and lack of discipline was never a problem.

In the summer of 1943 I was moved to Up Somborne, to the north-west of Winchester, in Hampshire. The site was on a hill above the village and was for 'jamming' only. The only equipment I can remember was a mobile SWB 4 transmitter. This was mounted in two furniture vans, the transmitter in one and the power supply/modulator in the other. A year later I was moved, with this particular equipment, to Flimwell to take part in the scheme to combat the V-1s and V-2s. The site was situated in 'Doodle-Bug Alley' and it seemed there was hardly a tree or hedgerow that was not blasted by them when they indiscriminately landed, causing such havoc and bloodshed. One that been damaged by either ack-ack or fighter aircraft narrowly missed the steel aerials on the site and crashed and exploded just beyond.'

W Priestnall (Marske, Yorkshire)
'I thought the security was a bit on the severe side. It was a case of "Halt! Who goes there?" and no fooling about. The guards did not have an easy time tramping round the field all night and not being allowed to take refuge in any of the technical huts as they were not allowed in. We had a couple of sets which had a system of air cooling for the output valves. Having done its job of cooling the valves the hot air escaped through a duct in the hut wall to be much appreciated on a cold night by the guard on duty who used it to warm himself.

We had a 'decoy fire' within two miles of us. We knew of its existence but did not find out until after the war what they did. A Wellington bomber crashed one night just a short distance away from our site and the lads brought the injured crew members into our control room only to be severely reprimanded by the CO the following day for allowing them into 'confidential' huts.

Colin Prior (Kimmeridge, Dorset)
'In June 1942 four of us, with a corporal in charge, were to open the outstation at Kimmeridge, on the coast about five miles west of Corfe Castle. We spent about two weeks kitting up the trailer which was to be our operational vehicle. The trailer was towed to the site, two of us were left in charge and the corporal drove off, casually suggesting that we find ourselves somewhere to live. We were on a ridge overlooking the Channel with Kimmeridge Bay below us to one side and Swyre Head on the other. There was not a house to be seen but a trace of smoke from a chimney in the far distance gave us an idea of a likely direction.

We finished up being taken in by farm workers at Blackmanston, a hamlet some half a mile from Kimmeridge. I was with a kindly, elderly couple who looked after me well. My host always shaved while wearing a bowler hat because, he said, of the draught.

Daily we toiled up the path to the site expecting the other two to return with more equipment any day. Like the grand old Duke of York we "marched up to the top of the hill, and we marched right down again" – for three months! Nobody arrived, nor were we advised of the reason for the delay, possibly because they hadn't an address to write to.

We decided in the interests of security it would be better not to inform anyone of our existence. This meant we wouldn't be bothered by official envelopes, but it also meant that we had no pay or billeting allowance. Fortunately I possessed a Post Office Savings Book so I was put in charge of pay accounts without opposition.

We dutifully went up to the site most days but now and then we visited the bright lights of Corfe Castle and sampled the heady delights of a paper shop run by a Mrs Holland. On one such day, in our absence, the strength of the detachment doubled and they brought with them a collection of crude transmitters which looked a bit like oversized gas meters.

George Rose (Flimwell, Kent)
'We jammed commercial European transmissions. The Germans used Radio Paris, amongst others, to superimpose a signal, usually in Morse, which could easily be identified by German aircraft and so used as a beacon ... When we re-transmitted the signal they would be unable to get a navigational 'fix' and so became hopelessly lost.

When we weren't meaconing we used the same transmitters as *Splasher* beacons for our own bombers. After we had been on duty all night for a 1,000 bomber raid we were all rather jaded in the morning.

Joe Russon (Parliament Hill, North London)
'I was employed on counter-measures against the *Y-Gerät*. During 1942 the Luftwaffe began to use the system with fighter-bombers. On one occasion I heard a German pilot start to scream and he continued to do so for what seemed hours until there was complete silence. Obviously he had been hit and had gone down. His ground station called and called telling him to come in and report, but there was no reply. Eventually they gave up.

It was normal practice each day to test our equipment before the raids began. Therefore we instructed the engineers at 'Ally Pally' to bring the transmitters up onto dummy load. This should have meant that the test transmissions would not be heard more than a mile or two from 'Ally Pally'.

One day I emulated an enemy transmission including a few instructions on the Morse key. I was amazed therefore to receive a telephone call from Radlett control asking if we had heard any strange transmissions on 42.5 Mc/s as a 80 Wing listening station in South Devon had reported some. Quite truthfully I told them that we had not *heard* any signals! I did not tell them I was the culprit and I made sure I did not do anything like that again.'

Joe Skinner (Windlesham and Epsom, Surrey)
'Each transmitter was manned 24 hours per day by one wireless mechanic. It was his duty to keep it going, repair as necessary, and take meter readings to measure operational performance etc. From 1942 onwards when German aerial activity dropped off, we were mostly on 'standby' with much 'care and maintenance' to keep us on our toes.

The local population certainly knew something was afoot in their midst for their wireless receivers were swamped when we were on the air. I never met any civilians who gave any hint that they knew anything, so the secret was well kept.

Being a small unit we did not have any catering or NAAFI facilities. We had tea rations from the NAAFI, and cigarette and chocolate rations were collected by van and later sold to us ... we called ourselves the Radlett Air Force and any resemblance to any other organisation with the same initials was co-incidental.

At Epsom the site was situated on the Dorking road, just out of the town ...

in the grounds of a convent. We only saw the occupants from a distance but they were kind to us. They left cakes and other goodies in tins outside our little hut which was rather touching.

Our Corporal Thompson was a Geordie. Most unusually for a serviceman he had a glass eye. It was a trifle disconcerting on switching on the light in the middle of the night to see it glaring at you when the rest of the body was fast asleep. He was a top-class tradesman though and we frequently had to call him out in the early hours when some technical problem had defeated us, which was extremely frequent believe me. He never complained.'

Anonymous Airman (Fairlight; Bonchurch, Isle of Wight; Dover, Kent)
'In 1942 I was sent to Fairlight, near Hastings. "Lantern House" they said, "Anyone will tell you where it is." I eventually found it! It was a mansion where I was directed by a servant girl to a distant corner of the grounds reached via the road to Fairlight Church.

I saw a wooden hut sticking up over a hedge. There were two planks over a ditch leading to a gap in the hedge where an airman was filling a bucket of water. Such was the secrecy of 80 Wing! I spent three months there learning the job … ours was the monitor station and the transmitters were down on the cliff edge a couple of miles away.

We moved from there to Bonchurch and had to build our own station. I was up a mast one day with safety-belt and all the gear, threading ropes through pulleys etc, ready to hoist the frame aerials, when I saw hundreds of ships pouring out to sea from every direction along the coast. It was D-Day.

After the landing our site became obsolete and we moved to Dover. I came out of Dover Priory Railway Station to the sound of shells falling nearby. I walked away from the town towards the countryside with absolutely no idea where I was going. Quite by luck I saw a wicket gate with a signpost pointing to 'RAF'. Taking a chance I followed the path up the hill to the top of what is known as Western Heights and found two large huts and RAF men peering across the Channel through a telescope. I had arrived.

One day, a fairly quiet one, a cargo ship was seen almost at the foot of Shakespeare Cliff, hugging the coast to escape enemy fire. The Germans did, however, fire a couple of shells which, fortunately, fell short. We knew they used radar to focus their guns so we turned on every jammer we had, focusing everything on the gun flashes the other side of the Channel until they were swamped. They did not fire again and the ship passed safely through. All very unofficial, of course.'

Off Duty

Gordon Barrow (Hindhead, Surrey)
'The site was at Gibbet Hill. It was at a cross-roads on the road to Petersfield and the South Coast. Right by the traffic lights was a corner cafe called the 'Queen of Hearts'. That was our base for a cup of tea and a bun when having a break.'

Frank Churchill (Mundesley, Norfolk)
'At first I was billeted with two others in a small terraced house. We lived in terribly cramped conditions. The lady, whose husband was away in the Army, had two young children and her father and sister-in-law staying there. We had no proper beds or bedding, and we didn't see much of our rations. Our landlady was a chain-smoker who dropped ash into the teapot!

After a week we complained and we were moved to individual billets. Mine was heaven after the first place. I was in a large detached house owned by a former Royal Navy man. He had been awarded the Iron Cross by the Germans earlier in the century when he had been part of the Royal Navy Unit which helped to put down the Boxer Rebellion in China. He was not allowed to wear it on his uniform in the First World War!'

L G Dunbar (Leiston, Suffolk)
'The 'billeting out' system proved an ideal means of integrating with local rural communities … At Leiston my cricketing interest led to a net practice. My first contact there expressed astonishment that a Scot would know any-thing about cricket. His eyebrows were raised when I told him I played for MCC. My moment of glory was brief, however, when I was obliged to tell him the initials stood for Minifieth Cricket Club, a village team in Angus, near Dundee.

I went on to play wicket-keeper for Leiston and football with Leiston Works Athletic Club, the latter experience leading to a rather shame-faced incident which occurred shortly after Arnhem. Having broken my leg dur-ing a football match I was taken to Ipswich Hospital and on release walked out on crutches and in 'hospital blues' (uniform of the service hospital patient). I was greeted by a dear lady of the WVS with a welcoming smile, a present of chocolates and cigarettes, and asked, "Where were you wounded?" To avoid further embarrassment I quickly replied, "Below the knee, Madam." My friend, who had collected me, told the local newspaper which produced a story bearing the headline, "Was Jock's Face Red!" My mother kept a copy of the story to produce on appropriate humbling occa-sions.'

*Vic Flowers (Flimwell and Hurst Green, Kent; Mimbridge and
Ashmansworth, Surrey)*
'The village people did their best to provide a homely atmosphere for their lodgers and many lasting friendships were made. Off-duty airmen were in great demand by the local farmers to help with hay-making but few stayed more than one day when they found it was extremely hard work in the sun for one shilling (5p) an hour.

Both sites witnessed many dogfights during the Battle of Britain with both friend and foe being shot down close to the villages. Some airmen played cricket for the local team but games became a farce due to interference from above. Once, when walking along the road I heard a whine and was shaken to see some bullets from an aircraft hit the road several yards in front of me. I could not hear any engines so they must have been fired a great distance away. From then on I was never keen to watch a dogfight.

Later I was moved to Surrey where the receiver site was at Mimbridge and the transmitters were located at Ashmansworth. I was billeted with a well-to-do couple who employed a full-time cook/housekeeper and a young girl as a trainee. We felt we were not wanted; the food was very poor with small helpings and, after lots of disagreements, we found lodgings with a couple both of whom worked on the local paper. The lady was Scottish and an excellent cook and we really felt part of the family.

We had a hut at Flimwell which could be used for leisure activities but obviously the public weren't allowed on to the site. During my visits to the 'Royal Oak' pub I saw a large wooden building (used for storing old furniture) and persuaded the landlord to allow us to use it. There were plenty of volunteers and the place was scrubbed clean, re-wired, and decorated. The floor was sanded and prepared for dancing. A small stage was built and Arthur Lord, a wireless operator, who before the war had been a well-known organist formed a band, and 'The Pavilion', as the hut was called, opened in style. The dances were a great success, also providing extra custom for the pub. Sadly, after a series of brawls and other disturbances, the police closed us down.

It is interesting to remember the money allowed for billeting (revised May 1943). Summer, according to the RAF, was from June to September inclusive for which a daily charge of four shillings (20p) was allowed for each man. During the other months of the year it went up to four shillings and two pence (21p) to compensate for extra heat and lighting. A standard rate of five shillings (25p) per week was paid to 'keep the bed' when an airman was on leave. I got friendly with the daughter on the landlady at one of the Hurst Green billets. Little did the landlady realise her daughter and I would be married after the war in 1947.'

Ernest Hackney (Eastleigh, Hants and Flimwell, Kent)
'I remember at Rogate, I think, the woman to whom I was taken for billeting flatly refused to take me, and the village bobby came to force her. It was very embarrassing for me but they quickly removed me to another billet.'

Ken Humphries (Stockbridge, Hants; Flimwell, Kent)
'I spent 2½ years billeted with Mr and Mrs Beauchamp at Little Somborne. He was a head cowman. It was an end-terraced house with no bathroom and the toilet was the bucket type situated in a shed away from the house. Mains water came from an outside tap which served all four cottages in the row. One of our chaps, Johnny Moyle, put a 'T' junction into the supply behind the tap and ran a supply into the house. You can imagine the pleasure Mrs Beauchamp got from this. She used a coal range and primus stove for cooking. Not only did she feed us well, she also did our laundry.

For baths we went to a nearby large house where the Pilot Officer and Sergeant were billeted (if sufficient water was available); or to the slipper baths at Winchester. Our Corporal bought his own house in the neighbouring village of Broughton and used to come to work in his own car.

We worked on farms in the early summer and at harvest time, and played football and cricket in the recreation ground next to the village pond, and tennis in one of the bigger houses. Dances were run in the village hall on Saturday nights – they were pretty good 'hops' too. The pub in Up Somborne was actually one of the rooms of a dwelling house. Service was provided via a hatchway from the adjoining room which served as the 'tap room'.

We had visits from the mobile canteen of the WVS and Salvation Army. They were most welcome for a cup of tea and, possibly, an increase in chocolate and cigarette rations.

When I was at Flimwell I was finally billeted with an elderly widow who, at one time, ran a laundry with her husband in Tunbridge Wells. I can tell you I wore the best laundered shirts with stiffened collars on the site.

The winter of 1944-45 was a very severe one in the Kent/Sussex area and I can still visualise the scenes of blocked roads, snow drifts under which the roads just disappeared; packed snow on the road and the bitterly cold moonlight nights with the frost forming on our greatcoats as we trudged our way home.'

Jack Leng (Mundesley, Norfolk)
'I was billeted with the village post lady. There is little doubt we were well received by the villagers and it could be said that, to a considerable degree, we took the place of the Mundesley boys who had departed to other spheres … Most of us seemed to acquire bicycles and we made frequent excursions to Cromer and North Walsham: even Norwich (21 miles) was considered to be within our reach … We became competent fishermen having been introduced by the locals to the art of laying out a line with about 30-40 hooks and bait at low tide and going out the following low tide to 'collect our catch'.

I married a local girl. Incidentally, this was not an isolated case. My wife's father owned the 'Coast Road Tea Rooms' in nearby Bacton. At the outbreak of war he turned it into a canteen for the troops stationed in the village. I remember a couple of the local trades people. The village shopkeeper never failed to amaze me. He was blind but could lay his hand on any commodity in the shop. And then there was the local hairdresser. Most of us were unimpressed with his skills and opted to cycle to Cromer to get a haircut.'

Cyril Lister (Potters Bar, Herts)
'I was billeted in Cotton Road, near the Police station. Our normal approach to work was via the Police station yard and over their back wall. Going on or off duty was simply a matter of hopping over the fence into the field to our signals caravan which contained an *Aspirin*, and a stand-by generator. I was married in the local Parish Church and my wife remained in Potters Bar until I returned from overseas duty at the end of the war.'

H Manton (Mundesley, Norfolk)
'It was alright living in the village but in winter it was terrible. The road would be thick with frost and ice. You couldn't ride a bike: you could barely stand up on it. The one bright spot was the village hall. We used to give dances, shows, especially at Christmas. The villagers' life was awful, they couldn't go anywhere – there were no buses. We had a bloke who used to be a cinema organist in Bristol. He gave performances in the village church,

much to the disgust of the local man who normally played the organ. Sometimes I'd go in there and hear the latest 'blues' music and 'Tiger Rag' – our man was a wizard! It was amusing to hear this sort of music in a church. Sometimes I had to keep the younger men from travelling down the road to moral ruin. They were 18/19 years old and I was 30 – an old man to most of them!'

Eric Masters (Windlesham, Surrey)
'The local ladies involved us in their bridge clubs and invited us into their homes. They were extremely kind and generous and groups of these ladies from the various clubs would organise small parties to London theatres and restaurants.

The majority of service establishments had their own 'home-made' off-duty entertainment – amateur dramatics, musical groups etc. No 80 Wing was no exception to this. Almost the first question asked of me on my arrival at Windlesham was, "Do you sing or play a musical instrument?" I did neither. On the incorrect assumption that as an ex air-gunner I just had to be a sharpshooter I was promptly enlisted into the small bore rifle team. I can only say I was marginally better at that than singing or playing a guitar. I was not in the team for very long!'

Arthur McAughtry (Longside, Aberdeenshire)
'The billets in Longside were hilarious to say the least. Three of us were billeted on the local Presbyterian minister and his wife in the Manse. The door was locked sharp at 10pm. We had an arrangement with the live-in servant girl who opened the door when we threw stones up at her window. It could also be said that within five minutes of ordering a pint at the local pub our landlady knew where we were. One of our number discovered where the Communion wine was kept in the digs and regularly topped it up with water after having imbibed – I don't believe anyone was the wiser!'

George Morley (Beacon Hill, Wiltshire: Parliament Hill, London)
'We were scattered in billets in various villages on either side of Beacon Hill over a large area of Wiltshire. My billet was a cottage occupied by a farm labourer and his wife. It had no electric light or gas supply. Lighting was by oil lamps and candles and a fire range was used for cooking and heating the water for the bathroom. I was later informed the bath was used for storing potatoes from October. Their son, who was about my age (20) went into the Army.

It must have been as difficult for them to accept a stranger into their home as it was for me to accept this way of life. After all this was just six months into my service life, and I had never before been away from home, apart from holidays. Getting used to this way of life in my new surroundings was a challenge. It was difficult to know what to talk about; work was out of the question. My coming and going on the various duties proved a problem and I had great trouble explaining the rota system to my hosts. Food was plentiful and different from what I was used to. Rabbits were available, rook pie, faggots, apple pie and lardie cake. Not my usual diet. Lighting a candle late at night to see my way up the stairs to bed took some getting used to.

In the October, with the thought of potatoes occupying the bath all winter, I moved to another billet in Amesbury, to the house of a man who was a security officer at Boscombe Down. The RAF connection was welcome and life certainly changed for the better. My Bulford landlady was surprised and relieved when I said I was moving. Social life was more lively in Amesbury than Bulford with pubs, a picture house, and dance hall, which were popular with the troops.

One of my billets when I was at Parliament Hill was at 50, Downshire Hill, the home of a Shakespearean actor and his wife. Mrs Rawson was an actress and both were well known in the theatre, Mr Rawson for his performances at the open air theatre in Regent's Park. He was also the Chief Air Raid Warden for Hampstead. After the war he said to me, "I don't know what you did, but when you were called out late at night I was always on duty early ready for the raid!"

This billet was beyond my wildest dreams, it was superb. The two housekeepers were detailed to look after me and because of my irregular hours it was decided that all my meals would be served in my room on a tray, rather than disorganise the dinner arrangements for the master and mistress.

Mrs Rawson, at my request, arranged for me to have some speech training lessons with a lady from RADA (Royal Academy of Dramatic Art). The fees were paid by the RAF. London was the place to be when air raids allowed. Buses took you to the centre of town for entertainment. I met my wife, who was a WREN (Womens Royal Navy Service), at the Paramount Dance Hall in Tottenham Court Road.'

Ken Myers (Harpenden, Herts; Up Somborne, Hants)
'At Harpenden I was well looked after by a kindly, homely and hard-working couple, Mr and Mrs Smith, in their cottage on the edge of the Werner Estate at Luton Hoo. Conditions were primitive … a pump in the back yard for washing in the summer, and a bowl in the kitchen in winter. The privy was at the bottom of the garden, nearby which grew excellent vegetables! I fondly remember returning from a visit to the local pub with Mr Smith to a supper of bread and cheese and pickled onions sitting around the table and facing the oil lamp, the heat from it and the strong onions causing perspiration to pour down our faces. It was a pleasure to grope one's way up the narrow stairs and fall asleep in a deep and supremely comfortable feather bed.

At the Hampshire site the Warrant Officer in charge was billeted in a most picturesque and modernised thatched cottage where I remember being hospitably entertained by the couple who lived there.

The Americans arrived into the area in vast numbers and this caused beer to be in short supply in the pubs. Even jam jars were used instead of glasses and publicans were charging when they were broken. Prior to D-Day, in 1944, there were huge fleets of gliders being towed overhead on 'dummy runs' before the actual invasion. It was a most impressive and unique sight.

One sad and upsetting incident occurred just after the invasion when a bereft and distraught village mother, who had learnt of her son's death in the invasion, berated us for being in his home village apparently doing nothing. As a young man it caused me to give thought as to what life was for. I had pondered previously when on watch on clear, starry nights, when one could see the vastness and order of the visible universe. How Mankind was so insignificant, and that Someone had caused it all to be there. I wondered why such terrible things were going on and if the Creator of the universe really cared.'

Colin Prior (Kimmeridge, Dorset)

'After leaving us at the Kimmeridge Site, Dick, with Bill the Corporal, dropped into a pub at Kinston, about a couple of miles on the Swanage side of the site. Closing time for them was about two years later since they persuaded the landlady to take them in. When they were not operational on the site they tended to be operational behind the bar, pulling pints for the locals!'

George Rose (Flimwell, Kent)

'On the whole we all had a good time. Dances in the local village hall, ghastly ENSA concerts and film shows as well. A friend and I used to cycle all over the place. In those days, of course, the roads were quite empty.'

Joe Russon (Capel-le-Ferne, Folkestone, Kent)

'Life at this outstation was not very hectic and we had to rely on the local 'carryings on' in the area to relieve the boredom. On one occasion some Canadian soldiers occupied a nearby field and they played some sort of ball game alongside our huts. The inevitable happened when one of them went over the edge down to the warren below, a drop of some 200-300ft. It was fortunate for him that the place where he had gone over was not a sheer drop but a very steep incline. When they retrieved him he was quite bloody but did not appear to be hurt badly.

For a time we also had an American anti-aircraft battery located right next to our huts. They took over the field, the old Dover Road, and part of the cliff top, announcing to us that this area was now part of the USA and we couldn't cross it. So to get to and from our billets we either had a long walk around their acquired land, or pick our way precariously along the edge of the cliff which, particularly in darkness, was not too clever. This was at the time of the 'Doodle-Bugs' which were crossing the coast in their hundreds. Even so we did not find the guns were fired very much in anger. In fact, when their radar man shouted, 'on target!' it was more than likely the guns were pointing directly at our huts, or so it seemed. One or two of us managed to gain from our 'neighbours' in the way of gum, fresh oranges and tinned fruit etc, Even so I think we were relieved when they were quickly moved away towards the D-Day invasion ports.'

Joe Skinner (Windlesham: Epsom, Surrey)

'I lived with Mr and Mrs McAthey the whole of my time at Windlesham and we became very close. I found out later that Mrs 'Mac', as I called her, wanted to adopt me! They lived in a tied cottage next to a large house owned by the Tennent brewing family. Ernie had been head gardener and was acting as caretaker of the house which was unoccupied in my time there. He had learnt his trade at Arundel Castle and, although semi-literate, knew every plant and flower by its Latin name. I spent many off-duty hours with him and learnt a great deal. He was one of the most contented men I have ever known. One weekend I met a dark 17 year old girl from Essex who was visiting my digs; she later became my wife.

We played a lot of cards at the site and were initiated into the mysteries of poker (and regularly relieved of our pay) by an interesting character named Johnny Johnson, an AC2 who bore on his shoulder the initials BLAV (British Latin American Volunteers). He was born and had lived most of his life in Argentina and had come over to help the old country. We often wished he hadn't bothered. He 'cleaned us out' of our pay every week and then lent it back to us. He was 'Sergeant Bilko' to the life, with a drawl and a permanent black cheroot in his mouth.

We did all sorts of jobs to earn money. I once helped to build up and dismantle a travelling fair at Bagshot and collected money on the 'dodgem' cars. When we helped a local farm to thresh corn all but two of us reported sick the next day with various aches and pains. We had to go to the local GP.

We also had a concert party. Many pre-war professional musicians were involved until the war intervened and there was a large exodus of our performers from the site to take part in Operation 'Torch' in North Africa.

When I moved to Epsom I was billeted with Mr and Mrs Field close to the Southern Railway Station in the town where he was Stationmaster. He ran his life by his pocket watch and was absolutely unyielding in his habits. After lunch he slept for exactly 8½ minutes, no more, no less, then sprang up and went to the bathroom, and then returned to his duties at the station.

There were many more attractions for our leisure time in a large town like Epsom, of course. There were 28 pubs in the High Street alone which meant that there was always at least one open.

Some of the lads did part time radio repair work for a local radio shop going out on calls to repair radios. My ambition or technical skill did not lie in that direction so I tried to earn a few shillings working at a racehorse stable on the Downs. As I was terrified of the highly-strung horses I was not altogether a success. On another occasion two of us ran a pub for a week while the landlord took a break. Quite an experience!'

Len Simmons (Wincle, Macclesfield, Cheshire)
Brian Simmons wrote: 'My father came from Stockwell, in London. After his initial training which, I think was at Compton Bassett, he was posted to the 80 Wing site at Wincle in the hills above Macclesfield in Cheshire, and was billeted on 'Butterlands Farm'. This was 1,500ft above sea level, and was bleak even on the summer's day when I was taken there as a child. My mother was a GPO telephone operator in Macclesfied main exchange. I don't know whether my parents met as the direct result of 80 Wing ... but certainly the RAF's telephones got priority when there was an air raid.

When my father arrived at the site there was heavy snow and he had to walk there. When the snow eventually melted he found he had been walking straight over the tops of hedges!

One night as he was walking up to the farm in the blackout he became aware of a pair of eyes six inches apart and about three feet from the ground... As the nearest German aircraft was probably hundreds of miles away he turned on his torch and saw only a fence and the gate post. He turned the torch off and there were the eyes again. They don't have glow-worms in Stockwell!

Another night he was pushing his bike up a very steep hill, when, close by, there was a blood-curdling cry like someone was being done to death. He jumped on his bike and cycled up the hill where he found nothing untoward. They don't have 'screech owls' (barn owls) in Stockwell either!

However he overcame these experiences and became quite handy around the farm. Both he and my mother could hand-milk a cow and on one particularly stormy night my father played a part in rescuing a cow trapped in a bog – it was pulled out by a tractor.'

Anonymous Airman (Dover, Kent)
'A billet had been reserved for me in some miners' cottages (the Kent coal field) along the main road. They were very friendly people but the accommodation was rather cramped. At midnight I awoke – in my bedroom in the front of the house – to a tremendous noise and a blaze of red streaking lights shooting past the window. These were the anti-aircraft guns. Elsewhere outside there were flames everywhere.

We were OK but the houses opposite were well alight. Hundreds of shells were being pumped into a dozen or more enemy bombers who were weaving about trying to dodge our night fighters. Fire engines and ambulances appeared with bells ringing. Something down the road exploded with an enormous crash. More flames; more din. I'm in the thick of it now, I thought. This was a scene from hell itself.

Just then I was grabbed from behind by my landlord and dragged down to the coal cellar, "We'll be safer here" he said, "Unless the roof falls in!" So we sat it out on wooden boxes and old chairs for about an hour until the bombers departed. The noise and flames continued but we managed to get some sleep.

Next morning the havoc in the road was enormous but familiar to me having experienced the London *blitz*. I wended my way through the mess past firemen, policemen, and other emergency workers to our site. Half the nine o'clock watch were late so the night shift stayed on. We made some tea. "What do you think of it?" they asked, "We are outside the bombing area up here on the site, they make for the town which lies between the hills." Most of the anti-aircraft shelling had been done by our gunners and US forces ranged along the cliff tops. I decided my billet was too near the town so I spent my spare time finding somewhere further out.

Shelling of the town by German guns from Calais was a daily event. Again, our site was fairly safe but if one was in the town then a dive into one of the dozens of shelters was often necessary. I believe there was a man on permanent look-out across the channel as the flash of the guns could be seen in clear weather and the shell took one minute to reach Dover High Street, time to sound the 'shell warning' and take cover.

One day I was in a Salvation Army Club having a cup of tea. Afterwards I left on the 20 minutes walk back to my billet. As I started out the shelling commenced. I later learned that the club I had been in had been destroyed by a shell soon after I had left it. Several WRENs lost their lives. Another time the shelling was so bad the police closed all roads into the town and pedestrians were forbidden entry.

Standing outside the hut on the site during one attack on the town I saw flames shooting into the air accompanied by whole rooftops and other debris. I've never forgotten that! When the V-1s began the Americans increased their gun teams and thanks to them many of these weapons were shot down into the sea. We used to watch them drop and explode. One or two hit the cliff face and blew up shaking up our outfit like mad – no work could be done while this was going on.'

Kingsdown, Deal,
Kent, April 1945.
J Russon

Chapter Fifteen

HERE AND THERE

As the Second World War developed, Allied commitments spread from Europe to other parts of the world. No 80 Wing took part in this expansion. Complementary to its UK-based activities it trained and equipped naval personnel for 'Meaconing' in northern Russia; undertook jamming and meaconing work in the Middle East; and followed the invading Allied armies into Europe.

Northern Russia

Allied convoys proceeding to northern Russian ports with the necessaries of war were being 'shadowed' by German aircraft. These aerial observers passed information regarding the convoy location to Luftwaffe units operating from Norwegian and Finnish bases, German capital ships based in the Norwegian fjords, and U-boats. They were a serious threat. Convoys taking much-needed equipment and supplies to the hard-pressed Russians, were pushed by the southern limits of the ice edge situated off the south east coasts of Greenland and Iceland, towards the danger area off the Norwegian coast where the Luftwaffe had several air bases where a large effective attacking force had been built up. This quickly achieved air supremacy over the convoys, and on two occasions, convoys were suspended due to successful attacks in which the Luftwaffe had played a major part. Of three convoys, which had sailed in the spring and summer of 1942, 15 merchantmen had been sunk. Seven had been claimed by the Luftwaffe. In the ill-fated PQ17 Convoy in July 1942, although it was the threat of the German battleship, *Tirpitz* which caused the disastrous order to 'scatter' to be given by the Admiralty the main damage, 23 ships sunk out of 33, was inflicted by U-boats and Luftwaffe dive-bombers. (See Figure 25.)

In June 1942 a meeting at the Air Ministry decided to set up a 'Meaconing' station in northern Russia to combat Luftwaffe activities on the convoy routes. The installation of equipment and training of the naval personnel would be the responsibility of 80 Wing; the Royal Navy would operate the station.

After being assembled and tested at Dollis Hill (*qv*) the equipment, contained in 37 cases, was placed in six separate escorting destroyers in a convoy which left Scapa Flow in the Orkney Islands towards the end of June 1942 (the ill-fated PQ17) with an officer and NCO from 80 Wing and 12 Naval ratings who had been trained in 'Meaconing'. Enemy action prevented the conveying ships from completing their journey and they were ordered to return to the UK.

A second attempt to take the equipment and men was successful and it finally arrived in Russia on 24th July 1942. Repeated loading and unloading plus stormy weather had damaged the equipment; the dearth of workshop facilities was overcome, the necessary repairs carried out and the equipment made serviceable.[1]

There were other problems, not least the difficult terrain throughout the region. Walter Brettingham served as a Royal Navy special telegraphist on 'Y' Service operations in the area:

The topography of the country thereabouts in all seasons was difficult to cope with. There were no roads and the landscape was broken up by gullies, ravines, lakes and many scattered rocks – mostly ironstone – which ranged in order of magnitude from the size of a football to that of a lorry, these being left in the oddest positions by the receding fields of the Ice Age.[2]

This was the environment, some 240 miles into the Arctic Circle, in which the commissioning party were required to operate. Sites had been obtained from the Russian authorities but these were found to be unsatisfactory. The Russians had assumed the installations were purely for jamming purposes and there were difficulties with the VHF link between receiver and transmitter sites.

Ultimately sites were found 30 miles north of Murmansk, near the Russian naval base at Polyarnoe. The receiving site was 1½ miles south of Navy House in Polyarnoe with the transmitter located at Vaenga, eight to nine miles away on the opposite side of the Kola Inlet. (See Figure 26.)

Difficulties were encountered with the receiver site:

The final situation of the receiving unit left much to be desired, due to the restricted area in which siting was permitted ... To avoid 'hill' screening, and to provide satisfactory VHF communication, this unit had eventually to be sited at the summit of the highest hill in Polyarnoe, which was almost a complete rock.[3] (See Figure 27.)

Tests were undertaken and after numerous breakdowns due to the inadequacy of the temporary power supplies supplied by the Russians, communication was established between the two sites on 19th September. Huts for billeting and technical purposes were not erected until mid-December.

The installation of the 'Meacon' station had been carried out, 'under conditions of extreme difficulty since the contours of the ground prevented the spaced vertical aerials being erected the required distance apart ... Power and co-axial cables could only be buried at infrequent intervals, wooden troughing being used to protect the cabling from the severity of the North Russian winter.' Due to the close proximity of the front line – the Germans had advanced to within three miles of Polyarnoe in 1941 – a radio telephone link could not be permitted between the sites and telephone communication between them was by means of the submarine cable across the Kola Inlet.

The ground and climate were not the only problems. Many obstacles were created by the various Russian authorities within the area, 'diplomatic, but firm, representations frequently had to be made by the British Naval authorities to the Russians in order to permit progress at all.'[4]

[1] PRO AIR 41/46, p.38.

[2] Letter to the author from W D Brettingham 27th January 1993, supplemented by various conversations.

[3] PRO AIR 41/46, p.39.

[4] Ibid.

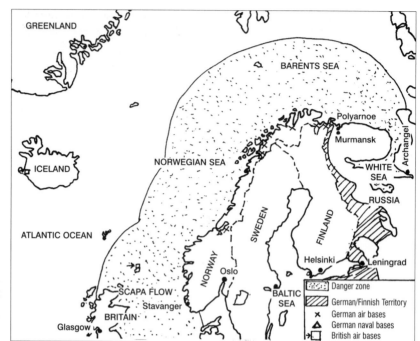

Fig.25
Map showing
'Danger Zone'
for Luftwaffe attacks
on Allied Convoys
to Russia.

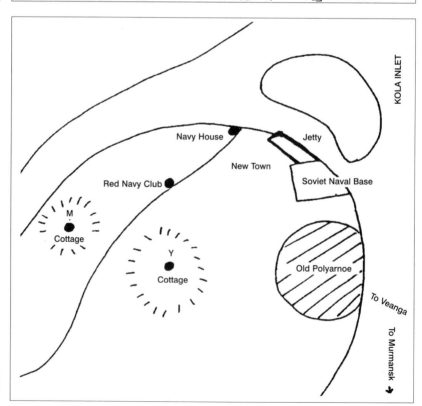

Fig.26
Sketch map of
Polyarnoe.

Fig.27
Drawing
of 'M' Cottage
(at top of hill)
and 'Y' Cottage
at Polyarnoe.
Walter Brettingham

Delivery of equipment was haphazard. Two vehicles housing a transmitter and alternator arrived in Archangel at the end of September 1942 and were transported far into the interior of Russia! When the equipment was eventually reclaimed two months later much damage had been caused. The lorry housing of the diesel-alternator received at Murmansk was badly damaged and the cylinder-block cracked. It was necessary to get replacements from the UK thus causing further delay.

There had been some doubts as to whether the enemy signals were sufficiently strong to be 'meaconed'. However towards the end of February 1943 it was found that they could be, although there were technical difficulties:

Radio reception in this area of North Russia is very freakish, some days providing a complete blackout, while on others it is just the reverse. Fading is extremely variable on all frequencies and the daylight reception on medium frequencies abnormally difficult.[5]

[5] Ibid.

The fragile alliance between the British naval authorities and local Russian officials was often tested. One misunderstanding occurred when the Russian customs sealed up all the equipment on both sites! The Senior British Naval Officer, North Russia, informed the Admiralty of his vexation:

The 'Meaconing Station' which has been under trials and which it was hoped to bring into operation for the next convoy has been impounded by the Russians on the grounds that the necessary permits for the introduction of the equipment into Russia had not been obtained. The result is that a technical device which might have been the means of saving our ships from air attack is, for the moment at any rate, out of service... This is by no means the only case of serious Russian obstruction to the operation of our convoys. However, it is intended to remove certain parts before confiscation![6]

[6] PRO ADM 199/604.

Diplomatic pressure was applied in London. 'If His Majesty's Government fail to attain what they consider the minimum standard of protection' wrote the First Lord of the Admiralty, A V Alexander, to Foreign Secretary Anthony Eden on 26th February, 'they will have to consider whether the Soviet Government attaches more importance to safe passage of convoys, or to pressing the policy of obstruction.' Eden promised to raise the matter with Mr Maisky, Russian Ambassador in London. This presumably was done and it was later learned that, 'the problem is under consideration by the highest Soviet authorities.' On 5th March the Foreign Office informed the Senior British Naval Officer (via the Admiralty) that permission had been granted for 'Meaconing' to take place, 'on condition that its work is co-ordinated with the Soviet Naval Authorities,' the wording of the permission being seen by the Foreign Office as, 'the Russians climbing down whilst saving face.'[7]

[7] Ibid.

At the end of March 1943 permission was given for transmissions to commence; the 80 Wing Technical Officer and NCO returned to the UK in mid-May. Walter Brettingham remembers visiting 'M' Cottage (as the receiving hut was called):

> *Once or twice we crossed the valley to the next hill to the west and visited 'M' Cottage. A small group of ratings led by Leading Telegraphist (Special) Roy Robbins kept a 'meaconing' watch on enemy air frequencies. The idea was to listen for reconnaissance planes, Focke-Wulf [Fw 200] Condors in the main, requesting a 'homing' course to their base and, as they transmitted for a bearing, the 'M' Cottage lads 'meaconed' the signal ... I don't know how efficacious they were, but they did claim to have brought down an aircraft by making it fly until its fuel was exhausted.*[8]

[8] Op cit [2]. The Luftwaffe, at various times during the war, operated from bases 30 miles away in Finland, and in Norway. (See Figure 25)

The Meacon Station was closed in July 1944 and the personnel transferred to other naval duties.

Middle East

No 80 Wing personnel operated in this theatre of war in an environment vastly different from Russia. Snow and ice gave way to sand and sun; tented accommodation often replaced billets. The job, however, was the same, protection of Allied convoys.

In June 1941 information had been received from Middle East Command that enemy 'homing' type signals had been picked up in the Alexandria region of Egypt. An investigative aircraft, two GEC jammers, and a technical officer from 80 Wing were sent out from the UK. Test flights were made in the area, including over Crete and the beleaguered island of Malta, and it was concluded that no threat existed. After local personnel had been trained in radio counter-measures (RCM) work, the aircraft and technical staff returned to the UK in August, the equipment being retained.

In November, following a request from the Middle East, a small RCM organisation was set up for 'watching' purposes under the responsibility of 80 Wing. Further jammers were despatched to form a reserve pool with another 80 Wing officer travelling to supervise any RCM activities. Towards the end of 1941 jamming of German tanks during army operations in the desert also took place. (See Chapter Six.)

At the beginning of 1942 No 80 Wing was instructed to produce a number of mobile meacon stations for possible use overseas. From February to September Dollis Hill (*qv*), at the request of the Air Ministry, carried out investigations to produce a 'completely mobile meacon unit for use in tropical climates.' The prototype unit was completed and tested at 80 Wing's satellite site at Bricket Wood, near St Albans, in Hertfordshire, in November 1942.

Ten were eventually built. Three were sent to the Middle East, (the remainder being adapted and used later during the invasion of North West Europe.) The following month No. 20 'M' W/T Station (Mobile Signals Unit), under the charge of an officer from 80 Wing, assisted by a senior NCO, was despatched to the Mediterranean; in March 1943, Nos. 21 and 22 Mobile Signals Units (MSUs) were sent to North West Africa. The climate was different but the work was the same:

... the primary function of these meacon units should be protection of convoys, by denying the enemy, to the maximum range possible, the radio navigational aids provided by his convoy-shadowing aircraft and the land-sited radio beacons along the coasts of Italy and Greece, and the islands of Sardinia, Sicily and Crete. This was to be consolidated by the use of aircraft meaconing against the extensive High Frequency and Medium Frequency ground direction finding organisations in order to prevent the accurate reporting of convoy positions. In order to meet these requirements the mobile units were deployed to sites in the Algiers, Benghazi and Cap Bon (north east of Tunis) areas respectively.[9]

A directive on 17th May 1943 from MAC [Mediterranean Air Command] stated Nos. 20 and 21 Units were to go into action immediately. Aircraft 'meaconing' was to be used 'as occasion arose' and 'action taken autonomously' as and when intelligence was received by them from MAC. There was some success:

[9] PRO AIR 41/46, p.50.

It was found that aircraft meaconing could be usefully undertaken during air raids on the North West African ports since extensive use was made of the enemy D/F (direction finding) organisation in these areas, particularly when Allied intruder aircraft were in operation over enemy airfields. The experienced meacon operators from the UK were soon able to appreciate the procedure in use and the results proved very successful.[10]

[10] Ibid.

As a result of the Allied advance into Italy, 20 MSU at Benghazi was closed. Nos. 21 and 22 were moved to Corsica and eastern Italy; both were ready for operations by February 1944 but the military situation made their 'meaconing' unnecessary. Early in March both stations were closed down and the personnel returned to the UK.

L G Dunbar went to North Africa with 22 MSU. Sailing from Liverpool on the *Arundel Castle* he realised he was no sailor:

Memories are imprinted of a landlubber's first, and then almost constant, feeling of seasickness, eating and sleeping 'hammock slung' between decks above mess tables, in what was common living, eating, and sleeping space, listening apprehensively to every strange external noise and metallic resounding echoes. Not quite the RAF life. 'God help the Navy types' was a persistent thought!

Access to the top-deck was limited. Constant blackout during the hours of darkness was restricting, the 'passengers' being unable to visit and get some fresh air. It was the same during the day, apart from morning boat drill when they participated in the demoralising pastime of 'counting the number of zig-zagging ships and the occasional, inevitable missing spaces.' Also remembered is an enthusiastic Highland piper 'airing his pipes with a few tunes on deck' as they neared Algiers his musical offering being abruptly halted by an authoritative, megaphone amplified voice testily bellowing from a neighbouring corvette to 'Cease the racket at once. Noise at sea is a security risk!'

There was no welcoming party at Algiers. Instead, as the ship passed the harbour wall, perched on its furthest extremity was a lonely Arab urchin, 'Go home, Johnnie!' he yelled across the water to those within earshot. Disembarkation was followed by a route march in full kit to the transit camp; 'just a few miles up the road,' they were cheerfully told. A whole day later they finished up on a disused racetrack. Acclimatisation followed after which the fully mobile transmitting station, complete with tents, moved out to an old football stadium in a French-Arab village. 'Activities were similar to Mintlaw,' Dunbar remembers, 'with four groups to cover the 24 hours. Three were employed on technical watches; one doing domestic/guard duties, which were shared on a rotational basis. All of us had been supplied with arms.' [11]

[11]
Letter to the author
from L G Dunbar,
22nd January 1994.

Bob Lowson was a member of 21 MSU. He kept a diary, and records they left Liverpool on 15th March 1943 aboard the *Johan Van Oldenbarnvell*, a converted Dutch-Java liner, part of an escorted convoy of troopships and freighters bound for the Middle East. After several U-boat alarms, a common occurrence in wartime seaborne movement in the Bay of Biscay – the ship behind them in the convoy was sunk – they passed through the Straits of Gibraltar arriving at Algiers nine days after the voyage began.

The MSU had arrived at Algiers – unfortunately its equipment was at Oran, a considerable distance to the west! A wait of a week for it to catch up with them and then a move on to Bordj Ménaiel, a small Arab-French town 80 miles east of Algiers and some eight miles inland. Vehicles were stored in the local sports stadium and a local unused school was commandeered as HQ and billets. The transmitting site was set up in a nearby field and the receiving station was installed seven miles away 'right out in the wilds' 500ft above sea level, five miles from Cap Djinet, a tiny village on the coast. Each site had a senior NCO in charge plus a radio mechanic and an electrician. Here the unit remained until 17th December when they were ordered to move elsewhere.

Passing through the Atlas Mountains and skirting the Sahara they travelled 588 miles to Bizerta in Tunisia having spent Christmas Day at Souk-el-Arba en route. On 6th January 1944, after a boisterous trip in high winds and a stormy sea, the MSU docked at Ajaccio on the west coast of Corsica, where they set up camp at the airport awaiting further orders. After almost a month they were told the unit was not required, the military situation had changed so rapidly. No 21 MSU's Mediterranean war was over and they were recalled to the UK arriving back in Liverpool on 16th March 1944. (See Figure 28.) Bob Lowson remembered his Mediterranean service in great detail:

The equipment we used was much the same as that in the UK, except it was all fitted onto vehicles and trailers. The transmitter site control hut and the receiver site hut were built into long cabins in articulated Commer lorries. (See Figure 29.) The receivers worked either from the 230 volt generator or a bank of batteries which were charged when the generator was running. In addition, there were a number of lorries used for other purposes, two BSA 350cc motor-cycles for messenger duties, two large water storage tankers, and a trailer workshop used for electrical and mechanical repairs. There was also a VHF link between transmitter and receiver sites and two portable transceivers (permitting both transmission and reception) for emergencies. The antennae were the same as were used on UK sites.

Fresh call-signs had to be conquered but the enemy were found to be using the same frequencies as in Western Europe which made things easier. With radio reception good throughout the Mediterranean and very little in the way of beams to deal with, nearly all the work consisted of the 'meaconing' of aircraft. A fair degree of success was claimed:

From my own observations it appeared we were particularly successful so far as Allied shipping in the 'Med' was concerned. German 'recce' planes when they spotted a convoy would transmit in Morse, 'QQQ' (Convoy sighted) followed by a series of 'As' so that the control station and satellites could take a bearing and so get a 'spot' position. This we 'meaconed' as effectively as possible and the position given would be nowhere near the convoy. We saved them a lot of trouble. So far as raids on the North African coast were concerned we put a fair percentage of enemy aircraft off their targets and occasionally prevented them from returning to base. Sometimes, to find out if the German ground stations were alert and listening, we would transmit a single 'dit' and 'dits' would come back from all around the Mediterranean. If there was no response we knew there would be no activity for several hours.

The airmen quickly learned to build upon the French acquired at school and the effort seems to have been worthwhile. Being a small unit they had to use nearly as much French as English when talking to the Arabs and the French Algerians. By the time they left North Africa all were pretty fluent, 'with marvellous Algerian accents and patois.' The unit quickly settled in, built its camp and began to absorb the local ambience:

We soon located the local 'pubs' ... and developed our education in French-Algerian wine ... we got on well with the locals, Arab and French, and made good friends amongst both.

There were off-putting moments. After setting up the receiver site five miles outside Cap Djinet, Lowson and the three members of his watch decided to walk to the town in search of leisure. There was, they were assured by the local Arabs, a bar (which rarely closed) situated in a wooden hut near the beach run by one, André, where they could obtain a relaxing drink. They found the place and entered:

The result was electrifying! At the sudden appearance of four uniformed men with Sten guns slung across their shoulders three Arab customers shot out of the back door like greased lightning and André, the proprietor, snatched a double-barrelled shotgun from behind the bar and pointed it at us. His face was a study!

Using their recently brushed-up French to full effect they explained who they were and were soon drinking Muscatel with André and quickly learning about the district. On the road back to base they were surprised by a Zouave (French-Algerian infantry) patrol whose job was to defend that section of the coast. A brief explanation was given and then all was well.

In the heat, swimming was a popular pastime but keen observation of the sea was necessary:

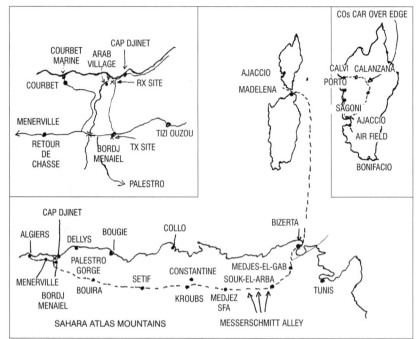

Fig.28
Map of the travels
of No.21 MSU.
(Bob Lowson)

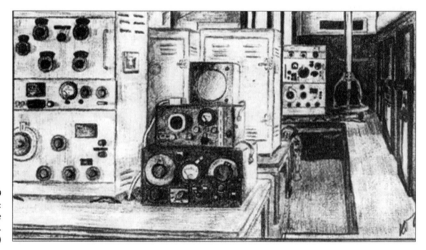

Fig.29
Drawing :
'Interior of the
Receiver Cabin'.
(Bob Lowson)

*One day, Jimmy Plenty, an Australian, and I were swimming back to the beach from a
group of rocks about a quarter of a mile out. When I was about 50 yards from the
shore, with Jimmy 100 yards behind me, two or three people on an otherwise deserted
shore started jumping up and down and waving their arms, and shouting in French,
that there was a 'big fish' in the water behind. I looked back and saw a big black fin
heading for me about 30-40 yards away. A shark! I've never swum so fast in my life!
Suddenly I seemed to be up in the air looking down, watching myself swim. I felt
nothing and was quite calm, and, judging my progress and that of the shark, which
appeared to be overhauling me, I thought I might just make it to the shore. I did, and*

shot out of the sea onto the sand with it just behind me. I shouted to Jimmy and pointed out the shark to him. His comments were unprintable! He swam diagonally away from it towards the shore whilst the French people and myself shouted and splashed to divert the shark's attention away from him. He reached the shore safely. For many years I never mentioned that 'out of body experience' afraid of not being believed. I later read it was not unusual and happened sometimes to people when they were in great danger.

Arriving in North Africa early in the year enabled the personnel of the unit to get used to the sun slowly; by mid-summer they were 'a rich mahogany colour' and contrasted markedly with new people posted from the UK. Thus, when four 80 Wing officers arrived clad in spotless new khaki shirts and shorts, sun helmet, and ghastly white hands, knees and faces, announcing they wanted to stay in a tent on the receiver site they were told of the disagreeable, unhealthy habits of the local natural life (snakes, scorpions, wild boars, locusts etc.). The officers still wanted to sleep under canvas:

We decided to prove we were not exaggerating. We collected various examples of the local fauna in boxes, bags and jars, and let them loose in the tent after 'lights out'. Huge locusts were soon climbing up inside it making a terrific noise and falling off onto the beds, half-a-dozen bullfrogs hopped around croaking their heads off, large glow-worms crawled up inside the tent switching their bright green lights on and off; several large tortoises ambled about the tents knocking things over. We waited – but not for long. There were several 'expressions of surprise' followed by a rapid opening of the tent flap and an exodus of the four officers!

The unit also witnessed the unusual sight of snow in North Africa:

Towards the end of November we woke one morning to find the whole countryside covered with several inches of snow, the first there, we were told, within living memory. The Arab kids had never seen it before, except in the far distance on the Sahara-Atlas mountains. We taught them to make and use snowballs! The snow had melted by just after midday.

New Year's Eve saw Lowson on a tank landing craft in Bizerta harbour waiting to travel to Corsica. The unit was travelling with 200 American soldiers:

...our cooks shared the galley with the Americans. They pooled rations. The 'Yanks' took one look at ours, told our cooks to put them away again, (or words to that effect!) and fed us all on their rations. For New Year we had turkey with all the trimmings, plum pudding, the US equivalent of Christmas Cake, mince pies and ice cream, wine, beer, rye whisky etc. We were fed right royally all the way to Corsica.

Arriving in Corsica No21 MSU travelled up the west coast road along a narrow rough track masquerading as a road. Progress was halted when they came to a stone bridge on a sharp bend over a deep gully. Most of the vehicles, carefully driven, made the crossing satisfactorily, except the two articulated Commers:

The radio cabins were about two feet wider than the power unit and protected on the front corners by curved metal sheets. These came up to the bridge parapets on both sides. Two 2-ton lorries which had made the crossing reversed to the bridge and, in line, were connected to each other and to the artic' on the other side. All three went forward in low gear and the artic surged over the bridge pushing both parapets down into the gully. This happened on several occasions travelling north!

The mountain roads often provided difficulties for the large vehicles – sometimes with hair-raising results:

Returning from Calanzana on the high inland road, which turned out to be no better than the coast road, we drove along several miles with a rock wall on the left and a sheer drop of two to three hundred feet on the right. The air-brakes on the 2-ton Crossley failed and it charged down the mountain! How it stayed on the road I'll never know. It skidded around sharp bends, somehow missed other vehicles, and eventually, collided with the CO's car knocking it over the edge; luckily it came to rest right way up in a tree growing out of the side 50ft down. The CO and the Sergeant were hauled up with ropes. The lorry driver brought his vehicle to a stop by scraping along the rock wall![12]

[12]
Letter to the author
from R O Lowson,
25th July 1994.

Continental Wing

As the Allies poised in mid-summer 1944 to take the battle to German-occupied Continental Europe, No 80 Wing prepared to play its part. Two mobile echelons of counter-measure units were formed at Bricket Wood which would quickly follow the invading army into Europe. These would be known as 80 Wing (Main), with Radlett becoming 80 Wing (Rear); the new units would supplement, with ground-based RCMs, the airborne RCMs already being carried out by 100 Group. The newly set-up units were to operate against enemy radar early warning systems, its fighter control communications network, air-to-air interceptions, and medium frequency beacons.

Supreme Headquarters Allied Expeditionary Force (SHAEF), worried about the interference likely to be caused by the Bricket Wood contingent to its other operational communications, gave control of the RCM organisation to the 2nd Tactical Air Force (TAF). It had the power to veto any RCM activities and certain frequencies were banned from use in radio counter-measures. It was envisaged that the Mobile Signals Units (MSUs) would spread on a front from Eindhoven in Holland to the Swiss frontier, with the radar jamming units 20 to 30 miles apart and the communications jammers 60 to 100 miles apart along the same front. Intelligence would be supplied by 'Y' Service.

Ajaccio, Corsica, 1944. No 21 MSU under canvas. The articulated Commer lorry used by the unit is in the background.
R Lowson

No 80 Wing (Main) set up a base at Wenduine on the Belgian coast north of Ostend, its HQ later moving to 'Château Brifaut' at Schepdael, eight miles west of Brussels. The first site was retained as, 'it proved invaluable as a transit centre where equipment could be overhauled if necessary after the Channel crossing.'

The movement of Echelon 'A', the first to travel from Bricket Wood, and its eventual establishment on the Continent has been described in an official daily diary[13] compiled by its CO, Squadron Leader D P Taylor. He conveyed simply, but effectively, the high-drama of the D-Day period:

[13]
PRO AIR 26/584.
Official diary for
month of June 1944
of Echelon 'A',
No 80 Wing (Main),
compiled by the
CO, Squadron
Leader D P Taylor.

5th June 1944 – Bricket Wood and Old Sarum
'Unit called at 0400 hours … the head of the column pulled out of the field at exactly 0730 hours. Assembly point was the Watford-Hatfield by-pass, about one mile from the camp site … A general feeling of excitement was noticeable throughout the unit, now that the 'great day' had arrived after so much hectic preparation and long weeks of training. At 0800 hours the first vehicle pulled away and soon the whole column of 23 vehicles was on the move. The first casualty occurred between Denham and Rickmansworth, where a Crossley transmitter vehicle had a puncture and fell out of the convoy … At Reading another vehicle broke down with mechanical trouble. A stop was made between Reading and Newbury for lunch, thick ham sandwiches previously prepared by the unit cooks and tea from an insulating container. At exactly 1630 hours the full convoy arrived in the Concentration Area at Old Sarum (near Salisbury in Wiltshire), the two defective vehicles now having caught up. All personnel with the exception of the drivers (who took the vehicles away for waterproofing) marched to No 6 Camp which was nearby … each man was given a palliasse, blankets and allotted tent space … The hardest worked people of the day were the despatch riders who had made an excellent job of keeping the convoy together, while passing through towns and heavy traffic.'

6th June 1944
'… Learned during the morning that today is D-Day, British and American troops having landed on the beaches of Normandy on the east side of the Cherbourg Peninsula. All personnel received £1 sterling, which was later exchanged with all surplus money into French francs … Escape kits (compass, hacksaw blade and linen map) issued to all officers and senior NCOs. A heartening sight was the large number of aircraft of all types passing overhead on their way to and from the beaches. In the evening an American airborne Division passed over in gliders. The camp is well organised and the personnel are enjoying the leisure after the hectic days at Bricket Wood.

After the initial excitement a period of idleness descended on the waiting RCM men, "nothing to do except write letters, visit the camp cinema, and sleep, occupations that were very much appreciated for the first few days but which now become less attractive as the days pass."'

Six days after D-Day the contingent moved on:

12th June 1944 – Old Sarum and Fareham

'Up at 0500 hours for an early breakfast and down to the 'hardstanding' where we rejoined our vehicles after being separated from them for several days. All kinds of strange additions have been made in the 'waterproofing process'. Large snake-like pipes emerge from the engine pass through the driver's cabs, and rear their ugly heads skywards, these pipes being heavily smeared with grease. In a short while the drivers resemble flies that have escaped from a fly-paper! Finally we moved off in convoy at 0800 hours, picking up four days rations to feed us 'over the water', and arrived at the Marshalling Area at Fareham (near Portsmouth) at 1400 hours. After being marched to a nearby camp, allocated tent space and given a meal, we were all issued with Bags, Vomit (ominous portent!), further rations and life-jackets. The drivers took the vehicles down to the 'hardstanding' in Fareham village where another stage of waterproofing was carried out. They are to live with their vehicles during our stay in the Marshalling Area.'

14th June 1944 – Fareham

'The second stage of waterproofing has been completed and another coloured stripe added to the wings of the vehicles, which are now beginning to resemble Jacob's coat of many colours.'

15th June 1944 – Fareham and Gosport

'As prophesied at the briefing we received movement orders when we least expected them. The morning being fine and warm a general decision was made to catch up on arrears of laundering. At about 1100 hours, when most of us had our one and only shirt well lathered, we had a Tannoy message to move off immediately. We were sent to Gosport … where we eventually arrived at the embarkation point. The whole unit was divided into roughly two equal parties and embarked aboard two landing crafts, LCT 609 and LCT 1070. Before embarking, the last touches of waterproofing were added to the vehicle engines, and the final stripe, this time *red*, added to the wings, to indicate that waterproofing was now complete.'

With a fairly strong south westerly wind blowing, the two vessels moved, when loaded, to a sheltered anchorage off the Isle of Wight and waited for a convoy to be formed. The sea was calm and 'Bags, Vomit have not yet come into their own.' The vast number of ships anchored in the Solent surprised the onlookers; 'everything from battleships to light loading craft.'

During the evening of the following day the 80 Wing contingent set off, with fourteen other LCTs, on the 'cross-channel trip'. The weather was kind but the voyage was not without incident:

17th June – At Sea – off Normandy

'Everyone out and about early, just after dawn to find that we (LCT 609) are the only vessel in sight! During the night a collision occurred in which our other LCT was involved, and in the confusion we lost the convoy. The captain cheered us all up immensely by assuring us that we were probably in the middle of a minefield … By about 0900 hours we had sighted the first of the ships anchored off the beaches; by 1000 hours we were passing through the midst of this most amazing collection of shipping, which stretched away as far as the eye could see in every direction. At 1100 hours we anchored about a mile off-shore to await instructions when to go in. The shore of Normandy could be seen quite clearly, a long low-lying shore, dotted with houses all of which showed signs of the damage incurred during the initial landings. The presence of mine sweepers at work and sundry wrecks, reminded us that all shipping had not had the pleasant crossing that had been our lot. At 1300 hours the anchors were weighed and we slowly glided in towards the beaches. This was the sign for general activity aboard and getting vehicle engines ready for the landings. Very soon the vessels bows grated on the sand and the bow doors were lowered into the water with a splash.

The first vehicle off was a Fordson three-tonner, which hit the water with a terrific splash, but which continued to move under its own power, and finally crawled out of the water onto the sandy beach. The second vehicle, a 15 hundredweight Fordson was not so lucky. When it was about a third of the way between boat and beach its engine died and it stayed there with the water level several inches above the level of the floor of the driver's cab. Fortunately it did not block the way for the remaining vehicles and was later towed out by a 'tracked' vehicle from the beach-party. It caught up the remainder of the unit at the 'Vehicle Assembly Park'. Here the waterproofing was stripped from all vehicles.'

Later, contact was made with the remainder of the contingent who had been in LCT 1070. Eventually both boat loads arrived at their given site destination, Tour-en-Bessin, a village to the north west of Bayeaux, near the front line, which was some ten miles to the south.

Two days were needed to establish the site. The diary entry for 18th June records that the Continental representatives of 80 Wing were. 'Busy getting "dug in" after a noisy night with considerable anti-aircraft gun activity from the beach-head … by evening all tents and masts were erected.. and contact established with Radlett.'

The following day 'after feverish activity': *… by evening all technical vehicles were in position and connected up and a signal sent to Radlett announcing that we were ready for operations… Have made arrangements with 83 Group for us to contact their radio station W.19 every hour. They have given us permission to radiate 'jammers' at our discretion. If interference occurs, they will send a code-word via W.19 on the 80 Wing frequency, and we shall cease radiation.*

An Operations Room was made from a Crossley three-ton lorry and field telephone contact established with all transmitters. Branches from nearby trees were cut and used to camouflage the tents and vehicles. All the work had been assisted by a spell of dry weather which enabled the staff to work long hours settling in. The enemy assisted. There was, at this time, 'Very little signs of enemy beam activity', the diary records. A week later the report is still the same, 'Weather again pleasant, an important factor as far as morale is concerned. No enemy beam activity has yet been received either here, or at 80 Wing, and we have not yet used our jamming transmitters since setting up camp.'

There was plenty of activity on the battlefields outside the site, of course, and some of the unit's personnel came close to it:

25th June
'Today the Commanding Officer, Squadron Leader Taylor and the Operations Officer, Flight Lieutenant Buckley went to the Cherbourg area to survey a site for Echelon 'B'. It was decided that the Delasse area five miles south of Cherbourg would be suitable. In the course of the search, the suburbs of Cherbourg were entered and the fighting lines reached, (The US 7th Corps did not capture the port area of the town until June 29th, after much bitter fighting). There were many enemy dead and prisoners in the area ... later ... we came across a pilotless aeroplane (V-1) launching site concealed in woods ... Later in the day we visited the ex-German radio station K10 on the west coast of the Cherbourg Peninsula near Carteret. The aerials had been damaged by blast from a nearby bomb, but we were able to make a sketch showing layout and dimensions. The entrance to the underground transmitter building was blocked by debris, access being gained several days later. The transmitter was found to be intact. This station is understood to have been evacuated the previous day by the Germans'. (See Figure 30.)

The camp had become established. Organised parties, under an officer, were allowed, from time to time, into Bayeaux to 'sample the cider and cognac'. Most of the shops were still closed but, 'the inhabitants were parading the streets in force, and seemed to be more friendly, having now, more or less, recovered from the shock of the invasion.' Sport was now a part of camp life. Inter-section soccer and touch-rugby matches were played, and two airmen, exercising splendid English eccentricity, were observed, less than three weeks after D-Day, busily 'rolling a cricket pitch, having borrowed the roller from a nearby farm!' Not quite equal to Sir Francis Drake and his game of bowls as the Spanish Armada approached, but heading in the right direction!

As the summer moved into July the Field Cashier of 83 Group was found, 'and relieved of several thousand francs... all the men are now wandering around with pockets full of notes – and nothing to spend the money on.' On 3rd July Bayeaux 'overcrowded with troops... all the British Army seems to be there,' was placed 'out-of-bounds'. This was revoked a week later but the overcrowding, the steadily rising prices and the limited parking space in the town produced limited enthusiasm for a visit from the 80 Wing men. Later in the month, personnel were allowed out of camp for the first time – apart from organised trips to Bayeaux – and, although they were not able to visit farms and villages in the immediate area which were 'out-of-bounds', enjoyed strolling around the lanes, 'after being cooped up in one field for three weeks.'

A detachment in charge of the captured K10 radio station at Sortosville-en-Beaumont near Carteret, on the Cherbourg Peninsula quickly became popular with the locals. One of the RAF men took his portable radio to the neighbouring village of St Pierre d'Arthéglise, 'where the whole population turned out to hear the French news.' Two days later on Bastille Day (July 14th), the airmen were entertained by local residents, 'with "vin blanc" (pre-war vintage!) and gateaux.' The Tricolour was hoisted to the top of a tower at K10, 'to much cheering by the French population.' The war caught up with this small detachment two days later when the US Army arrived, 'to clear K10 site of mines!' They returned to the main unit on 22nd July after dismantling the equipment at K10.[14]

On 18th September, 80 Wing (Main), as it was now known, moved to Wenduine. It had its problems 'en route'. Firstly, it managed to extricate itself from a meeting with an American convoy of 35 vehicles coming in the opposite direction along a narrow country lane. Then there were several breakdowns and the convoy only travelled 30 miles on the first day. When they crossed the River Seine at Vernon the pontoon bridge sank by one foot due to the weight of the vehicles. However, the 80 Wing convoy eventually reached its destination, 'amid torrents of rain … but tonight, at least we shall be dry.'

Although the building, which had been a tuberculosis sanatorium before the war, had been left in an untidy state by the German Navy there was no shortage of accommodation which 'was quite luxurious'. It was a popular location and 'the town's many cafes are thronged every evening. The airmen enjoy a glass of beer after living in the dry land of Normandy for so long.' Good relations were established with the local inhabitants.

On 28th September Echelon 'B' arrived. Great difficulty was experienced parking their vehicles as the grounds surrounding the building had not been entirely cleared of mines, but they managed to find space for them: 80 Wing (Main) was growing; fortunately there was sufficient accommodation.

Early in October 1944 several soldiers had been killed by 'booby traps' (antipersonnel bombs) left by the Germans in the town. All fortifications on the sand dunes had been placed out of bounds; care was also taken to keep away from the hotels where similar traps had been placed. In the middle of the month an Australian pilot of a Supermarine Spitfire crashed near the site but pronounced himself, 'after a double whisky, to be fully fit!' In November evacuees, driven from Antwerp by the V-1s, were entertained and a party was held in the village to raise funds for them.[15]

Philip Colehan was with 62 MSU, part of Echelon 'B'. He remembered a noisy November afternoon at Wenduine:

One signals vehicle was placed right on the coast alongside massive concrete coastal fortifications … One November afternoon just as it was getting dusk a German E-boat came speeding along the coast shooting up any military installations. We stood outside the cabin watching the 'fireworks display' with great interest, until the tracer bullets came whistling past, then we dived for cover! We, and the signals vehicle were unscathed, but an ammunition ship further down the coast off Ostend was not so fortunate.

The MSU was engaged in trying to pick up signals from V-1s and V-2s; signallers with forward troops were asked to send the Morse letter 'X' if they saw the launch of any of these weapons. As this arrangement brought no useful result 62 MSU was moved up closer to the enemy in the Ardennes, just behind the American front line, now close to the German border:

[14]
PRO AIR 26/584.

[15]
PRO AIR 26/585.

No 62 MSU at Wenduine, Belgium, 14th May 1945, prior to returning to the UK. Chalked/painted on the canvas cover of the lorry are the names of their European 'bases': 1944 Nijmegen, Asche Verviers, Gulpen, Prum,Aachen; 1945 Cologne, Remagen, Liege, Leende, Wenduine.
P Colehan

We were near Malmedy in December 1944, in a deserted farmhouse. One morning an American liaison officer came to tell us the Germans had launched a counter-offensive. Nobody seemed concerned as it was assumed that the Germans were just about beaten. The liaison officer returned to say that the attack was coming our way and, as a non-combatant unit, we ought to move back.

We started to pack up and move out and then we saw, in the distance, German Tiger tanks moving menacingly towards us. We were rapidly making ourselves scarce when someone remembered that the safe had been left in the farmhouse. We backed up the lorry and Bert Downey ran into the farmhouse. Normally it took four people to carry the safe but Bert Downey, a Newfoundland lumberjack in civilian life, heaved it into the back of the lorry and we went tearing off back to base. The attack by the Germans was von Runstedt's push, which became known as the 'Battle of the Bulge'. We were well out of it. We lost the keys to the safe. Several weeks later, not knowing what to do with a safe we couldn't open, we quietly went down to Zeebrugge harbour one evening and dropped it into the sea!

Still trying to find locations close to where the V-2 rockets were being launched, in March 1945, the unit followed up the US Army's capture of the bridge at Remagen by taking over Schloss Rheineck which overlooked it:

The battle was still raging over the other side of the Rhine and there were remnants of the German Army behind us. It was eerie to be on duty in the castle's tower, which we had made into our signals room, particularly at night. We lived on 'K' rations for several weeks, and life was bleak until we found the keys to the wine cellar!

Peter Giles served in the same unit as Philip Colehan. The preparation for overseas duty was, he recollects, unusual and tough. Sent to North Creake, near Great Walsingham in Norfolk, there was a bleak and inauspicious start to his time there. The countryside was still gripped by cold winter, 'snow had fallen, the power had failed, and we ate our meal by the light of two hurricane lamps placed on each table.' Here he took part in a three week course:

This 'backers-up' course was essentially basic weapons and field-training, plus a toughening up regime. The idea was that we would be able to assist the RAF Regiment in the event of enemy attack. This was a pleasant change from watch-keeping. We practised firing several weapons, including the Twin-Browning anti-aircraft gun on a 'Stork' mounting. The guns would rear up in our inexperienced hands, so after a twin stream of tracer was seen heading for Walsingham Church, the mounting was tied down to the horizontal. Our unit developed a strong team spirit, and one expects that others did too... Later we returned to Bricket Wood where we continued to practise the survival skills learnt at North Creake.

Eventually he reached the Continent:

Shortly after our arrival at Wenduine a party was selected to go to a 'Forward area' under Flight Lieutenant Buckley (ex-BBC Birmingham, I think, who had also been in charge at Flimwell in 1941). They went to Liège and Aachen and came back in a hurry when the 'Battle of the Bulge' broke out. (See Philip Colehan's story above.)

This battle gave rise to another event not likely to figure largely in the annals of 80 Wing – we took two prisoners! A mile or two down the road to Ostend we had a listening post. I was not on duty myself at the time but, apparently, one afternoon early in 1945 two German soldiers knocked on the door and asked to surrender. One of them spoke enough English to explain that they had become separated from their unit and had taken a Jeep in the hope of out-flanking the battle zone and rejoining their forces. They were hopelessly lost, cold (there was four inches of snow on the ground), hungry, and exhausted. The main site was informed and a well-armed party drove down to make the formal capture.

At the end of March 1945 Giles was transferred to 60 MSU which had earlier set up operations in a church tower at Vught a village near Hertogenbosch, Holland, north of Eindhoven. A couple of weeks later he was sent to Kleve, just inside Germany and came across a piece of radio counter-measures history. Here a detachment under Flight Lieutenant Arnabaldi had encamped right beside the *Knickebein* transmitter from which the first signals had been traced back in 1940 which led to the setting up of 80 Wing:

On arrival at the site I was aware of its significance, being as I thought THE 'Knickebein' ... the aerial array, as I recall it, was like a big signal-gantry. It had a central-pivot and its outer extremities had been placed on bogies so that they could run on a circular railway track ... I was sitting by one of these bogies after breakfast on 13th April when I heard the news that President Roosevelt had died. Apart from the 'gantry' I saw nothing else in the nearby buildings - which had a 'temporary' look about them - to suggest any technical operation. (See Figure 31.)

The 'Knickebein' site was on gently-rising ground on the Kleve-Nijmagen road, about two miles west from Kleve. The height made it conspicuous above the lower slopes. A nearby German frontier D/F site was also being examined. The D/F site was another three miles along the road almost into Kranenberg. This was a pylon structure supporting a cabin about ten feet square which was about 25ft above ground level. The cabin contained nothing that I can recall, but the remains of radio units were scattered in the surrounding mud. Unlike the 'Knickebein', this site was on low-lying ground beside the road. The area had been badly flooded when British and Canadian troops captured the region early in February, and was still treacherously boggy. The connection between the D/F and 'Knickebein' sites was never explained to me. (See Figure 32.)

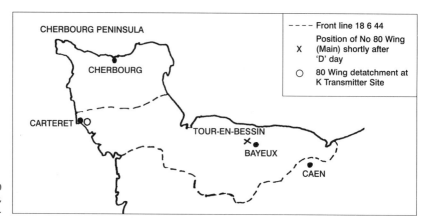

Fig.30
Map of Normandy,
1944.

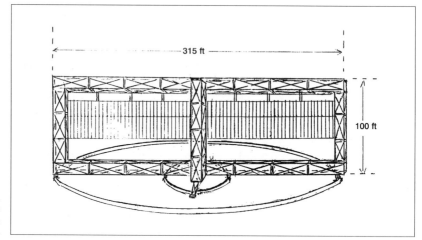

Fig.31
Sketch of *Knickebein*
Transmitter at Kleve,
(Peter Giles).

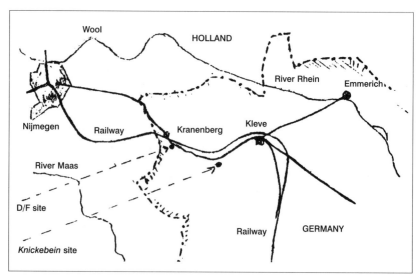

Fig.32
Sketch map of
Kleve *Knickebein* site
and surrounding
area. (Peter Giles).

POSTSCRIPT

... you must be one of the beam-benders then ...

In 1940 No 80 Wing had been hastily set up with a staff of just over 200. Five years later it was just as quickly disbanded. On 24th September 1945, 80 Wing ceased to exist. The personnel, which had increased ten-fold during the Wing's lifetime, went their separate ways. Most were demobilised, many continuing in radio work in civilian life where a significant number were eventually to achieve senior positions. The equipment was either disposed of as 'war surplus' or placed in store at RAF Watton in Norfolk, under the care of the Radio Warfare Establishment, (the successor to 80 Wing) which had been set up under George Baillie, one of the Scientific Analysis Team from Radlett. This new organisation worked independently of the main RAF Station and was known locally as 'Baillie's Castle'.

How can the work of 80 Wing be assessed? Initial impressions are that it was a triumph of organisation as well as achieving considerable operational success. Much of the credit for this must be given to its first CO, Group Captain Addison who, it seems, always seemed to know where to go for resources and who to ask for knowledgeable and highly skilled assistance. Equipment was obtained quickly from the various radio manufacturers, and the positive help, knowledge and adaptability, of the Post Office's Radio Branch at Dollis Hill and the Telecommunications Research Establishment (TRE) cannot be stressed too highly.

Complementary to this was the excellent support given by 'Y' Service monitors, Air Ministry Intelligence, and the *Enigma* decoders at Bletchley. To augment the strength of the RAF signals personnel employed on counter-measures, other already radio-educated staff were obtained. Fifty BBC radio engineers joined the Wing and, with its Secretary acting as a Recruiting Sergeant, the Radio Society of Great Britain, the organisation for amateur radio enthusiasts, also provided many of its members for the unit. Commenting on the Wing many years later, Sir Robert Cockburn, who, as Head of the Radio Counter-Measures (RCM) Group at TRE had been a major contributor to its efforts reflected:

Within a year, starting with no equipment or trained personnel and under difficult 'blitz' conditions, 80 (Signals) Wing built up, throughout the country, a fully deployed system of jamming and monitoring... Although during its formation the demands from the Wing received very high priority, nevertheless, its rapid development under most difficult conditions was a notable performance.[1]

[1]
IEE Proceedings,
Volume 132, Part A,
No 6, October 1985.

Security was always likely to be a problem in such a highly secret unit but, it was, in general, implemented with intelligence. It does, however, appear to have been both a strength and weakness. The offer of a conducted tour to 'see my shelter' by a lonely *Starfish* site member, and the airman who was surprised to be told by an RAF flyer, a travelling com-panion on a railway train, 'Oh, you must be one of the beam-benders then', seem to have been exceptional experiences. In the main the important secrets were kept. Most personnel realised that for 80 Wing to perform effectively it was necessary for its operational activities to be kept closely confidential.

On the other hand free movement of information, and discussion between the people taking part could have increased efficiency. The Special Wireless Operator's view that 'tight security and a general reluctance to encourage discussion about the job... led to unforeseen trouble', and the Post Office Engineer's opinion that lack of knowledge of what his Branch had been doing may have resulted in 'unnecessary re-invention' by others carrying out similar work, are valid points.

The technical work of 80 Wing meant that a considerable amount of the enemy's scientific resources was taken up in an effort to combat it. The expertise acquired also provided a springboard for the offensive counter-measures later in the war by 100 Group. The Foreword to the Air Historical Branch's History of No 80 Wing states that, after the war:

Very senior German officers admitted that at the time when the Germans most sorely needed to concentrate the endeavours of their scientists and radio engineers on the tasks of inventing and developing new radio apparatus with which to defend their country, a large proportion of those efforts had to be diverted to overcome the efforts of our radio counter-measures.[2]

[2]
PRO AIR 41/46.
AHB History of No
80 (Signals) Wing.

Lack of full and accurate statistics means the full story of 80 Wing's contribution to the successful prosecution of the war will never be told.

'I don't recall any occasion where 100% success was claimed.' wrote a former member of the unit, John Whitehead, many years later, 'the best we could hope for was a thin spread of bomb damage over a wide area as a substitute for what otherwise would have been heavy damage and loss of life'. Although these remarks relate to the early defensive counter-measures undertaken in the two vital years at the unit's beginning, they summarise the general philosophy behind all the RCM unit's operations throughout the war. There were failures as well as successes but there is plenty of evidence to show 80 Wing rose to the challenge, in whatever way it manifested itself, on many occasions.

Perhaps the last word may be left with the key figure in the Wing's history. In a lecture on 'The Radio War' given at the Royal United Services Institute for Defence Studies in November 1946, Air Vice-Marshal Addison, who had organised and administered 80 Wing in its early, crucial period, summarised the work undertaken. He had this to say about its effectiveness:

There can be but little doubt that the air defences of this country were aided, in no small degree, by the work of this counter-organisation at a time when our means of warding off heavy night attacks were meagre in the extreme. Moreover, the valuable experience we gained during this defensive phase was to stand us in very good stead when out turn came to deliver bomber attacks in great strength on the Germans.[3]

[3]
RUSI Journal,
February 1947.

FROM HULL HELL & HALIFAX
An Illustrated History of No.4 Group, RAF 1937-1948

Chris Blanchett

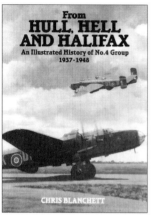

This is the story of an incredible effort by the Yorkshire-based No. 4 Group of RAF Bomber Command, over an eleven year period that encompassed the Second World War. Backed by loyal ground staff who toiled for exceptionally long hours, sometimes in atrocious weather conditions, many hundreds of courageous young men set out, night after night, in their Whitleys, Wellingtons and Halifaxes, to take the war to the enemy.

Aircraft of this Group were the first to fly over Berlin – much to the annoyance of Goering – and the first to bomb Italy. The casualty rate was horrific in the early years of the war; a bomber crew rarely completed a tour of thirty operations.

This profusely illustrated history of No. 4 Group, 1937-1948, is printed on a high quality gloss paper. It features many first hand reports and a good proportion of the photographs are published herein for the first time.

The full cover laminated cover features a specially commissioned painting by Keith Woodcock GAvA.

Hardback
282 x 213mm, 240 pages
330 b/w photographs plus maps etc.
0 904597 81 4   Published 1992
£24.95

BRITISH AIRFIELD BUILDINGS OF THE SECOND WORLD WAR – a pocket guide

Graham Buchan Innes

The world of airfield buildings is one of constant fascination to enthusiasts. Until now, references on this subject have been the domain of very specialist works, or to be partially found within high price books. All of this has conspired to put off a whole army of people who have a thirst for such knowledge.

British Airfield Buildings is the answer to this need and in a genuinely pocket-size form. From control towers, to hangars, to defensive strongpoints, barrack blocks, maintenance buildings to the humble latrine, it provides an illustration of a *surviving* example, highlighting details and other styles of similar building.

Over 200 illustrations with brief but informative captions take the reader for an excursion through a typical wartime station.

British Airfield Buildings has received wide critical acclaim and provides an ideal primer to a subject close to the heart of all enthusiasts.

Softback
148 x 105 mm, 128 pages
230 b/w photographs
1 85780 026 5 Published 1995
£6.95

AVRO MANCHESTER
The Legend Behind the Lancaster

Robert Kirby

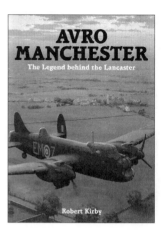

History has not been at all favourable to the Manchester, which is all too easily written off as a failure and a death-trap. Although its twin Vulture engines proved to be its downfall, when introduced it was the only Bomber Command 'heavy' capable of taking the 4,000lb *Cookie* bomb.

Anyone claiming to have a complete library on the Avro Lancaster and Bomber Command is in error unless they have *Manchester*. The true story of the son is impossible to appreciate without looking at the father's deeds.

The book provides the 'unwritten' chapters of the Lancaster's career via a rich combination of technical development interwoven with nail-biting accounts of raids deep into Europe in an aircraft that was as good as dead the moment an engine played up. A testimony to the achievements of air and ground crews and to a design team that learned from their interim solution to produce a legend, and including more Manchester photos than have ever been between two covers.

Hardback
282 x 213 mm, 208 pages
217 b/w photographs plus drawings
1 85780 028 1   Published 1995
£29.95

**ROYAL AIR FORCE
BOMBER COMMAND LOSSES
of the SECOND WORLD WAR**

W R Chorley

**THE BOMBER COMMAND
WAR DIARIES** – An Operational
Reference Book: 1939-45

Martin Middlebrook & Chris Everitt

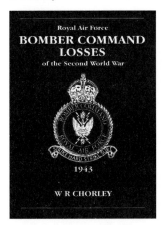

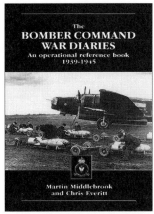

**Further (post free) titles from
Midland Counties Publications –**

A much respected researcher is
producing a series of books designed
to cover the whole of the Second
World War, on a day-by-day basis,
identifying units, aircraft and crews, as
well as the circumstances behind each
of the 9,000-odd aircraft losses in the
European Theatre of operations.

Appendices include loss totals by
squadron and aircraft type for each
year; Group loss totals; Squadron
bases by group, bomber OTU losses
by unit and type, PoWs, escapers etc.

This series is an ideal complement
to *Bomber Command War Diaries*.

Available in 234 x 156mm sbk format:

Volume 1: 1939-40
Details 1,217 aircraft losses; 160pp
0 904597 85 7 **£9.95**

Volume 2: 1941
Details 1,515 aircraft losses; 224pp
0 904597 87 3 **£12.95**

Volume 3: 1942
Details 2,035 aircraft losses; 318pp
0 904597 89 X **£15.95**

Volume 4: 1943
Details 3,100 aircraft losses; 494pp
0 904597 90 3 **£18.95**

Volume 5: 1944
Details c3,500 aircraft losses; c544pp
0 904597 91 1 **£19.95**
Due for publication 1997 (4th qtr)

Some books acquire the 'classic' label
without really deserving it. Others
become classics and don't need to
advertise the fact.

Bomber Command War Diaries is
firmly in the latter category – essential
reading matter for all interested in
Bomber Command and its campaigns
during the Second World War.

Bomber Command War Diaries
provides a concisely-worded review of
each raid and its background.
Operational statistics provide unit and
group sorties against aircraft lost –
which range from 1% through to 18%.

Copiously indexed, this is a
balanced testament to Royal Air Force
Bomber Command, its men and
rationale.

This latest Midland Publishing
edition includes a new appendix on the
survival of aircrew from shot down
bombers, plus minor amendments and
observations, but essentially *War
Diaries* continues to be what it has
always been, an icon in aviation
publishing – the essential classic.

Softback
234 x 156 mm, 808 pages
65 photographs
1 85780 033 8   New edition 1996
£19.95

**AIR FORCE MEMORIALS OF
LINCOLNSHIRE** (4th edition)
Mike Ingham. Sbk £8.95

**THE BATTLE OF BRITAIN
MEMORIAL FLIGHT**
Bill Taylor. Sbk £9.95

**FIGHTER COMMAND LOSSES
OF WW2 - Vol.1 1939-41**
Norman Franks. Sbk £12.95

CRANWELL - RNAS & RAF photos.
Green, Hodgson and Taylor. Sbk £7.95

LEGEND OF LLANWROG
Story of the airfield and the birth of the
RAF Mountain Rescue Service.
Edward Doylerush. Sbk £4.95

NO LANDING PLACE
Aircraft Crashes in Snowdonia.
Edward Doylerush. Sbk £4.95

OCEAN BRIDGE
The History of RAF Ferry Command
Carl Christie. Sbk £30.00

SILKSHEEN
The History of East Kirkby Airfield
Geoff Copeman. 2nd edn. Sbk £6.95

WINGS OVER LINCOLSHIRE
Peter Green, Mike Hodgson and Bill
Taylor. Sbk £7.95

INDEX